Thomas William Shore

A History of Hampshire

Including the Isle of Wight

Thomas William Shore

A History of Hampshire
Including the Isle of Wight

ISBN/EAN: 9783744717748

Printed in Europe, USA, Canada, Australia, Japan

Cover: Foto ©ninafisch / pixelio.de

More available books at **www.hansebooks.com**

POPULAR COUNTY HISTORIES.

A

HISTORY OF HAMPSHIRE,

INCLUDING

THE ISLE OF WIGHT.

BY

T. W. SHORE, F.G.S., ETC.

LONDON:

ELLIOT STOCK, 62, PATERNOSTER ROW, E.C.

1892.

PREFACE.

THE history of every county has been affected to some extent by its natural features, and this is especially the case in respect to that county whose history is sketched in this volume. The County of Southampton or Hampshire has been much favoured by nature, and its natural advantages must have commended it to its early inhabitants, whose connection with it are traced in these pages.

The surface of the county consists largely of well-wooded plains or valleys, and dry chalk hills which stretch across it in a broad belt, having on the north and south of them two other broad areas of clays, and sandy loams. Hampshire is, and always has been, a woodland county, and its forests have been much concerned with its history. Its natural features have had a great influence on the growth of its forests, for oak grows on the clay lands in all parts of the county, while beech flourishes on the loamy soils lying upon the slopes of the chalk hills, and upon similar soils in the north and the south, and those areas which contain more sand than clay can be distinguished by a growth of pines and firs. Much of the land on the chalk hills was formerly old downland, a great part of which was the common pasture-land of the ancient manors until the time of the inclosures, since which time most of it has been broken up and cultivated in large fields, under the modern system of sheep farming.

A considerable part of the land in the south of the county rests on a substratum of gravel which keeps the soil dry, and has in modern times assisted in attracting a large residential population.

Its landlocked harbours, its double tides in South-ampton Water, an estuary which stretches into the interior of the land, and leads into the long valleys of the Test and the Itchen, and the many eligible sites for occupation, must have invited settlements at as early a period as any part of Britain.

The materials for the History of Hampshire are more abundant than those of most English counties, as will be seen in the following pages. No county offers a richer field for the study of prehistoric or medieval archæology. A peculiarity in its history is the great part it has played in national history, and especially during the Saxon and Norman periods.

Its history has not been adequately written. An attempt was made more than twenty years ago to produce a reliable history of this county, and the late Mr. B. B. Woodward collected valuable material for it and began the work; but he resigned the undertaking. The publishers of the proposed history asked the late Rev. T. C. Wilks, to continue Mr. Woodward's work. He did so, and was assisted, in respect to the part relating to the Isle of Wight, by the late Mr. C. Lockhart. Their work was issued in three quarto volumes in 1870 in an incomplete form, for many places in the county of great historical interest are not even mentioned. In the preface he wrote, Mr. Wilks acknowledged its many imperfections. Probably the magnitude of such an undertaking and the cost of its publication has deterred other students from attempting to write a comprehensive history of this county. The materials for its history have greatly increased since the date of the above-mentioned publication, and every year is adding to the bulk of this information. Owing to the increase of historical knowledge, the time for attempting to write the history of such a county as Hampshire, in one comprehensive work, may have passed away.

Some valuable contributions to Hampshire history have been published within the last few years, such as the 'History of the Parish of St. Mary Bourne,' by Dr. Joseph Stevens; and the 'History of Basingstoke,' by the Rev. Dr. Millard and Mr. F. J. Baigent.

Two county societies are now engaged in collecting and publishing historical and antiquarian information relating to Hampshire—viz., the Hampshire Field Club, which is concerned with Archæology as well as Natural History, and whose annual papers and proceedings are awakening a great interest in the county antiquities; and the Hampshire Record Society, which is engaged in printing its hitherto unpublished MS. treasures. It is intended by the Record Society to publish the episcopal registers preserved at Winchester, the chartularies and other MS. remains of the abbeys, priories, and other religious houses, some of the MSS. of the ancient municipal corporations, of the old Hampshire Courts, and other valuable historical matter.

It is hoped that the large and valuable historical MS.

collections relating to Hampshire, and especially to its ecclesiastical affairs, made by Mr. F. J. Baigent, of Winchester, may be published under that gentleman's direction. Their publication would be of service to all historical students, and would be welcomed by all who are interested in the history of this county.

CONTENTS.

HISTORY OF HAMPSHIRE.

CHAPTER I.

PREHISTORIC HAMPSHIRE.

THE earliest inhabitants we can trace in this part of England are those who made rude stone implements by chipping flints into the form of hatchets, spear-heads, and other weapons, and are known as the Palæolithic people, or men of the Early Stone Age. They have also been named the River Drift men, from the circumstance that these relics are found in beds of gravel, which have been formed by the drifting power of rivers and floods that have washed the gravel down from higher parts of the country. The beds which contain these implements in Hampshire are found capping the sea-cliffs at Barton, Hordle, Stubbington, Hill Head, Lee-on-Solent, along the shores of Southampton Water, and in similar situations, in some instances as high as 100 feet above sea-level, so that the water which deposited the beds of gravel must have flowed at a greater elevation, a circumstance which points to a further extension of the land seawards than occurs at present, the rivers probably flowing down a gentle slope to their outlets, or junction with a larger river further out, where the English Channel now is. Other beds of implement-bearing gravel are found inland, in terraces along the courses of the streams, or those of former rivers. Near Southampton some of these terraces are 100 feet above the present level of the rivers, and examples of the stone implements which have been found in them are to be seen in many of the principal geological museums in England. The gravel-beds on Southampton Common, and at Highfield, about a mile to the eastward, have yielded many fine examples of implements, of various shapes. Similar worked flints have been found in gravel-beds higher up the Itchen, near Winchester and Alresford. They have also been discovered in the terraces along the course of the Test near Romsey, Stockbridge, and St. Mary Bourn. They have been found along the course of the Avon, near Christchurch and Fordingbridge. They have been also met with along the course of the Loddon, and in other parts of the county.

Palæolithic man has left us nothing in Hampshire except his stone implements and weapons. No caves, such as he may have used in Devonshire, have been found in this county, for the chalk and most of the other strata in Hampshire are so soft that caverns could not have been formed in them by natural means as in harder limestones, and, if formed artificially, would not under ordinary circumstances have lasted long.

The remains of some of the animals which lived in this part of the country contemporaneously with Palæolithic man have, however, been found. The teeth of the early elephants (*Elephas antiquus* and *E. primigenius*), a horn of a reindeer, and another of an ibex, have been obtained from the gravel near Southampton, or found below the peat in the new dock excavation there. Elephant remains have also been found near Winchester, Romsey, and Freshwater.

The Palæolithic period is so remote from our own, that England at that time must have been very different from what it is now. It was probably connected with the Continent, or had not long been separated from it, otherwise the animals whose remains are found could not have migrated so far.

The valleys through which the Hampshire streams now flow were then only in process of formation. These streams have since that time deepened their channels, and rain and local floods have smoothed down the valley slopes. The rivers in the Palæolithic period all flowed at higher elevations than they do at present, and the whole surface of the country was higher than it is now. Considerable modifications of the surface and the extent of the land have occurred since the time when the River Drift man, who probably lived by hunting, roamed over that part of England which, after many thousands of years of gradual change, we now call Hampshire. No traces of language or customs which can with any certainty be ascribed to so ancient a people as the Palæolithic race have yet come to our knowledge.

The bones of the people of the Neolithic or Newer Stone Age are the earliest human remains which are found in Hampshire or the adjacent counties. There are still remaining in this county nearly 400 barrows, or tumuli, which were reared at various times by its prehistoric inhabitants over the remains of their chieftains and other distinguished dead. Most of these barrows are round in shape, and vary somewhat in the details of their construction, while others are what archæologists call long barrows, and which were formerly known among the country people as giants' graves. The long barrows which remain are few in comparison with the round ones; not more than about twenty or thirty of these exist in this county. They consist usually of a great mound of earth of an elongated shape, and higher at one end than the other. The examination of barrows of this kind has shown that the people who made them buried their dead in a contracted position, the legs being drawn up towards the head. This is perhaps the most ancient mode of disposing of the dead which is known, and examples of this method of inhumation have been met with in many parts of the world. In those parts of England where stone could be obtained in large slabs, the builders of the long barrows made roughly constructed chambers, with a roof and entrance formed by large stones laid horizontally on the edges of others set vertically, and afterwards heaped up the earth on this structure, thus forming a chambered long barrow. Such chambered long barrows often contain stone implements, and they were the mausoleums where the Neolithic people buried their distinguished dead in a common sepulchre, groups of skeletons having been found in them. In Hampshire, where suitable blocks of stone do not occur, the long barrows were constructed without such chambers, as far as known, but it is probable they were also used as common sepulchres for distinguished persons among the Neolithic people, and that openings were made into them when required for the remains of such individuals to be deposited in cists, roughly made with flints, or cut out of the chalk or other strata beneath the barrow. Perhaps it was for such a reason as this that these barrows were made so large. Hampshire has its folklore concerning the giants that lived in the land in very olden time, and it is natural that these long mounds should have been regarded as their burial-places. Such a tradition must itself be very ancient, probably as old as the time of the Saxons.

The burial-places of a people so ancient as those of the Newer Stone Age must have been considered by the Anglo-Saxons and early English people to have belonged to a far older world than their own. These great grave-mounds were inexplicable to them, except as evidences of the Heroic Age in Hampshire, when men did all kinds of marvellous feats in war and in peace, such as were beyond the ordinary powers of the men of their own time. Hampshire must have had its giants, for here in these great mounds they were buried. Such was the folklore which connected the burial of the renowned Bevois of Hampton with a large barrow that existed until the beginning of the present century on Bevois Mount, Southampton, where his name survives unto the present day. The renown of Bevois was shared by another giant, Ascupart, his former antagonist, but afterwards his faithful companion-in-arms. When the barrow on Bevois Mount was opened, some human bones of a man of unusual stature are said to have been found. Similar legends of the age of the giants probably gave rise later on to that of the Danish giant, Colbrand, who was slain at Winchester by Guy of Warwick, and to the legend of Onion, the giant of Silchester, whose name, in the mediæval folklore of the county, was given to Roman coins found among the ruins of that city, these having been known to the country people in Camden's time as Onion's pennies. The name and some of the achievements of another giant, called Dun Drovy, still hang about the neighbourhood of Woodcot. Another giant is traditionally remembered in the Isle of Wight, and certain large barrows on Breamore Down and at Charford are still spoken of as graves of giants.

Some of the round barrows have a circular ditch or bank round them, and are called ring-barrows. Others are shaped somewhat like an inverted bowl, and are called bowl-barrows. Others are higher and somewhat like a bell, and are called bell-barrows. Other burial-places are marked only by a ring of earth and a ditch, surrounding in some instances a slight elevation of the ground, and these have been described as disc-barrows.

These round tumuli belong to an age subsequent to that of the long barrows, and the sepulchral remains which are found in them differ from those of the long barrows, in showing in the great majority of cases evidences of cremation.

The barrows of Wiltshire, including many on the Hampshire border, were systematically explored by the late Sir Richard Colt Hoare in the early years of the present century, and later on by Dr. Thurnam, but no similar systematic investigations of the barrows of Hampshire have been made. Many have, however, been opened in the Isle of Wight, in the New Forest, and other parts of the county. There is every reason to believe, from the evidence of these sepulchral mounds, that the custom of cremating the dead was almost universally adopted during the age to which the round barrows belong, and there can be no doubt that time was during the Bronze Age, when the use of stone implements and weapons had for the most part been superseded by others made of bronze.

In some cases two interments have been discovered in round barrows, and where this has been the case the primary use of the mound was to mark the burial-place of some distinguished individual, who probably lived before the custom of cremation had been commonly adopted ; for such remains are found in cists cut out of the chalk or other beds beneath the surface, in some instances as deep as nine feet, and the bones in these cases are found in a contracted position, showing that the early mode of burial had not yet been discontinued. The secondary interment in such a round barrow, when it is found, is of quite a different kind, for the remains of this second burial usually consist of fragments of burnt bones and ashes in an urn, placed on a floor of flints, the urn being commonly found in an inverted position, and the mouth of it covered with a thick layer of clay. These buried urns have been usually found in such cases above the level of the ground, showing that the round barrow was opened at the top and the cremated remains placed in it. This practice, which does not appear to have been very common, saved the trouble of making a new tumulus, the sepulchral monument being used of an earlier time, the traditions of which, and of the chieftain it commemorated, had perhaps long been forgotten.

A considerable number of instances occur in Hampshire in which the people of the Bronze period chose the neighbourhood of the burial sites of the people of the Stone period for their own interments, the round barrows being found close to or not far from the earlier long barrows. Such instances may be seen on Crawley Down, on Beaulieu Heath, and elsewhere. A sanctity thus appears to have been attributed to these burial-places of the Neolithic people by the people of the Bronze period who followed them.

Nothing is more characteristic of differences in race than differences in the shape and dimensions of the skull, and fortunately a sufficient number of round barrows in the South of England have been found to contain skeletons for these to be examined, and their skulls to be compared with those found in long barrows. Many examples of these have been examined and compared by Thurnam and others, and it has been found that the skulls of the people of the round barrows are broad and round, the breadth being more than four-fifths of the length ; that is, having an index of breadth above 80, in some instances nearly 90, while the skulls of the people of the long barrows are long and narrow, the breadth being less than three-fourths of the length, or having an index of breadth less than about 74. One of the best examples of a broad skull from a prehistoric interment in Hampshire which has come under my observation, was found with the skeleton in a contracted position, in a cist nine feet deep in the chalk at Wherwell, when a railway was being made there some years ago. This skull has an index of 87, and its discovery, with others of a similar kind in other parts of the county, shows that burial by contracted inhumation was practised by the early Celts of Hampshire as well as by their predecessors. From the remarkable differences in the dimensions of the skull, the people of the Stone Age are said to have had dolico-cephalic, or long-headed, skulls, and the people of the Bronze Age to have had brachy-cephalic, or broad-headed, skulls.

This conclusion is of the utmost value to the archæological student who desires to unravel the threads of information concerning the prehistoric condition of the people of Hampshire. The skulls and burial customs of these prehistoric people point to the existence of two races, who apparently succeeded each other in the possession of the valleys and downlands of this county, after invasion and war, and probably after a period during which the survivors of the people of the Stone Age became blended with, and more or less absorbed into, the people of the Bronze Age, and the earlier customs and modes of burial were gradually changed, cremation following the custom of contracted inhumation.

The dawn of history in this part of Europe cannot be placed earlier than about the fourth century B.C., when the Greek mercantile colony settled at Marseilles sent out the exploring expedition under Pytheas, who visited the coasts of Britain for trade purposes, and more especially for accurate information concerning the sources of and trade in tin. The European nations at that time had long been passing through their Bronze Age, and we may reasonably conclude that a knowledge of the manufacture and uses of bronze reached the southern parts of England later than the date of its use among the civilized nations of the Mediterranean shores. Tin was a necessity in bronze manufacture to mix with copper and give it the requisite degree of hardness for hatchets, knives, spears, swords, and articles of domestic use, and the tin trade was consequently one of great importance. Tin was found in Devonshire and Cornwall, and a trade in it developed many centuries before the Christian era. The rise of this trade may perhaps be assigned to the time when a knowledge of the manufacture of bronze first came into Britain. That period probably marks an era of conquest, the date of the conquest of this and the adjoining counties by some branch of the great Celtic race.

Although Hampshire has never produced tin, the trade in that metal is the earliest example of commerce connected with its ports which we can trace, which apparently arose before the fourth century B.C., and survived, probably without any very considerable break, until the time of the Venetian traders, who shipped tin at Southampton as late as the fifteenth century.

The articles which have been found in the long barrows in the South of England are stone weapons of the later Stone Age and implements of various kinds, sometimes found broken, and also broken pottery of a very rough kind.

Stone implements have also been found occasionally in round barrows, but not so commonly as articles of bronze manufacture. The round barrows have yielded a variety of pottery, in addition to the funeral urns, such as drinking-cups and food vessels.

Although no thorough examination of the barrows of Hampshire has been made, such as those made in Wilt-shire, yet many barrows have been opened by different explorers in various parts of the county. The late Mr. J. R. Wise, author of 'The New Forest : its History and Scenery,' opened a considerable number on the New Forest heaths, where they are common, and the results of his investigations are detailed in that volume. Many barrows have been opened in the Isle of Wight, and some of their contents are preserved in the Newport Museum. Some round barrows were opened in 1882 on Cranbury Common, near Chandler's Ford Railway Station, and the remains of several of the urns found there are now pre-served in the museum of the Hartley Institution. Barrows have been opened and examined at Arreton Down, Nun-well, Brook Down, Freshwater, Shalcombe Down, Chessel Down, Vittlefield, Bowcombe Down, Brixton Cliff, and Ashey Down, in the Isle of Wight. The articles found in these tumuli were all of the usual general character, the con-tents pointing to the Bronze Age as the probable date of most of the interments in the round tumuli.

On Chessel Down and at Nunwell, in the Isle of Wight, the barrows which were opened were heaped up over cists cut out of the chalk, into which the dead bodies were placed in sitting postures, such characters denoting early inter-ments.

In and near the New Forest funeral urns and implements of stone or bronze have been obtained from barrows at Minstead, Burley, Buttsash, Shirley Holms, Bratley Plain, Fritham Plain, Hilly Accombs, and Sopley. Some of these barrows were opened without finding any urns, only the remains of cremated matter and charcoal. Many of these New Forest tumuli are made of heaps of gravel, the loose nature of which would be more permeable to water than the clay and earth on the chalk downs, and consequently their contents would perhaps not be so well preserved. In many parts of the county the remains of interments have been met with without cinerary urns being found—a circumstance which perhaps points to an early date for such interments, the use of the urn being a refinement in the way of preserving the ashes.

Barrows of both shapes have also been opened on Wonston Down; round tumuli in Hackwood Park, at Broughton, Winchester, Upham, Hoe, near Bishop's Waltham, Weavers Down, Old Winchester Hill, Chalton Down, and elsewhere.

Some of the most remarkable groups of tumuli in Hampshire at the present day occur on Petersfield Heath, where within a short distance nearly twenty are to be seen. A large number exist on Beaulieu Heath, between Beaulieu and the Southampton Water, where as many as twenty-four are found within a distance of about eight miles. On the New Forest heaths, between Beaulieu on the east and Brockenhurst and Lymington on the west, about twenty-four more still remain. Most of these are round barrows.

Hampshire contains some remarkable groups of barrows, seven in number, known locally in each case as 'The Seven Barrows'—such as, the Seven Barrows south of Burghclere, the Seven Barrows west of Stockbridge, and the Seven Barrows of South Tidworth. Before the inclosure of the common lands of Basingstoke, a group of seven barrows also existed on the common south-west of that town.

The inclosure of the Hampshire commons must have led to the obliteration and gradual destruction of many of the burial-places of the prehistoric inhabitants of the county. This is much to be regretted, for these prehistoric burial sites, once obliterated, have gone for ever. Some of them have existed for thousands of years, for the date of the introduction of bronze weapons and tools into Britain, such as have been found in these tumuli, cannot be placed at later than about 1400 or 1200 B.C.*

At the present time the plough is annually passing over both long barrows and round barrows in this county, and in the course of time, unless something is done to arrest this destruction, these monuments of the distinguished dead of prehistoric times will be entirely lost, as certainly as it is known that many others have already been obliterated. This destruction of British barrows did not go on in Hampshire in earlier periods of its history. In the Anglo-Saxon pagan time they appear to have met with all the respect which races of ancient people have so commonly been known to show to the burial-places of their predecessors of another race. In the early Christian centuries in this county they were also respected, for in charters relating to boundaries of land in Hampshire from the eighth to the eleventh century the old barrows are sometimes mentioned as places of 'heathen burial.' These great mounds of earth are far more permanent monuments of the dead than any other forms of sepulchral monuments which have succeeded them. Priories, hospitals, chantries, and other institutions of beneficial use to the people, established in Hampshire to commemorate their founders' piety, or their great and noble deeds in war or peace, many centuries after the barrows were raised to mark the burial-places of the unrecorded names of British chieftains, have long since passed away, or been so transformed and reorganized that their original purposes are only recognised by antiquaries; but some hundreds of these monuments of prehistoric times in this county still remain, although we cannot now read their long-forgotten stories.

The British barrows of Hampshire were apparently selected in some instances, on account of their indestructi-

* Dr. J. Evans : 'Ancient Bronze Implements,' p. 473.

bility, during the early centuries of its history, to be its landmarks—in some places of the shire, as at Baughurst Barrow in the north of the county, Knap Barrow on Rockbourn Down in the south-west, and the barrow on Long Hill, South Tidworth, in the north-west ; in other places of the hundred, as at Popham Beacon ; and in other places of the original manors, as in the cases of the barrow at the corner of the parishes of Hursley, Farley Chamberlain, and Sparsholt, the Millbarrows at the boundary between Cheriton and Corhampton, and the tumulus near Leckford Hut, close to the eastern boundary of the parish of Leckford.

It is to be regretted that the explorations of such Hampshire tumuli as have been opened were not conducted on some general scientific system, such as was the case in Wiltshire ; but sufficiently accurate observations have been made in Hampshire to show that the contents of the tumuli in this county point to the same general conclusion as prevails elsewhere—namely, that the long barrows are the sepulchres of the Neolithic people, a race with long and comparatively narrow skulls, and that the round barrows are the sepulchres of their successors, a race with broad and comparatively round skulls.

These distinctions of ancient races of men are found to prevail on the Continent, as well as in Britain. So many conquests have passed over Western Europe, and so many ancient races have been replaced by their conquerors in various parts of it, that there is but one small race in Europe at the present day whose cranial characteristics correspond with those who lived in Britain, and probably also occupied the whole of Western Gaul, during the Neolithic period, and this is the Basque race of Southern France and parts of Northern Spain. These people are a small race of men of dark hair, having long, narrow skulls, corresponding to the skulls of the ancient Neolithic people. From these circumstances, and from peculiarities in their language, it is believed that the Basques are descended from the same ancient stock as the Neolithic race, who have consequently been named the ancient Iberians.

The more we study the prehistoric antiquities of Hampshire, the more convincing becomes the chain of reasoning which points to a very great antiquity for the date of the settlement in this part of England of the long-skulled people of the later Stone Age. When Britain last arose from the sea, or emerged from that Glacial Drift period which perhaps followed its previous occupation by Palæo-lithic man, the surface of the land in Hampshire must have resembled its general outline at present. Its hills must have been a little higher, its valleys not quite so deep, and its coast-line a little further out in the English Channel. Since that time rain, rivers, and floods, which have been modifying its surface, have left their furrows on its face, and the marks of old age upon its landscape. These gradual changes have been going on during thousands of years—how many we cannot say—since the men of the later Stone Age first took up their quarters here.

How many centuries of human life and settlement are unrecorded in this county before the time of the Greek traders we cannot say, any more than we can say how many centuries passed over the native races of America before the time of Columbus. The settlements in Hampshire all appear to have come from across the Channel. The Iberians were followed by a great Celtic immigration, which pushed the long-skulled race further inland, or assimilated the remnants of that race in their own, as the great Celtic invasion of Gaul did the same there. The mouth of the Loire in the time of Pytheas was the boundary of the Iberian or Aquitanian population, and the limit southwards of the Celtic advance. These Aquitanian people were ultimately driven into the regions of the Pyrenees, on both sides of which we find their descendants, the Basques, at the present day.

The ancient custom of burying the dead in a sitting posture in cists, or in dolmens made of flat stones placed on others, set vertically, can be traced from England, through France and Spain, to North Africa, in parts of which countries many hundreds of such sepulchres still remain. Some of the races of North Africa at the present time, such as the people living near the Gulf of Cabes, have also similar cranial characters to those of the ancient people buried in long barrows and dolmens in England, so that it is probable that the people who constructed these burial-places were descended from the same primitive stock as the ancient Iberic or Neolithic race.

The Hampshire barrows and tumuli have afforded some evidence that the prehistoric people who made them believed in a future existence. The belief in a spirit world is perhaps the oldest of all beliefs, and exists among races in all stages of civilization in various parts of the world at the present day.

The barrows and tumuli of this and the adjacent counties have in numerous instances been found to contain fragments of broken pottery and other articles. A widely-spread idea appears to have prevailed in prehistoric time in Britain, similar to that which prevails among many semi-civilized tribes at the present day—that when man goes to the spirit world it will be useful to him for his family or clan to send with him what may be termed the spirit of the articles which he found useful in his life here; and that if his drinking-cups, food vessels, and weapons are buried with him, the spirit or essence of these articles will go with him to the unseen world. This belief may be the explanation of the custom of burying such articles with the dead, and of breaking them to set the spirit of them free. Broken pottery and broken weapons have been found in Hampshire, either in the barrows or in such situations as make it probable they have been brought to the surface through the destruction of such barrows by modern agricultural operations.

At a later time, if not during the Neolithic period itself, the remains of the dead were often deposited on the watersheds or near to water sources, and in some of these burial sites broken pottery has been found. Such customs were probably widely spread throughout the ancient world, and may be similar to those which are referred to in Ecclesiasticus : 'Or ever the silver cord be loosed, or the golden bowl be broken, or the pitcher be broken at the fountain, or the wheel be broken at the cistern, then shall the dust return to the earth as it was, and the spirit shall return unto God who gave it.'

CHAPTER II.

THE FIRST CELTIC CONQUEST.

THE settlement of the Celts in Hampshire, whatever the precise date of that event may have been, was marked by the introduction of the knowledge and use of bronze into this part of England. The conquest of the old Iberic people was probably not effected all at once. Successive settlements were probably made by the invaders on the coast, as the increase of the Celtic population on the opposite side of the Channel made it necessary for some of that race to seek for new homes across the sea. The invaders probably arrived in Hampshire by crossing the Channel at its narrowest part and sailing westward along the coasts of Kent and Sussex, which was also probably the route by which the long-headed Neolithic people had arrived ages before. This was certainly the route also along which subsequent invasions took place.

With the arrival of the Celts we are able to unravel the threads of prehistoric inquiry better than in the preceding ages. We have still remaining in Hampshire some few place-names chiefly relating to water sources, which must in all probability be ascribed to the language of the Iberic people, but we have a large number of such place-names which are undoubtedly of Celtic origin. We have local customs still remaining, or which have only ceased to exist within the last few centuries, which may have had their origin among the Iberians, but which certainly must be as old as the time of the Celts. We have camps and other defensive earthworks still remaining in Hampshire, some of which were probably constructed by its ancient Iberic inhabitants, seeing that flint implements and abundance of flint flakes have been found within them, and which probably were the strongholds of the land before the Celtic invasion, but which were certainly adopted subsequently by the Celts as their own castles of refuge. Among the folklore and legends of Hampshire there are some traditions which may have had their origin in the time of the Iberians, but which cannot be of less antiquity than the time of their Celtic conquerors. The traces of ancient Celtic mythology which may be recognised in Hampshire and the neighbouring counties at the present day may, in part at least, have been derived by the Celts from their predecessors in this part of England. Even race characteristics after thousands of years may occasionally show themselves in individuals, and the people of Hampshire, who are mainly of West Saxon descent, must have derived a considerable admixture from the Celtic race, which centuries before was probably considerably blended with the more ancient Iberic people. The survival of some few place-names and customs, and the variations in cranial and other race characteristics which may still be recognised, all point to the probability of this fusion of races.

The Iberic people were probably nomadic in their habits, wandering over the downlands with their herds of cattle and flocks of goats, while the Celts were a typical branch of the great Aryan race, who tilled the land, and consequently were more stationary. With the introduction of bronze hatchets the Celtic inhabitants of Hampshire would be able to begin the systematic clearings in its primeval forests, an undertaking probably beyond the power of the Iberians, who had nothing but stone axes, very liable to fracture in such a work. Such clearings as the Neolithic people were obliged to make they probably effected by burning the trees.

The bronze tools and weapons which have been found in Hampshire comprise examples both of the earlier and later ages of bronze manufacture in this country.   Daggers, plain wedge-shaped axes, and other articles which mark the early part of the Bronze Age, and swords, spears, palstraves, and socketed celts which mark the later part of the period, have been found.

Such bronze articles have been discovered together in hoards on Arreton Down, in the Isle of Wight, at Blackmoor, near Selborne, at Hinton, near Christchurch, and in Woolmer Forest.   Implements and weapons of various kinds have also been found on Ashey Down, in the Isle of Wight, at Bere Hill, near Andover, Liss, near Petersfield (where bracelets were discovered with bronze weapons), in parts of the New Forest (where hatchet-heads have been met with), on Rockbourn Down, at Ropley, Bishopstoke, Southampton, St. Denys, Tachbury, near Eling, and other places.

The number of bronze tools, weapons, and domestic articles used by the Celts in Hampshire during the Bronze Age cannot be estimated by the number which have been found and recorded since the beginning of the present century, or since the time when such antiquities began to be preserved.   Previously, no doubt, ancient articles of bronze found from time to time during many centuries commonly went into the melting-pot.   After the general disuse of bronze for tools and weapons, it was used for many centuries for various artistic and useful purposes, and there must consequently have been a considerable demand for this metallic alloy in the arts and in various trades during the Middle Ages.   Whenever ancient bronze articles of long-forgotten shapes and uses were found, such articles would probably be regarded as of a certain value, like old copper articles at the present day.

The introduction of the use of bronze into Britain having been in all probability the result of the Celtic conquest, we may conclude that, as this conquest proceeded from the south towards the north of the island, bronze was used in Hampshire at as early a date as in any part of Britain. Dr. John Evans has assigned the date for the beginning of the Bronze Age in Britain at about 1200 or 1400 B.C. He has arrived at this conclusion from historical references to the use of bronze by the people of Gaul and other parts of Europe, by the ancient nations settled on the shores of the Mediterranean Sea, and many other considerations in relation to ancient trade routes, and the shapes and decorations on various articles of bronze found in Britain compared with similar articles found in other countries.

At certain seasons of the year, at least, some of the Neolithic people appear to have frequented the coast and the shores of Southampton Water for fishing purposes, for their polished stone weapons have been found in these situations. The migrations of these people were determined by food supplies, and it is certain that the early settlements of the Celts in Hampshire were influenced by similar considerations. The valleys through which the chief streams flow, their dry upper continuations, and the lower slopes of the hills which form the watersheds, show signs at the present day that they were the parts of the county which were first occupied by a settled agricultural race.

The proofs of such early occupation consist of the earthworks, which were constructed to serve as castles of refuge for the tribes or clans around them, and in the fact that it is in these valleys and on the lower slopes of the hills that such articles of bronze as have been found apart from the burial sites have been picked up.

There are in Hampshire at the present day the remains of more than forty prehistoric defensive earthworks.

It is not possible, within the limits of a volume such as this, to describe these old Celtic fortifications in detail. They are of various kinds and shapes, and, where they inclose areas and form the so-called camps, they are of widely different dimensions. Most of them are hill-fortresses, either situated on the tops of considerable hills, or on rising ground conveniently near to the districts which they were intended to protect. There are also marsh and peninsular fortresses, and in the New Forest one, if not more, examples of insular mound refuges, as a defence for one or more small communities, exist in bogs. In one case, a mound, known as Black Bar, at Lynwood, is situated in what was formerly a small lake, and which might easily be reconverted into a lake at the present day.

The surroundings of the ancient Celtic earthworks in Hampshire at the present day help us to arrive at a right conclusion as to the purposes they were intended to serve. The forests which existed near them have for the most part passed away, but the variations in hill and dale which we see now are the same, and the geological conditions connected with the dry chalk hills, or with the chalk streams and the alluvial meadow-land through which they flow, are the same as in prehistoric time. As we stand within the area of any one of these entrenched inclosures, and consider the probable purposes it was intended to serve, the natural features of the country in which it was placed, and the geological circumstances connected with these surroundings, will be found to be very important considerations. These camps could scarcely have been permanently inhabited sites, for very few traces of dwellings or articles of common domestic use, such as have been found abundantly elsewhere, have been found within them. They could not have been constructed by passing bodies of armed men, for the labour involved would have been far too great for a passing shelter.

There is but one other object, so far as I can see, for which they could have been constructed, that is, as strongholds of defence, or places of refuge in case of sudden attack, for the people who lived near them. If this was the purpose of their construction, then these entrenched areas must have had a distinct reference to the number of

people required for their defence, and also to the number of
people and the head of cattle they were intended to shelter.
We can scarcely think that any old Celtic community
would construct a defensive earthwork, such as one of these
Hampshire camps, larger than their requirements for
shelter, or larger than their power of defence. Otherwise
such a large camp would be a source of weakness to
the people attacked, instead of a tower of strength. From
such considerations we may perhaps draw some fairly
correct inferences as to the relative number of people in
parts of Hampshire in the time of the Celts. Early writers
tell us that Britain was a populous country, and the
evidence which remains in this southern county points to
the conclusion that during the time of the Celts a large
population must have lived in the valleys and such other
cleared parts of the forest-lands of Hampshire as contain
these defensive earthworks within reach of their villages
and homesteads.

The largest Hampshire camps are placed where large
open areas must have existed, and the smallest of them are
in situations from which we can see even at the present day
they could have had no great clearings near them, and
documentary evidence concerning the extent of the ancient
forests confirms this. The smallest of the earthworks which
remain are but forest forts, while the largest are on some of
the highest positions of the chalk hills, with extensive areas
of downland, and generally also of meadow-land, near
them. Water-supply for the hill-fortresses must have
been an important consideration. I have only met with a
few instances of wells, or their remains, within the British
camps of Hampshire, such as occur at Ashley, at Wood-
garston, and Bury Hill, near Andover. In other cases, the
earthworks on the hills, especially on the highest hills,
were probably supplied with water, as flocks of sheep are
commonly watered on these hills at the present day, by the
construction and use of dew-ponds. This primitive method
of collecting water on the chalk hills of Southern England

is probably a survival of a practice which has been handed down from age to age from the time of the Celts. A pond is made and puddled, or made water-tight with clay carefully placed round its sides. It is then found that, if the situation of the pond is carefully chosen, sufficient water will accumulate in it, from the rain and evening mists which hang over the hills, for the requirements of flocks of sheep. Many of the dew-ponds on the Hampshire hills are never dry.

The largest of the old British earthworks of Hampshire is Walbury, at the north-western corner of the county, half of it being in this county and half in Berkshire. It overlooks the extensive valley of the Kennet, and is constructed on the high ridge of chalk down between this valley on the north and the dry valley of Combe and Netherton on the south. It has a natural scarp as a defence on three sides. Its dimensions are 550 yards from north to south, and 783 yards between the two gates, or openings from east to west. Its area has been cultivated as arable land, but has lately been left in the condition of waste, or rough downland. It is covered with an immense quantity of flints, such as would form an inexhaustible source of material for sling-stones and flint weapons. Stone implements of various kinds, such as neatly-trimmed spear-heads, cores, flakes, and arrow-tips, have been found within its area, and other implements of the later Stone Age have been found in parts of the country within easy reach of it, both in the Kennet Valley and on the chalk downs and valleys on the south, thus leaving no doubt that the district was occupied during the later Stone Age. This does not necessarily prove that the earthwork itself was made during that period, for flint-flakes and the cores from which they were struck have been found on many of the hill sites of Hampshire, where no traces of old British earthworks have been discovered; but it shows that the Neolithic people frequented this site, chipped some of their flint tools and weapons here, and made use of the site perhaps for defensive purposes, on account of its commanding position. Whether these earlier people threw up any earthen defences here or not, it is certain that the Celts used it, for it is constructed with an inner bank and an outer ditch, and the line of defence follows the natural line of the hill in the way which is so characteristic of Celtic fortifications. It contains within its area, or just outside its ditch, several dew-ponds at the present day, and it would have formed a refuge in case of attack for many hundreds of men and women and their cattle.

General Pitt Rivers, in his investigation of Cissbury Camp, in Sussex, has computed the probable number of men such a camp would require for its defence. He has taken the lowest computation according to modern warfare —viz., two men for every yard of parapet, and one-third more as a reserve. Under such a calculation, as Walbury has about 2,100 yards of parapet, it would require a force of 5,600 men to garrison it; and if we allow that the women would have helped in its defence, it still is reasonable to suppose that several thousands of men would have been assembled here for defensive purposes, when their homes within reach of this great fortress were threatened. Such considerations concerning the people within reach of this camp of refuge show that there must have been a large Celtic population in parts of Hampshire and the neighbouring counties. When we compare the sizes of similar earthworks in different parts of the county, and survey the extent of open country within reach of each, we are able to draw some approximately correct conclusions concerning the relative density of the population of Hampshire in the Celtic period. A good example of this kind will be obtained by comparing the extent of the fortress on St. Catherine's Hill, near Winchester, with that of Walbury. The earthwork on this hill is a large camp, but not so large as Walbury. It has more than a thousand yards of parapet, and, according to General Pitt Rivers' calculation, based on considerations of modern warfare, it would require 3,300

men for its full defence. If we allow a smaller number
than this, and consider that some of the women would help
in various ways in its defence, we can scarcely place the
force of men necessary to hold it against an enemy at less
than 2,000.

I think that a Celtic tribe able to find 2,000 or
3,000 men for the defence of St. Catherine's Hill could
have found subsistence for themselves and their families in
the Itchen Valley north and south of this fortress, and
within reach of its defences in case of need. I think the
Celtic tribe which lived around Walbury was greater
than that which lived in the Itchen Valley, round St.
Catherine's Hill, from considerations connected with the
size of the camp, and also from considerations of food-
supply ; for the contracted valley of the Itchen, near St.
Catherine's Hill, could scarcely have supported so large a
population as the more extensive Kennet Valley and the
open country round Walbury.

Perhaps the best example of a British camp in Hampshire, conveniently situated as the stronghold for its district,
is that of Old Winchester Hill, in the valley of the Meon.
This is the only earthwork in the district, and the upper
part of the valley which it overlooks has a winding course
from East Meon to Droxford. The stream first flows
north, then west, south-west, and south, and the earthwork
known as Old Winchester is conveniently placed on the
highest and strongest position in the district—650 feet
above the sea—and, owing to the winding of the valley,
about equidistant from different parts of it on the east,
north, west, and south-west. This was one of the parts of
Hampshire subsequently occupied by the Jutes after the
conquest of the country by their allies the West Saxons.
Old Winchester, in the upper part of this valley, was clearly
the stronghold of the British tribe that preceded the Jutes.
Its ramparts are about 1,000 yards in length, and no doubt,
like the ramparts of the other Celtic fortresses, were
stockaded for the purpose of strengthening the defences.

If we apply the same lowest modern computation to this ancient fortification, we shall find it would require a force of 2,666 men for its defence. From a careful survey of this part of Hampshire, I have no doubt that this valley could have supported a tribe sufficiently numerous to muster 2,000 men for the defence of this fortress.

In some instances in Hampshire the Celts formed their castles of refuge by fortifying peninsular sites, such as that at Hengistbury and at Bransbury. This latter, at the junction of the Micheldever stream with the Test, is a fortification of much interest, inclosing a considerable area by a single entrenchment, consisting of a deep outer ditch and an inner bank thrown up from marsh to marsh ; and as we may consider that the marshes of the Test and its tributary stream were probably impassable in the early Celtic period, there must have been a population sufficiently numerous at least to have been able to defend these ramparts.

In some parts of this county we have unmistakable traces of communal arable fields close to the old British earthworks, probably also close to the sites of old British villages, and remote from the nearest existing villages. In one instance at least the hill fortress for the defence of the district appears to have been preserved for defensive purposes from the Celtic period to the early Anglo-Saxon time —viz., that of Burghclere, anciently Boroughclere, a place which derived its name from one or both of the old British camps, on high hills on either side of the narrow valley which forms the only natural pass for many miles from the Berkshire country into the north of Hampshire, and which was a place where toll was taken as late as the date of the Domesday Survey. The existence of the Burghclere earthworks, the only large camps between Silchester and Walbury, proves, I think, that the clearing in this part of the great northern forest of Hampshire round these earthworks, whether wholly natural or partly artificial, is as old as the time of the Celts, and that a population which we may estimate by the size of the earthworks lived within reach of them. On several sides of these camps the remains of many small communal fields may still be traced on the hill slopes, and in one of the valleys much black earth, resting on chalk, and probably derived from habitations here, may be seen close to the outlines of the ancient communal fields. Close here also, on the south, are the well-known Seven Barrows of North Hampshire. One of the most ancient roads in the county also leads from these camps direct to Walbury Camp, in the north-west of the county.

There are many traces of the Celts to be found in Hampshire in addition to the remains of their earthworks. There are traces of their religion and customs, of their villages, of their communal life, of their trade and industries, of the form of their small houses or huts, of their agricultural operations, of the roads and fords they used, of their language, and of the coins they struck during the centuries immediately preceding the Roman occupation. The life of the Celts in Hampshire during the many centuries they remained in occupation of the land was probably marked by frequent wars among themselves, during which the clans invaded the territories of other clans, according to a system of warfare very much like that which prevails at present among some of the tribal people of Africa. These wars were often raids by one clan on another, brought about probably by an increase in their numbers and their food requirements. When food necessities were pressing among the people of any clan, a cattle-raiding expedition into the territory of a neighbouring clan, in such a country as Hampshire, on the other side of the forest-land, which divided the tribal settlements in one valley from those of another, would probably be the means adopted for averting famine; and during such raids other commodities, as well as cattle, were no doubt carried off. The Celtic earthworks of Hampshire appear in part to have been designed to protect the people living round them from such raids, for these camps were evidently places of refuge for the cattle as well as for their owners.

CHAPTER III.

THE CONQUEST AND SETTLEMENT OF THE BELGÆ.

THE first Celtic conquest was followed some centuries later—how many we cannot say—by a second invasion from the Continent of a race of people also descended in part from the primitive Celtic stock, and known as the Belgæ. They were a Celtic-speaking people, descended either from a fusion of the Gauls with Iberians, or from a fusion of race between the Gauls of what is now Belgium with northern tribes of dolico-cephalic or long-headed people. The Belgæ are believed to have been a tall and rather long-skulled race, a character which would be sufficient to distinguish them from the earlier Celtic tribes of Britain, who were marked by broad skulls. This second invasion and conquest of the country, which extends from Kent to Somerset, by the Belgæ, is one which is recorded in history.

They appear to have been impelled forwards to their conquests in Britain by a pressure of population among themselves, or advancing hordes of enemies behind them on the Continent. The name of the race survives in the modern name of Belgium, and an ethnological frontier survives to the present day in their original Continental home, where marked racial differences can be detected between the Flemish people and their neighbours the Walloons.

In considering the condition of Hampshire in Celtic times, it is necessary to keep in mind this second Celtic immigration ; otherwise we shall fail to understand why we find among the surviving Celtic place-names of the county two distinct varieties of Celtic words. I have already mentioned that we find in the round tumuli examples of two kinds of sepulture, and in some instances both examples in the same tumulus, the oldest at the bottom—viz., that of burial of the body in a contracted position—and above this the later form of cremation of the body, and the interment of the ashes in the mound, either in a rudely-made cist or in an urn.

At some time, therefore, during the Celtic period in Hampshire, a change in the burial custom of the race, from contracted inhumation to cremation, occurred. This widely-spread custom of cremating the dead is shown in the Celtic sepulchres of Hampshire at the present day, not only by the occurrence of burnt human remains in the barrows, but by similar traces of cremation in small circular pits, which are constantly being brought to light in this county by agricultural operations, and by excavations for building sites, for chalk-pits, railway-cuttings, and other purposes.

The Belgic invasion occurred several centuries before the Christian era. It happened early enough for the whole Celtic people of Hampshire and the adjoining counties to have become blended into one of the most powerful of the tribes of Britain before the time of the Romans. This Belgic invasion may also have been the means by which a knowledge of the art of the metallurgy of iron was introduced into the southern parts of England, after which the use of bronze for weapons and implements of warfare and peace became gradually superseded. It is interesting to trace the conquests of the Belgæ from an iron-producing country in Belgium and North-Western Gaul into Kent, Sussex, and Hampshire, all of which produced iron ore in sufficient quantity in Cæsar's time and long afterwards to supply the native forges, the sites of which can still be identified. Cæsar tells us that 'iron is produced in the maritime parts of Britain, but the quantity of it is small '—a statement which the geology of Hampshire and its border counties at the present day fully confirms. It must, indeed, have been more abundant in the time of the Celts than at present, for in Hampshire it commonly occurs as nodular masses of clay ironstone in the Tertiary beds; and in that period there must have been an accumulation of lumps of such ironstone lying on the surface of the ground, and especially on the shores of the Solent, washed out of the Tertiary beds by the denuding forces of nature. It is less than a century since the last of the old iron forges on the shores of the Solent ceased its operation, and even now lumps of ironstone rich in the metal are gathered from the waste of the cliffs, and occasionally sent for smelting purposes to South Wales.

If the manufacture of iron was not introduced into Hampshire on the arrival of the Belgæ, it is certain that it followed soon afterwards. A race from the iron-producing part of Gaul would not long remain dependent on foreign importation for supplies of iron while the native ore lay at their feet.

We do not find in Hampshire, or in any other parts of England, the remains of the early weapons and implements of iron, as we find those of stone or bronze, for iron rapidly oxidizes and passes into the condition of peroxide, in which state it does not differ from the abundance of peroxide of iron with which the clays, loams, and sandstones of this county are stained.

The name Belgæ, which has come down to us from remote antiquity, is perhaps one which had some reference to their funeral customs. The Belgæ appear to have reverenced fire as part of their religion, as many tribes do at the present day, and as many more are recorded to have done in ancient time. The worshippers of Baal will at once occur to the reader as an example. Baal-worship was the sun and fire worship of Eastern countries, and the name Belgæ was perhaps understood by the Anglo-Saxons in the same sense. 'Bæl' in Anglo-Saxon is a funeral-pile,

'bælstede' a funeral-pile place, and 'bælwudu' the wood of
a funeral-pile. We find the remains of the funeral-piles of
the Belgæ in all parts of Hampshire, and we find in the very
ancient custom, which has only within a century or two
become extinct in this county, of lighting fires at midsummer, and in other customs of the Middle Ages which can be
clearly traced, indications that the ancient inhabitants of
Hampshire paid reverence to the sun.

Tacitus says that 'the Belgæ reared no great laboured
monuments to their dead. They burnt the bodies of their
chiefs with fire, and they sacrificed horses.' Horses' teeth
have been obtained from places of interment at Nursling,
Otterbourn, and elsewhere, and they have been found
among the remains of cremation in the round barrows in
other parts of the county. Tacitus, in mentioning monuments, must have meant sculptured stones or other memorials, and probably did not regard the tumulus so
commonly reared over the burial site as a monument in
this sense. In any case the tumuli were reared, and some
hundreds of them after the lapse of thousands of years still
remain to mark the burial sites of the chiefs of the Belgæ
or of their Celtic predecessors.

Cæsar tells us that the Belgæ worshipped the sun, moon
and fire, and Tacitus says that they also worshipped
Hertha, or their mother-earth, by which he must, I think ﹍
have meant to include springs and fountains issuing from
the earth and giving fertility to the land. The traces we
find of the religion of the Belgæ in Hampshire confirm
the statements of these ancient historians. Close to the
ancient border of Hampshire, which at one time appears to
have included Amesbury, is Stonehenge, the most remarkable structure connected with the worship of the sun in
Britain. Whether it was built by the Belgæ or the Celts
of the earlier immigration is of little consequence to our
present consideration. It was certainly reverenced by the
Belgæ. The barrows which lie so thickly around it have
afforded unmistakable evidence of the later Celtic, *i.e.*, the

Belgic interments, and we know that certain outlying stones at Stonehenge point to the positions of the sun at sunrise and sunset, not only at the summer and winter solstices, but if tangential lines be drawn to such stones from the outer circle, instead of from the central dolmen, the directions of the sunrise at the beginning of May and November may also be indicated. These four seasons were the sacred times of the Celtic year. The Yule-time of antiquity has survived in the Christian mid-winter festival. The midsummer fires, which have ceased to be lighted in Hampshire, are still customary in Ireland. Mid-summer games existed in this county as late as last century. The May festivities have lasted down to modern time, and the survival of one maypole in Hampshire at the present day shows that the ancient May games were long continued. All Hallows' Night also is still spoken of by the peasantry in parts of Hampshire with all that reverence and respect which comes from ancient traditional usage, and which tends to show that there was probably a continuous commemoration of ancestors at the beginning of November from the Celtic pagan time until the Christian form of this commemorative festival of the dead had become established.

Stonehenge must, therefore, be regarded as an elaborate symbol of the religious sentiments of the Celtic race in Britain, and especially of the Belgæ of the later Celtic period, who perhaps inherited their religious customs not only from the forefathers of their race, but partly from the older Iberic stock both on the Continent and in Britain. As these people expressed their deep religious conviction by such an elaborate symbolic structure as that of Stonehenge, we can feel no surprise if we should discover in some other remains of the race other symbolic traces of their religion. These traces, I think, we may find in Hampshire in regard to some of the places they selected for burial sites.

Many of the barrows are on the watersheds. A good

example is that at Crawley Clump, where you may stand
near the tumuli there, and, looking north and south, see
that the site is on high ground, close to the dividing line of
the water-drainage between two branches of the Test.

In his lectures on ' The Origin and Growth of Religion,'
Rhys tells us that ' the Celts of the British Isles had
sacred mounds, which were known as the gods' mounds,
the god being designated the chief of the mound,' and I
think there can be no doubt that some of the mounds
which remain in Hampshire were of this character.

The evidence pointing to a fusion of part of the Celtic
population of Hampshire with their Saxon conquerors is
so strong that we are justified in alluding to it in connection with the Celtic survivals concerning the early
mounds.   A number of ancient churches in Hampshire are
built upon artificial mounds.   One of these at Corhampton
has a Saxon church on the mound.   The mound at Burton,
which was flattened, had a church upon it dedicated to
St. Martin, a Gaulish saint, and was known at St. Martin's
Hill.   Higher up the Avon a mound may be seen, on
which the church of Sopley stands.   Another example
is that of Cheriton, which has an artificial mound occupying
the greater part of the present churchyard.   Very near the
site of this mound we find some of the most remarkable of
the permanent springs of this branch of the Itchen, which
circumstance is an additional argument in favour of its
Celtic origin.   The Saxons appear to have utilized sacred
Celtic mounds for Christian purposes.   It is, of course,
possible that these mounds were first adapted to Christian
uses by the early British Christians.   These sacred mound-
sites of the Celts certainly appear to have had a continuous
reverence paid to them down to the time of the conversion
of the Saxons, and we know that the early Christian mis-
sionaries in England were instructed to adopt the sacred
pagan places as sites for Christian temples, and to substi-
tute Christian festivals for those of pagan origin.

The Celts who occupied Hampshire have left behind

them some remains of their language. To this day many of the water-names in the county—the names of springs, rivers, ponds and lakes—have been derived from the names which the prehistoric races gave them. These words may be said to speak to us in the language of two, if not more, of the races or tribes of Hampshire previous to the Roman occupation. The last settlers from the Continent before the conquest by the Romans, *i.e.*, the Belgæ, have, as might be expected, left a larger number of place-names behind them than the earlier Celts who were their predecessors, and who are believed to have spoken a language somewhat like the Gaelic. The earlier Celts have consequently been called Goidels, or Gaels, while the Belgæ are considered by Rhys and others to have been Brythons in speech, the linguistic ancestors of the Cymri, or Welsh. Welsh may be considered to be a language which is a detritus from the ancient Celtic tongues spoken in Hampshire and other parts of our country. We must not expect, therefore, to find ancient place-names in Hampshire which are precisely the same as existing Cymric place-names in Wales. The same considerations apply to those names which more resemble the Gaelic languages of Scotland and Ireland at the present day than the language of Wales. As successive races of men occupied Hampshire, and after a certain number of centuries were succeeded by other races, a blending of their languages must have taken place, as well as a blending of the races themselves. As we may well believe that some of the blood of the old Iberic race was blended with the blood of the Goidelic or earlier Celtic race, and this with that of the Belgæ, so we may expect that part of the language of the earlier races became blended with and incorporated into that of the latter. Philologists tell us that traces of the old Iberic speech can be detected in the Gaelic language, and as the Gaels, or Goidels, were their immediate successors in Hampshire and the adjoining counties, this is what we should naturally expect. This fusion of language, as regards the place-names of Hampshire, was not confined only to the prehistoric races of the county, but the same transmission of words and blending of place-names took place between the Romano-British or post Romano-Celtic people, and their West Saxon conquerors.

The old Gaelic or Irish word *lin*, a lake or marsh, occurs in the place-names Linwood, Lyndhurst (anciently Lin-hest), Dublin, Lin Brook, Linford, Lyne's Copse, Linstead, and in the name London, of which Hampshire has about twelve small places so called. Of other Gaelic words—

Cor, round hill, occurs in Corhampton,

Lann, a house, in Lainston ; *larrock*, a house site, in Laverstoke (anciently Lavroch-stoke),

Derry, a wood, in Derry Copse,

Knock, a hill, in Knock Wood, Kitnox, and Noclei (the Domesday name of Nutley),

Lochan, a lake, in Lockerley, Lockerwood, Locks Lake, Lockswood, and Lockhams,

An, or *ean*, a spring, in Andover, Andwell, Ampfield (anciently Anfield), Anmore, Anbury, Terstan (the ancient name of the Test), and Icenan (the ancient name of the Itchen),

Eannagh, a marsh, in the ancient Domesday name of Anna,

Bun, the bottom or end, in Beckton Bunny and Chewton Bunny, in Christchurch Bay,

Liss, a fort, in Liss, and probably Lusborough, and

Rine, a watercourse, in Rinewede, the Domesday name of Ringwood, corresponding to Rinawade, an ancient ferry in Ireland.

The Cymric word *pen*, a hill or head, occurs in Penton, Pennington, Peniton, Penley, Pens, and Penwood.

Gwy, or *wy*, water, occurs in Wyeford, the ancient name Pharwy, or Pharwyse, Wymering, and the rivers Wey, of which Hampshire has two. Of other Cymric words—

Ac and *ach*, a spring or water-source name, occurs in Ashe, Ashley, Ashlet, Ashbridge, Ashford, Ashdell, Ashfield, Ashley Head, Ashholt, Ashford Hill, Andlers' Ash, Shootash, Ashes Bridge, all at the sources of springs, or water places.

Ox, ex, ax, other syllabic water-names, occur in Oxney, Oxenbourn, Oxlease, Oxey Marsh, Exbury, and Axford.

Wysg, another water-name, occurs in Isington, Ismans, Isnage, and perhaps in Tisted, anciently Isted or Ystede,

Ouse, in Owlesbury (locally Usselbury), Hurstbourn (locally pronounced Husbourn and Husselborne in the fourteenth century), and

Ar and *yar,* in Harbridge, Yarmouth, and the Yar rivers, of which two exist in the Isle of Wight.

Cwm, a hollow between hills, occurs in the Hampshire place-names Combe (in the Isle of Wight), Combe (in the north-west of the county), Chilcombe, Compton, the Combes, Combe Copse, Compton (near King's Somborne), Combe Farm (Alresford), Combe Bottom (Ashley), Combe (East Meon), Cockscombs Hill, Combe Wood, Stancombe, Nettlecombe, Kitcombe, and Testcombe.

Rhyd, a ford, occurs in the names Rudley at Soberton and Rudley at Southwick, and

Rhuime, a marsh, in Romsey, Rumbridge, and Rumseys Hursley, marked on the manorial map of 1588 preserved at Hursley.

Man, a district, occurs in Mansbridge, Manhode (east of Hayling Island, submerged since the Middle Ages), and perhaps also in Manydown.

The Celtic word *ache* has probably become sounded as *etch* under Teutonic use, as in Germany, or *itch* as in the Hampshire names of Itchen, Itchingswell, Itchell, Tichborne, Titchfield, Itchall, and Ytene (pronounced Ychene), the ancient name for the district of the New Forest.

Cuid, a wood, appears in Quidhampton.

Dur, water, occurs in Durley, Esteddurle and Westedurle (the ancient names of East and West Tytherley), Dur Wood, and Durdens.

Dufr, a word of similar significance, occurs under the

form of *dover*, or *dever*, as in Andover, Candover, Michel-dever, the Dover (St. Helen's), and the Dover (Ryde).

Both the Celtic words *dur* and *dover* may, however, have been incorporated into the ancient Celtic language spoken in this county from an earlier source. The word *ur*, or *our*, appears to be a Basque word for water, as in the name of the river Adour, in the Basque country of Southern France, and the names Andover, Candover, and Micheldever occur in ancient documents as Andeure, Candeure, and Michel-deure. These place-names, therefore, and others in *dur*, may have been derived by the Celts from the old Iberic tongue. Other names derived apparently from the same source occur in Overton (anciently Ouerton), the river Oure, Ower, the river Stour, Westover, and Woodcot Dower.

The Celtic word *ock* occurs in Ocknell Pond, Hockless Hole (Burghclere), and Ockhangre (now Oakhanger).

The Celtic *pwl*, a pool, occurs in Poleshole, Pollack, Pol-hampton, Paultons, Paulsgrove, Polsden, Poland, Red Poles' Pond, and Poulner.

CHAPTER IV.

THE COMING OF THE ROMANS.

THE invasions of Julius Cæsar did not affect Hampshire. Whether the Belgæ marched to the assistance of their neighbours along the valley of the Thames and in Kent, in withstanding the Roman advance under Cæsar, is uncertain ; but it is known that he did not come into this county. The Roman invasion of this county took place about the year A.D. 43, under Aulus Plautius, whom the Emperor Claudius had sent from Gaul to subdue the island, and who subjugated a great part of Southern Britain. The landing-place of the Roman General is uncertain, but it has been assigned by some to the neighbourhood of Southampton—among others, by Dr. Hübner,* who has given much attention to the subject. It appears certain that Aulus Plautius did not land on the same part of the coast as Cæsar had landed a century earlier. The topography of the campaign indicates that the Roman army made its way to some higher part of the Thames rather than the lower tidal estuary, and, after a series of engagements, moved down the Thames Valley and drove the British army over the tidal part of the river. As the great forest of Anderida, almost an impenetrable area for an army, stretched from the open chalk downs of Kent to the open chalk downs of Hampshire, it appears probable that

* See Article by Hübner, 'Das Romische Heer in Britannien, Hermes xvi., p. 527 ; and 'Celtic Britain,' by J. Rhys, p. 76.

the estuary of Southampton Water was chosen by the
Roman General for his landing-place, and that this invasion
of the country took place on the same lines of advance
along the coast as those which marked the conquest of
the Celts and the Belgæ centuries before. With Aulus
Plautius came Vespasian as the General's lieutenant.
Vespasian, in this war, is said to have reduced the two
most powerful tribes in Britain, to have taken more than
twenty towns, and also to have subdued the Isle of
Wight ;* which last circumstance makes it certain that
part, at least, of the Roman fleet came along the coast.
The Roman historian does not mention the names of the
two most powerful peoples of Britain subdued by Vespasian,
but, as his campaign included the Isle of Wight, there can
be no reasonable doubt that the Belgæ, whose ancestors
had conquered the older Celtic inhabitants of Southern
Britain some centuries earlier, must have been one of these.
Titus served in this campaign with his father Vespasian,
and on one occasion is stated to have rescued him when he
was hemmed in on all sides by the British forces.

If we may conclude that the landing of the main body of
the Roman army took place in the sheltered parts of
Southampton Water, its march must have been northwards
up the Itchen Valley, through that great natural vent or
opening in the chalk hills which the Romans themselves
named either at this time, or subsequently, Venta Belgarum,
the site of the city of Winchester. Beyond Winchester,
their route northwards to the Thames would be across a
fairly open country, over the chalk downs for about
twenty-two miles, until the edge of the great northern
forest was struck about two miles north of Basingstoke. It
is probable also that their way would be past the site of the
city they subsequently built at Silchester, for the remains
of the extensive British earthworks, which may still be
seen at Silchester, prove that it must have been a great
Celtic stronghold before it became a Roman city.

* Suetonius, 'Vespasian,' chap. iv.

Hampshire, in common with the neighbouring counties, appears to have been brought into the condition of a Roman province, and by the year A.D. 50 this change was probably completed. The early Roman coins which have been found show that it was occupied at a time when such early coins were current. The absence of records of the establishment of the Roman authority in this part of England probably denotes the quiet way in which this change of government was accomplished.

A certain British prince, known as King Cogidubnos, appears to have made himself useful to the Romans as an ally in the southern counties, and Tacitus* informs us that he remained faithful to the Roman Emperors. He was permitted to rule as a subordinate prince, and probably Hampshire, or some part of it, was included within his government, for about a century ago an inscribed stone in his honour was found at Chichester, on which he is described as 'Tiberus Claudius Cogidubnos, King and Lieutenant of the Emperor in Britain.'

After the establishment of the Roman government, the higher culture of the empire began to influence the ruder civilization of the British people of Hampshire. These people, at the time when they passed under the Roman rule, were much more advanced in the arts of life than their early Celtic predecessors. Considering their isolation from the rest of Europe, their civilization was very considerable. They met the Roman invasion with organized troops, a fair proportion of which consisted of cavalry, the horses being of a small size, resembling the New Forest breed at the present day, which is not improbably descended from this same aboriginal stock. The remains of the small horses of this period are found in the Hampshire peat-bogs. It is recorded that the British tribes had a large number of war-chariots with scythes as offensive weapons protruding from their sides, that these chariots were driven furiously, and that the drivers possessed extra-

* 'Agricola,' 14.

ordinary skill in managing them. The British weapons were daggers, long iron swords, short spears, bows, darts, slings, and other missile weapons. In battle they used large shields, some of them as high as a man, and wore cuirasses made of plaited leather or chain mail, or parallel plates of bronze. They also wore helmets, on some of which were carved figures of birds and faces of animals, these representations perhaps denoting the distinguishing marks of their clans.

The chiefs and other high personages appear to have worn collars and torques of gold, such as have been found in this county. About fifty years ago a gold torque was ploughed up at Ropley, probably from the destruction of some British burial site. This fine ornament weighs 5 oz. 17 dwt. 11 gr., and was exhibited by Mr. Lilly-white, on whose land it was found, at the meeting of the Archæological Institute at Winchester in 1845.* A few years ago it was still preserved at Ropley. A similar gold torque was found at Romsey.

Some of the British people, at the time of the coming of the Romans, used woad for dyeing the skin ; and, if we may judge by the figures on the medals of Claudius, the men and women wore a somewhat similar dress. The women's heads were uncovered, and their hair tied in a knot on the neck, but the male figures are represented as wearing what appears to be a soft head covering.†

At the time of the Roman conquest the inhabitants of Hampshire must have been numerous, and distributed through the valleys of the county as I have shown else-where,‡ governed under a system of clans, the chiefs frequently at war with each other, and consequently they fell an easy prey to the Romans. It is probable that many

* See description in the ' Proc. Arch. Inst.,' Winchester, 1845.
† Elton, ' Origins of English History,' 110.
‡ Paper on 'The Distribution and Density of the Old British Popu-lation of Hampshire': 'Journal of the Anthropological Institute,' vol. xviii.

of the existing Hampshire villages were sites of British settlements at the time of the Conquest, or soon afterwards, for Roman coins have been found in or quite close to a considerable number of them. Much of the arable land near such villages was probably cultivated for corn-growing before the coming of the Romans. The British system of agriculture was of a primitive kind, but in some parts of the country, at least, barns existed for storing and threshing corn, for Pytheas says that the corn was collected in sheaves and threshed in large buildings. In other parts of the country the older method of cutting off the ears of corn from the stalks, such as was the custom in the Bronze Age, appears to have survived. This was done with a short reaping-hook, in shape like those shown in the collection of bronze antiquities in the British Museum. In some parts of the country the corn, after it was threshed, was stored in underground granaries, such as that discovered at Nursling, near Southampton, on a Romano-British site, where a considerable quantity of wheat, black with age, was found in such a store.

The corn which was grown was wheat, barley, and oats. The farms were laid out in fields without fences, a plan which survived for many centuries, until the time of the enclosure of the common arable lands. Before the Roman occupation the British people had learnt to make a permanent separation of arable land from pastures, and to apply manures. The plough was of the wheeled kind,* which superseded the older overtreading plough held down by the driver's foot. The system of marling or chalking land was practised in much the same way as it is still practised in Hampshire. The ancient chalk-pits of this county, some of which are of enormous size, such as that at Odiham, bear witness to the extreme antiquity of the agricultural operation of marling land, which Pliny tells us was practised in Britain. Some of these chalk-pits in Hampshire are so large in comparison to the annual quantity of

* Elton, 'Origins of English History,' 116.

chalk ever likely to have been taken from them, that they
probably mark the sites where the Belgæ first began to dig
for marling purposes.

On the slopes of one of these old chalk-pits, now overgrown, at Sherborn, near Basingstoke, Roman coins have
been found. The cattle were of two kinds : (1) the Celtic
shorthorn, *Bos longifrons*, the bones of which have been
found with other remains on Romano-British sites in
various parts of Hampshire ; and (2) a larger kind of ox,
probably descended from the *Bos primigenius*, whose
remains have been found in the peat of the recent dock
excavation at Southampton. The Celtic sheep appears to
have been a horned variety, such as is common at present
in the North of England. Wild boars were common, and
from them was probably derived the old breed of hogs
which was at a very early period identified with this
county, and from which its jocular name of ' Hoglandia '
was derived. The forest-land of Hampshire, which is
so considerable at the present day, was of much greater
extent in Romano-British, and even in mediæval time,
and these forests have always afforded pannage for a
large number of hogs. Traces of the ancient breed still
remain in the swine of the New Forest. The red deer,
Cervus elephas, also roamed through the woods and fed in
the open glades. Their horns have been found in almost
every peat-bed in the county, and, until the general removal
of the deer from the New Forest about fifty years ago,
herds of them were preserved there. The Romans introduced the fallow deer and the pheasant, and it was under
their influence that the hornless sheep first appeared on the
Hampshire downs.

No county in England is better adapted than Hampshire
for the acclimatization of trees of warmer latitudes, and it
is probable that the chestnut, sycamore, box, laurel, walnut,
pear, medlar, quince, damson, peach, cherry, mulberry, and
fig, all of which flourish in this county, and which were
introduced by the Romans, were at that time first planted

in Hampshire. They also brought in the vine, and although we have no vineyards, at present, there is unmistakable evidence that they formerly existed. In the Middle Ages there were vineyards at Winchester, Hurstbourn Priors, Beaulieu and East Meon.

The Romans found the British people dwelling in small round huts of a mean kind, formed at best of wattle and dob, and under their influence a great advance must have been made in the building arts. They brought in a knowledge of the art of brickmaking, for the manufacture of which both the North and South of Hampshire contain an abundant supply of clay. In Roman times the clay-beds in the south of the county appear to have been worked for making bricks, tiles and pottery at Rowland's Castle, Fareham, in the New Forest, and elsewhere.

Wherever a Roman building or inhabited site has been explored in this county, bricks, and in many cases flanged tiles, have been found. Some parts of Hampshire, such as the neighbourhood of Rowland's Castle, Fareham, and Bishop's Waltham, which are noted brickmaking places at the present time, appear, from the discoveries which have been made, to have been utilized for the same purposes by the Romans. At Fairthorn, near Botley, heaps of débris of Roman bricks and tiles still remain under the surface soil, and London clay is found on the surface at no great distance. This firm clay and the passage-bed between it and the Lower Bagshot beds, were probably both used by the Romans in this neighbourhood. The flanged tiles, which were made for building purposes, exhibit a flaky structure, as if a firm clay was selected for their manufacture. The Roman bricks found in the north as well as in the south of the county, at Silchester, Crondal, Fairthorn, Rowland's Castle, and many other places, all show that the British people of Hampshire under Roman tuition became very skilful in the art of brickmaking.

The Romans also taught the early people of Hampshire the use of the potter's wheel. The Celtic tribes in this county made pottery before the Roman conquest, but it was of a rougher kind than that which was subsequently manufactured, and shows no trace of having been made by the aid of the wheel. The Celtic pottery is gritty in texture and thicker, and so is easily distinguished from that of Romano-British date, which is of a closer texture, more delicately made, more artistic, and well burnt. Extensive Romano-British potteries have been discovered at Crock Hill, Panshard Hill, Sloden, Anderwood enclosure, and other parts of the New Forest, specimens of which are exhibited in the British Museum and in the Hartley Museum, Southampton. This New Forest ancient pottery is a ware much resembling the Staffordshire stoneware.* In some of these places the remains of the ancient kilns have been found, and in 1889 a potter's kiln of the same date was discovered in Hall Court Wood, near Shidfield.

A specimen of pottery discovered at Shidfield is exhibited in the Hartley Museum. Romano-British potteries of an extensive kind have also been found at Rowland's Castle, and others at Brixton and Barnes, in the Isle of Wight.

The Romans also appear to have introduced the art of glass-making into Hampshire, for the late Rev. E. Kell discovered several Roman glass-works near Broughton, on a site which was close to the Roman road from Winchester to Old Sarum, and near the place where an old British road from the north to the south of the county crosses it. This site was in the ancient forest of Buckholt, in a favourable situation for procuring sand and flint for the manufacture, and plenty of charcoal for the kilns.

The art of charcoal-burning has survived in Hampshire from the time of the Romans, or earlier, until the present day, there being a few charcoal-burners, who will probably be the last of their kind, still following their craft in the New Forest. This old industry must have been in a flourishing state when the New Forest potteries and other

* Birch, ' Ancient Pottery,' p. 550.

industries, such as the glass manufacture, in which charcoal was useful, were in operation in Romano-British time.

Another ancient industry, that of basket-making, which was a native British art, supplied an article of export trade during the period of the Roman occupation. It is still followed in parts of Hampshire near to the osier-beds, at places along the courses of the rivers, in much the same way as it must have been carried on in the Romano-British period, when articles of this manufacture were sent to Rome, and, according to Martial,* were adopted for use there. The skill of the Celtic people of Britain in making baskets was probably of ancient date, for the earliest accounts we have of their boats tell us of coracles, or boats made of a wicker framework, and covered with skins.

The most enduring remains which the Romans have left in Hampshire are the ruins of their cities and their villas, and the remains of their great roads. The chief Roman cities were Silchester, Winchester, and Porchester. These were all strongly-fortified stations, the walls of which still remain at Silchester and Porchester, and probably also in part at Winchester. In addition, there was a station at or near the present site of Southampton, known as Clausentum, which appears to have been the port of Venta Belgarum (Winchester), of the country beyond it as far as Calleva Attrebatum (Silchester), and of Sorbiodunum (Old Sarum), and of the country beyond it. Ships coming up to Clausentum would be as near to the great city of Silchester as they would be by sailing up the lower part of the Thames. Clausentum has commonly been described as a place situated on an island in the Itchen. On the tongue of land on which Bittern Manor House now stands, and which was formerly an island, there was undoubtedly a fortified Roman station ; but the island was small, and for convenience of landing, whether for trading or military purposes, other parts of the Itchen or the Test, which wash the peninsular site on which Southampton is built, would have been more

* Martial, ' Apophoreta.'

advantageous for goods or troops proceeding inland to other stations. For the shipping of any export commodities, such as corn, it is obvious that a site on the mainland would have been much more convenient than an insular station. Roman remains, such as coins and pottery, have been found in various parts of the mainland between the Itchen and the Test, on which Southampton is built.

On the west side of the Itchen also, on the higher ground of Portswood, opposite to the site of Bittern Manor House, many Romano-British remains, such as coins, pottery, and sculptured stones, have been discovered. Roman pottery has been dredged up in the Southampton Water, opposite to the present town, or found in the mud during the dock excavations. The name Clausentum appears to denote an inclosed port, such as Southampton now is, and such as the Roman port was. The earliest name of Southampton which we can trace is Hantune, which perhaps refers to its situation, from the Celtic word 'an,' water, of which we have many other examples in the county.

In the early Venetian map* of 1436, published in the State Papers, Venetian series, Southampton is marked under the name of Antona, and it is probable that the Venetians derived their maps and charts from earlier sources than any in this country.

From these considerations I think we may identify the Roman Clausentum with the port of Southampton, and not merely with the fortified island in the Itchen, which was no doubt its military station.

Silchester, the largest of the Roman cities of Hampshire, was reared on the site of an immense British fortification, some of the earthworks of which still exist. As it was built in the region of the Attrebates, it was called Calleva Attrebatum. The name Calleva possibly meant a town in a wood.† An allied Welsh word is 'cell-i,' a wood or copse,

---

* 'Chart of the British Channel,' by Andreas Bianco, 1436, from the original in St. Mark's Library, Venice.

† Rhys, 'Celtic Britain,' p. 279.

and the simpler form 'cell,' a grove. The name of the place in Domesday Book is Cilcestre, probably pronounced by the Norman-French scribe Celcestre, a name also implying a chester, or fortification in a wood. Its name spelt Cilchestre occurs in official records as late as the fourteenth century.*

Silchester is the most remarkable of all the Roman remains in Hampshire. Its wall, built largely of nodules of flint washed out of the chalk by ages of denudation, is still almost complete round the area of the city. The wall is 2,670 yards in length, rather more than a mile and a half, and the area it encloses is about 100 acres. Some remains of several of the gateways of the city still exist, and within the area many objects of Roman manufacture—brooches, pins, glass, pottery, buckles, tools of various sorts, and domestic articles of all kinds—have been picked up for centuries. A large number of coins have been found here, and latterly a collection was made by the second Duke of Wellington, which, together with a Roman eagle, a fine tessellated pavement, and other interesting remains connected with the stately buildings of this city, are preserved at Stratfieldsaye. The excavations which have been conducted on its site by the late Rev. J. G. Joyce, F.S.A., and lately by the Society of Antiquaries, have laid bare the site of the city forum, some of its baths, a temple, the remains of fine pavements, of mansions or villas, a number of other floors made of tesseræ, carved stone capitals of buildings which must have been imposing, and a large number of other objects connected with Roman city life in Hampshire. That city life included the diversions of the amphitheatre, the remains of which still exist outside the north-eastern part of the wall.

Although its massive walls have become partly decayed by time and by demands made on them for building and other purposes, they remain for the most part entire, and impress the visitor with their grandeur even at

* Inq. p. m., 34 Edw. I.

the present day. The site of the city has long been tra-
versed by the plough, and has probably been cultivated as
arable land since the Middle Ages, by which time we may
suppose that the vast débris of its ruined buildings, for
centuries used as a quarry for building material, had been
cleared away.

The remains of elaborately-constructed Roman villas
and other buildings have been found at Winchester,
Twyford, Porchester, Thruxton, Abbot's Anne, Bittern,
Bramdean, Crondall, Itchen Abbas, Carisbrook, Brading
and other places.

Stones with Roman inscriptions have been found at
Winchester, Bittern and Silchester.

Other Roman remains, such as the foundations of
buildings, interments, domestic utensils, ornaments and
coins, have been discovered in so many places in this
county, that the details of these discoveries and of other
traces of the Roman occupation would be a very long
story—far too long for this volume.

CHAPTER V.

THE WEST SAXON CONQUEST.

WITH the coming of the Saxons the recorded history of Hampshire begins, like that of the rest of England. We have no longer to grope our way in the dark, gathering up scraps of ancient history here and there, and laboriously piecing together circumstantial evidence to learn what we can of the Iberians, the Celts, the Belgæ, and the half-Romanised Britons; but we have the light of the English Chronicle to guide us, and although this was not begun until about the year 855, it is of great value, as it embodies the floating historical lore and information which existed concerning Britain, and what happened for several centuries before its date. Some of this must be regarded as erroneous, but the chronicle may be accepted as embodying the historical knowledge of the ninth century, which had been handed down from the time of the earliest Saxon settlements. If we make allowance for the creeping in of legend and fable here and there, such as those of Port and Whitgar among the verities of early Saxon history recorded in this chronicle, receiving what will stand the test of modern criticism, and rejecting those statements which are at variance with overpowering evidence, we yet shall have in this early record much that is of great value, and it will always be one of the most interesting literary associations of this county that the early part of this chronicle—one of the earliest examples of English literature—was written

4

in the city of Winchester. In addition to the chronicle, there is much that can be learnt about the early wars and customs of the Saxons from the traditions preserved in their old poems and Sagas, which constitute the literature of their heroic age.

The earliest Saxon attacks on the British people of this part of England began in the year 495, when Cerdic and Cynric landed at the mouth of the Itchen. This appears to have been a raid for plunder, and the invaders came along the coast of Sussex, which had been already occupied by the South Saxons under Ælla. All the invaders of Hampshire, Celts, Belgæ, Romans, Saxons, and Danes, appear to have come along this route. In 501 Cerdic and Cynric attacked Porchester, but do not appear to have captured it. In 508 a more determined attack on the Hampshire coast was made by a combined force of Gewissas, known subsequently as West Saxons, aided by the Jutes of Kent, and the South Saxons, and the English chronicle tells us that a battle ensued in which five thousand Britons and their leader fell. No permanent occupation of the country, however, was made until the year 514, when Southampton Water and the country adjacent to it passed from the British to the Saxon rule. Porchester and Clausentum must have fallen at this time, and probably the first Saxon settlement was made on the tongue of land between the Test and the Itchen, which they named ' Hampton,' or their home town, although it was known also as Hanton, or Hantona, perhaps a modified form of its older name of Clausentum, for many centuries later. We cannot say with certainty what was the later sequence of events between this time and the final overthrow of the British power at the great battle of Charford. Whether Winchester was taken before that battle or subsequently is not quite clear. Cerdic and Cynric are said to have landed in the year 519 at Cerdices-ora with another force, which must have come from over the sea, and they were probably joined by their countrymen already settled here.

Cerdices-ora, or Cerdic's shore, has been identified by some historians with the shore near Calshot, formerly called Calchesore; by others with the mouth of the Hamble, on the eastern side of Southampton Water. What may be considered as certain is that in this year the final defeat of the Britons of Hampshire took place. The reinforced Saxons drove the Britons to the west through the woods which now form the northern part of the New Forest. I see nothing improbable in the tradition which assigns this landing of an army of Saxons on the western side of Southampton Water. Such a force would be supported by a force already established on the northern part of the estuary, and it should be remembered that a good Romano-British road existed, along which the invaders could readily pass from Lepe, near Calshot, to the north-west of Eling, where it joined another Roman road from Clausentum which crossed the Test at Nursling. A study of the topography of this campaign will make it clear that, wherever the Saxons landed at this time, the place where they were mustered for this final attack on the Britons must have been at or near the junction of these Roman roads west of Nursling. The Romano-British way from Lepe can still be followed across the lonely waste of Beaulieu Heath, where it exists in part as a raised causeway. As the Britons retreated westward, the Saxons pressed on them, until the final struggle took place at the ford of the Avon since known as Cerdic's ford, or Charford, where the Britons were defeated with great slaughter, and where the site of this decisive battle was traditionally known as late as 1759 by the name of Bloody Marshes.*

'On that day,' says one of our old historians,† 'a great blow fell on the dwellers in Albion, and greater yet had it been but for the sun going down; and the name of Cerdic was exalted, and the fame of his wars and of the wars of his son Cynric was noised throughout the land.'

* See Map of Hampshire, by Isaac Taylor, 1759.
† Henr. Huntingd., II., 17.

4—2

After this victory all the southern and middle parts of Hampshire were occupied by the Saxons, who did not pursue the remnants of the British forces beyond the Avon, but apparently returned to the neighbourhood of Southampton and Winchester to consolidate their power. If Winchester had not fallen into their hands before the battle of Charford, it must have fallen to them immediately afterwards. Then began the kingdom of Wessex, under Cerdic and Cynric, its first kings.

In the following year, 520, the Saxons crossed the Avon and advanced into Wilts and Dorset. A few miles beyond the river they must have met with a line of British hill-fortresses, the formidable earthworks of which still exist at Clerbury, Whichbury, and Dudsbury. These and others in their course into Dorsetshire they probably took, until they reached Mount Badon, now called Badbury. Here the Britons made a successful stand, and the Saxon army met with a crushing defeat. They retreated across the Avon into the country they had made their own, and no further western conquests were attempted. The present south-western border of Hampshire may be taken to represent roughly the dividing-line between the Saxons and Britons for many years after this time.

During the war which resulted in the Teutonic settlement of Hampshire, the Saxons were assisted by Jutish allies, and these, after its subjugation, were provided for by the northern shore of the Solent between Southampton Water and Portsmouth Harbour being assigned to them, and also the long valley of the river Meon, which extends from the mouth of the river, two miles below Titchfield, northwards into the county as far as East Meon. They also appear to have occupied the eastern part of the shore of Southampton Water as far as the present parish of Hound, and also a part of the New Forest around Canterton. These districts, however, were not large enough for the Jutes, and consequently in the year 530 Cerdic and Cynric subdued the Isle of Wight in the interests of their allies, and that island then became a Jutish province.

During the thirty years which followed the defeat of the West Saxons at Badbury, this conquest of the Isle of Wight was the only enlargement of their kingdom ; and although the island was occupied by Jutes, like the valley of the Meon, these Jutish settlements were not dependencies of the kingdom of Kent, but Jutish provinces in the kingdom of Wessex. During these years the small West Saxon kingdom did not even include all Hampshire. The Britons still held their own in the northern forest, which stretched from Crondall and Odiham across the country to the north of Andover. Their chief stronghold was the great city in the forest, Calleva Attrebatum, or Silchester, and they appear to have held all the country through which the Roman road from Silchester to Sorbiodunum, or Old Sarum, passed. Old Sarum was still British, so that the expansion of the Saxon kingdom westward or northward was for a time arrested. Cerdic died in 534, and Cynric his son became the second king of Hampshire. It is interesting to look back on this small West Saxon kingdom during these thirty years. Its internal organization must have been developed during this period, and the home kingdom firmly established. Then must have begun also that blending of the original West Saxon race with the remnants of the old British people, and it is significant that this period was just long enough for a new generation of warriors to rise, desirous to emulate the victories of their fathers.

The history of Hampshire during the early years of the West Saxon settlement is not merely that of the growth of an English county, but the history of an infantile kingdom.

Then were laid in Hampshire the political foundations of that state which, after many struggles, subsequently became the dominant State of the Saxon heptarchy, and which ultimately developed into the kingdom of England.

In 552 Cynric marched along the Roman way from Winchester, and captured Old Sarum. This added the whole of southern Wiltshire to his kingdom, and a settlement of colonists from Hampshire appears at once to have occupied it. In 556 he marched along the north-western Roman road from Winchester over the hills of the county into Wiltshire at Conholt Hill, and onwards to Marlborough, the Roman Cunetio, which he took after a great battle at Barbury Hill. This capture of Marlborough led to the annexation of the northern part of Wiltshire, and also the greater part of Berkshire. The downland of Berkshire was separated from Hampshire in those days by the forest along the valley of the Kennet, some miles across ; but when Cynric had captured Marlborough, he had only to follow the fine old British road eastward, called the Ridgeway, which still exists, and runs along the northern crest of the Berkshire downs for many miles, and the whole upland country of Berkshire would be open to him. This territory he added to his kingdom, and, advancing southwards, probably captured and destroyed the Romano-British town of Speen. Certainly, a new town, fortified in the Saxon manner, began to grow close by, under the name of Newbury. This place must have been of great importance at this early period before the capture of Silchester, for the only natural pass through the chalk ridge of north Hampshire and the forest beyond is that between the Burghclere Hills, which the road from Whitchurch to Newbury now follows. The West Saxons were thus firmly established north of the great forest belt of the Kennet valley. Old Sarum was theirs, and the greater part of Wiltshire, but their kingdom did not yet comprise the whole of Hampshire, for the north-eastern forest, in the midst of which Silchester was situated, was still British. The Saxons could, however, attack it from the north, as well as from the south, and about 566 or 568 it was taken, probably by Ceawlin, who succeeded his father Cynric in 560.

Silchester was probably burnt ; it certainly became a waste. Among the charred wreckage of one of its houses the figure of an eagle, now preserved at Strathfieldsaye, was found, such as was used as a legionary standard, and perhaps used for the last time in that final struggle. Even if some part of the city and some of its inhabitants were spared, and were not reduced to slavery, after the departure of the old civilization and the commerce to which they had been accustomed, the ruins of Silchester could not have afforded them a subsistence. What the Saxons spared of the city must have been left for the weather to finish, and the ruins gradually crumbled away, except the massive walls, which have lasted to the present time.

The expansion of the West Saxon kingdom went on under Ceawlin, Cutha, and Cuthwulf, sons of Cynric, until it extended as far as Bedford in one direction and Gloucester in another. During this time Hampshire remained their home province, on which they fell back when checked in their progress of conquest. In this province there must have been a seat of government, and I see no reason to doubt that that seat of government was Winchester, even in this early Saxon time. The Saxons, on their settlement in Hampshire, formed their numerous country tuns, or townships ; and although their government was in the main local, and their custom of life essentially rural, they must have had some place from which the central government of their State could be administered. They would need a seat of government of some sort as much in the sixth century as in the ninth, and I think Winchester never ceased to be the governing centre, but that, when the Saxons captured it from the Britons, they adapted it to their own requirements. That they destroyed the chief public buildings of the city is probable, but there is no evidence to show, as some historians state, that Winchester was completely destroyed and made a waste chester by the Saxons. There is strong circumstantial evidence pointing to the opposite conclusion. Its situation

is a natural centre for a province, and its advantages in
this respect must have been as apparent to the Saxons as
to their predecessors the Belgæ.   The Saxons required
roads for the communications of their kingdom, and their
further conquests, and we know that they used the great
Roman highways which radiated from Winchester like
spokes from the centre of a wheel.   If they burnt and
destroyed Winchester, they must at once have set to work
and constructed new dwellings of their own on its ruins,
and it is not likely they would thus destroy a city in order
to rebuild it.   They probably destroyed such buildings as
were repugnant to their own customs and ideas, and
utilized the others.   They certainly made great use of the
Roman roads, and they could not have done this without
constantly crossing and recrossing the site of the Roman
Venta-Belgarum.   The remains of the pavements and
streets of Venta Belgarum are found eight feet below the
level of the modern city, but this does not prove any
sudden destruction of the Roman town, for the streets and
general level of every old town have risen in the same way
by the accumulations of centuries, and the débris arising
from the repair of roads and the necessary repair and
rebuilding of houses.

The early Saxons in Hampshire disliked the life of cities,
and lived for the most part, as their forefathers had lived,
in hamlets scattered along the banks of the rivers or in the
glades formed by the forest clearings.   The British towns
and fortified places were for the most part abandoned by
them.

The island-fortress, commonly identified with Clausentum, does not appear to have been occupied in any way
after the coming of the Saxons until many centuries later,
when the Bishops of Winchester built a country-house on
its ruins.   The Roman Porchester probably shared a similar
fate, so far as its occupation in Saxon times was concerned.
It became simply a waste chester ; and it was not until the
time of the Normans that its Roman walls, which were left

standing like those of Silchester, on account of the difficulty of demolishing them, were utilized as part of the defences of a Norman castle.

After the country had become settled according to their semi-barbarous Teutonic customs, these new occupiers of Hampshire gradually advanced in civilization. They could not always live apart in isolated hamlets and village communities; for national interests of various kinds would make it necessary for them to assemble in their moots, to deliberate on the affairs of their state, or to resolve on further conquests. Consequently Winchester must, at a very early period after the Saxon settlement, have become the chief tun in the Hampshire kingdom. Its alternative name of Winton appears to have been given to it by the early Saxon settlers, who formed their tuns in all parts of the county. Such places as Hamtun, Winton, Aulton, Broughton, Houghton, Kimpton, Thruxton, Overton, and others, were probably among the earliest of the primitive West Saxon townships.

Similarly such places as Odiham, Fareham, Stoneham, Ellingham, Greatham, Waltham, and Upham, probably mark the sites of some of the earliest Saxon hams or homesteads.

Some of the earliest settlements by the fords are denoted by such place-names as Alresford, Forde, Droxford, Leckford, Reodford, Twyford, and Warnford.

Similarly some of the most important of the early settlements by the ings, or places where extensive meadowland prevailed, suitable for grazing cattle, are marked by such place-names as Allington, Avington, Basing, Bullington, Eling, Wonsington, and Wymering.

The early settlements where the land was closed in round the homesteads, and therefore known as worths, are marked by such names as Worthy, Emsworth, Beauworth, Bentworth, Chilworth, Tidworth, and Tunworth.

The early settlements whose names were compounded from wick—a dwelling-place or habitation—can be distinguished by such names of places as Southwick, Wickham, Wyke, and Rotherwick.

The early settlements by the bourns are denoted by such names as Tichborne, Hurstbourn, Somborne, Holybourn, Selborne, and Sherborne.

The settlements by the springs are marked by those place-names terminating in or compounded with the Saxon word well—a spring—as Andwell, Maplederwell, and Itchingswell.

The settlements in the open forest-glades, where cattle could lie and which the Saxons called leghs or leys, are marked by such place-names as Botley, Bramley, Crawley, Tytherley, Eversley, Grateley, Headley, and Baddesley.

Other forest settlements are distinguished by places whose names contain the words hurst, holt, or wood, as Lyndhurst, Brokenhurst, Holdenhurst, Buckholt, Linkenholt, Sparsholt, Woodcot, Wootton, and Woodmancot.

The settlements formed by the clearings of the forest-land are denoted by the word clere, as Burghclere, Kingsclere, Highclere, Clerwoodcote ; and also by the numerous place-names terminating in the word field (Anglo-Saxon, feld), where timber was cut down, such as Anfield, Winchfield, Froxfield, Sherfield, Stratfield, and Titchfield.

The settlements by streams and marshes, where it was necessary to make some artificial passage-way in order to cross either stream or marsh, are marked by the words compounded of stoke or stock, as Alverstoke, Basingstoke, Itchen Stoke, Oldstoke, Bishopstoke, Stockbridge, Longstock, and Laverstoke.

One of the results of the Saxon conquest of Hampshire was a general re-naming of the British villes and other dwelling-places. Although the conquerors may have disliked the life of towns, and so did not hesitate to destroy those which it did not suit their purposes to hold, yet they must have found in Hampshire many British homesteads ready made for them, which they utilized for their own settlements. Such old hamlets and villages appear, for the most part, to have been named anew by the Saxons in such a way as to make their names intelligible to themselves. Some of these old village sites are those on which Roman coins and other indications of Romano-British occupation have been found ; so that in such instances there can be no doubt as to their previous occupation.

Only a few village or town names in Hampshire are entirely Celtic names. Such names as Candover, Andover, Appledercombe, and Meon, may have been the names of the places they now denote in Romano-British time. Such names would certainly have been more intelligible to the Celtic population of Hampshire than to the Saxon; and the survival of such Celtic names, and many others such as Maplederwell and Itchingswell—which subsequently were made intelligible to the Saxons of Hampshire by a syllable of their own language being added to the old Celtic root-word—probably points to the survival of part of the conquered race at or near to these places.

In addition to such village place-names ending in tun, ham, ing, worth, ley, etc., as those mentioned, that mark the early West Saxon settlements in Hampshire which afterwards grew into villages, there are scattered over the county many examples of isolated farms, homesteads, and hamlets which have similarly significant names, many of which must have had an origin quite as early, but which never grew into villages. These are, perhaps, better examples of what most of the original Saxon settlements were like than the larger hamlets or villages which many of them subsequently became. These quiet homesteads in the valleys, lying in the midst of hedgerow, orchard, and meadow, or these lonely farm-houses on the hills, often sheltered from the wind by a ring of trees, and commonly only inhabited now by a bailiff or labourer, must be on the sites of many of the primitive West Saxon settlements ; and the deeply-worn old lanes and hollow ways which lead to some of these early homesteads and farms of Hampshire must be the same lanes and roads which the Saxons used, and some of them may be as old as the Romano-British period.

One class of early Saxon settlements in Hampshire has a special interest, namely, those which were known by names terminating in bury or don.   These were on or quite close to many of the old Celtic fortresses, and although the earthworks themselves have in many instances become obliterated, yet these distinctive place-names remain, denoting that a bury or fortification existed at such a place. Many of the existing Celtic fortifications are still called by names ending in bury, such as Walbury and Tidbury; and there is no reason to suppose that such names were given for reasons different from those which caused similar names to be given to such villages and places as Owlesbury, Holbury, Exbury, Tachbury, Timsbury, Cranbury, Bransbury, Hiltonbury, Rooksbury, Stanbury, Egbury, Woodbury, Colbury, Aytesbury, Westbury, and Bucksbury.   At some of these places Celtic earthworks still exist, and remains of Romano-British date have been found at others.

In a few instances similar early Saxon settlements appear to have been made near old Celtic earthworks at Hambledon, Dunwood, Dummer (Dunmer anciently), and Bullingdon; and these names have retained the Celtic termination dun.

CHAPTER VI.

EARLY WESSEX.

THE earliest Saxon organization for local government, defence, and the administration of law which can be traced in Hampshire, is that of the Tithing (A. S. téothing), a union of ten freemen for mutual security. These tithings were village communities, under which the ten men not merely bound themselves together for security, but for co-operative agriculture. The institution of tithings is therefore closely concerned with the institution of common pasture-lands, and a common or co-operative system of farming.

It is probable, from the prevalence of a similar system of early agricultural communities among the people of Wales, that some such system prevailed among the Celts and the Romano-British people of this county—a question which I have discussed elsewhere.* It is certain that co-operative agriculture was the main bond of union between the men of the tithings. A headman of the tithing was elected annually and known as the tithingman. Notwithstanding the changes which have occurred during more than fourteen centuries, the tithingman is still annually elected in numerous tithings and parishes of Hampshire. In many instances in this county, in which the organization of the tithing became merged into the later organization of the parish, the ancient tithingman has not ceased to be

* Paper on 'Early Boroughs in Hampshire.'—*Archæological Review*, vol. iv., No. 4.

elected. In many other instances in Hampshire, in which large manors or parishes were subsequently formed by the union of a number of tithings, the earlier divisions of the tithings still prevail. This is the case at Fordingbridge, which has seven tithings; at Hambledon, which has four; at Christchurch, which has seven; at Buriton, which has four; at East Meon, which has eight; at Amport, which has two; at Bramshott, which has three; at Selborne, which has two; at Warblington, which has two, and formerly had three; and at Ringwood, which has ten. Ringwood affords a good example of ten tithings being united to form a hundred. There are grounds for believing that some organization resembling the later Saxon organization of the hundred, and perhaps more resembling the cantrefs or cantreds of Wales and Ireland, prevailed among the Celtic people of Hampshire before the coming of the Saxons; but the tithing, as it has come down to us, much changed in the course of centuries, is a venerable institution of our early Saxon forefathers.

The traces which remain in this county of the primitive boundary-marks of the West Saxon settlements are among the most interesting of its early antiquities. These boundaries were in many instances denoted by marks cut on trees; in other cases they were well-known stones—probably greywether sandstones; in other cases, well-known springs; in others, the Roman roads or the Celtic tumuli; and in numerous other instances the limits of the settlements were denoted by the deans or dens, which marked the limits of the forests.

The marked boundary-trees have long since perished; but some of their positions can be traced by such names as Cutted Thorn or Cut-thorn, which marked the northern boundary of the land belonging to the tun or town of Hampton—a boundary which still exists. A similar name, Cuttes hern (or horn), occurs on a map dated 1588, of the manor of Merdon; and the name Cuthedge survives at Longparish. Marke oak and Mark ash are old names connected with the New Forest, and probably older than its afforestation; and Mark ash row occurs between Cadland and Fawley. The thorn which was cut by the Saxons was probably the holly-tree—still called a thorn in remote parts of the county. Boundary trees have in some cases apparently been replanted as the older ones have become decayed; and examples of such occur in the cases of the Bound oak of Dibden, Cadnam oak, and the Bound oak north of Silchester, and the hundred oak of Heckfield.

Primitive marks of some kind are denoted by such names as Four marks, where the parishes of Chawton, Ropley, Farringdon and Medstead meet; by Lee marks, Alverstoke, Marks lane, east of Stubbington, Markwell wood, north of Finchdean, Worting mark, Mark Lane, Mottiston, West mark, Petersfield, and Markfield, Bishops Sutton.

The limits of the forest-land in Hampshire at the settlement of the Saxons can be traced by the numerous names, dean and den, which they gave to various localities. These names occur all over the county. Such as Borden, Hatherden, Redenham, Biddesden, Vernham's Dean, and Soresden, near Andover, and which relate to the early limits of the forest of Chute. Chidden, Gledden, Denmead, Horndean, Finchdean, and Hoyden, refer to the eastern limits of the forest of East Bere; while Longwood Dean, and Dean, near Bishops Waltham, refer to its western limits. Bramdean, Ropley Dean, and Derdean, are names which relate to the ancient forest of mid-Hampshire. Dean, Deangate, Clyds-dean, Pidden, relate to the northern forest; while Nordens, Highden, and Dean, near Sparsholt, are old boundary names relating to the forest of West Bere.

When the Saxons conquered what was afterwards known as Hampshire, their recognition of kingship was of a primitive kind. Such kings as Cerdic and his son Cynric appear to have been elected chieftains, and to have commended themselves to the West Saxons by special qualities which made them eminently fitted for their position as leaders of men. Cerdic, like the kings of other Anglo-Saxon states, claimed descent from Woden, or it was claimed for him; and as Woden was the central deity in the Saxon mythology at the time of the conquest of England, it is clear that the worship of ancestors was part of the religion of the Saxons at the time of their settlement in Hampshire.

The settlements of the West Saxons, known also as the Gewissas, beyond the home settlement in Hampshire, appear to have been, at first, those of independent bands who migrated from Hampshire or came across the sea, and who governed themselves mainly according to the democratic ideas to which the race had been accustomed on the Continent. Although they were willing to combine for warlike purposes, the West Saxons of Hampshire and the extended settlements were for two centuries after the death of Cynric under the alternating headship of kings not strictly hereditary, but descended from more than one of the grandsons of Cerdic. Cynric left three sons: Ceawlin, Cutha, and Cuthwulf, who all became kings conjointly or in turn. Subsequently Ceol, or Ceolric, a son of Cutha, was accepted as King of the Gewissas, who settled in Gloucestershire and Worcestershire after a great defeat of Ceawlin; and then began a struggle for the hereditary kingship of the race between the descendants of Cutha and those of his brother Ceawlin, which lasted for about two hundred years with alternating success to the rival houses. The Saxon history of Hampshire, the home county of the West Saxon people, was necessarily much concerned with these rivalries. Between the date of the conquest under Cerdic and the consolidation of the West Saxon power under Egbert, Wessex had twenty kings, whose headquarters were in Hampshire, viz., Cerdic, Cynric, Ceawlin, Cutha, Cuthwulf, Ceolric, Ceolwulf, brother of Ceolric; Cynegils, grandson of Cutha; Cwichelm, brother of Cynegils, who shared the kingship with him; Cenwealh, Escwin, Centwine, son of Cynegils;

Ceadwalla, of Ceawlin's line ; Ina, Ethelard, Cuthred, and Sigebert, all of Ceawlin's line; Cynewulf, of Cutha's line ; Beorhtric, son of Cynewulf; and then Egbert, of Ceawlin's line. The authority of these successive potentates, who all ruled more or less over Hampshire, varied in degree. At several periods, such as during the time of Ceawlin, Cutha, and Cuthwulf, and during the time of Cynegils and Cwichelm, the kingship was held jointly, but all these rulers were real men, not legendary kings, concerning whose existence there can be any doubt. Some of them were great warriors and able rulers, who did much to consolidate the kingdom of Wessex, and whose work and influence affected the history of Hampshire for centuries.

The reign of Ceawlin ended in defeat and disaster. An alliance between some of his discontented subjects and the Welsh was formed against him, instigated, perhaps, by Ethelbert, king of Kent, who had been defeated by him at Wimbledon in 568, during a war between the Jutes of Kent and the West Saxons. Ethelbert was very young at that time, and had aspired too soon to that nominal leadership of the Saxon states to which he succeeded on Ceawlin's defeat. The coalition against the West Saxon king was too strong for him, and in a great battle at a place called Woddesbeorg, in the Anglo-Saxon Chronicle, probably Wanborough, on the Marlborough Downs, overlooking the Vale of White Horse, near Swindon, he was defeated with great slaughter, and shortly afterwards was exiled and died. This battle took place in 591. By the end of the sixth century Wessex had been restored in power and importance by Ceolwulf, a son of Cutha, and nephew of Ceawlin, who raised the fame of his state by his wars against the Angles and Welsh, and against the Picts and Scots. He died in 611, and was succeeded by Cynegils, in whose reign Christianity was first preached to the West Saxons of Hampshire by Birinus. Cynegils was baptized by him at Dorchester, on the Thames, a place

5

closely connected with the early history of Wessex and its ecclesiastical centre before the removal of the early bishop's seat to Winchester. Cynegils had been king for twenty-four years before he was converted to Christianity. This was in 635, when Oswald, king of the Northumbrians, was godfather at his baptism. This conversion was the beginning of the change in the religion of the people of Hampshire, a change which was probably a very gradual one, seeing that Anglo-Saxon paganism can be clearly traced in this county centuries later.

The chief divinities of the Anglo-Saxon pantheon were Woden, Thunor, Frea, and Tiu. These leading divinities were the same, under different names and with modifications, as those recognised by the ancient civilized nations of Southern Europe. Woden corresponded to Mercury, Thor or Thunor to Jupiter, Frea to Venus or Aphrodite, and Tiu to Mars. In addition, it is clear that the Saxons, like the Celts, reverenced the sun and moon, seeing that they gave the names of these luminaries to the first two days of their week, Tiu, Woden, Thor, and Frea having the succeeding days assigned to them. In addition to the common worship of the sun and moon, in which the Saxon mythology corresponded to the Celtic, they certainly had, in common, midsummer and midwinter festivals, also that of May day, and that of November for the commemoration of their ancestors; for under other names and in modified forms they have come down to our own time, or can be traced in this county within the last few centuries.

In addition to the central figures in their pantheon, the Saxons had a large number of lesser gods and goddesses, heroes and heroines, and much lore concerning them all.

In the folk-lore, legends, and customs of Hampshire we find much that would be unintelligible to us, without such explanations of their origin as a survival of the mythological lore of the Anglo-Saxons and Norsemen gives to them. Within the recollection of people now living, old folk in parts of this county have been heard to talk glibly about herbs under the sun, and herbs under the moon, of wizards and witches, charms and enchantments, elves and fairies, divination and invultation, water and land spirits, and similar lore, which must have filtered down through the Middle Ages from their heathen forefathers. There must, however, have been among some of the pagan Saxons of Hampshire a much higher conception of their mythology than the lower material ideas of it which prevailed among the common people; for in one of the Sagas the Edda asks: 'Who is the first and eldest of the gods? He is called the All-fader in our tongue. He is the living and awful Being, the author of everything that exists. He lives from all ages, and rules and directs all things great and small. He made heaven and earth, the lift (sky), and all belongs to him, and, what is most, He made man and gave him a soul that shall never perish, though the body rot to mould or burn to ashes. He, the Ancient, the Eternal, possesses an infinite power and a boundless knowledge. He cannot be confined within the enclosure of walls, or represented by any likeness to the human figure, and can only be worshipped in the awful silence of the boundless forest and the consecrated grove."* This higher conception of their religion must have been known to the noblest of the West Saxon race, and perhaps helps us to understand why the earliest converts to Christianity were those of the royal race, and not the common people.

Cynegils, the first Christian king of Wessex, shared his kingdom with his brother Cwichelm, and in this joint rule we may see how imperfectly the later idea of kingship prevailed in these early times. Soon after their accession the Britons invaded the northern part of their kingdom, and were defeated with great slaughter at Bampton, in Oxfordshire. This was in 614, and from this time to 626 no great events occurred. In that year Cwichelm sent an

* Thorpe's 'Northern Mythology,' I., p. 229. Dasent's 'Norsemen in Iceland,' p. 187.

envoy to Eadwin, king of Northumbria, who, during an audience, made an attempt on the life of that king. Eadwin revenged himself by invading Wessex, and the Chronicle tells us that he killed five kings, probably princes of the royal house, and slew a great number of the people. As a consequence, Cynegils and Cwichelm submitted to the overlordship of Northumbria, and for eight years, from 626 to 634, Hampshire was thus under the influence of the Northumbrian rulers.

Then arose a remarkable king in Mercia, named Penda, who subsequently exercised his lordship over this part of England. Christianity was in the meantime spreading, and the wars which occurred were perhaps partly the result of the struggle of the new faith against the old. In 627 King Eadwin of Northumbria was baptized. In 628 Cynegils and Cwichelm fought against Penda, of Mercia, defeated him at Cirencester, and afterwards made a treaty with him.

Cynegils appears to have lived until the year 643, when he was succeeded by his son Cenwealh. The Chronicle tells us that he commanded the old church at Winchester to be built in the name of St. Peter, and that he was baptized in 646. Penda, the pagan king of Mercia, appears to have been at this time the most powerful of the Saxon monarchs, and he drove Cenwealh for a time out of Wessex. He appears, however, to have regained his kingdom by abjuring Christianity and marrying the Mercian king's sister. From this time the Mercian king was the overlord of Wessex. Penda died in 655, and his son Peada died two years later. Then Wulfhere, another son of Penda, and a Christian, became king of Mercia and asserted his overlordship. He defeated Cenwealh in 661 in a decisive engagement, and dismembered his Hampshire province. His authority was recognised by the South Saxons of Sussex, and their king was baptized by his persuasion in 661. As a reward for this submission, Wulfhere took away all the Jutish settlements of Wessex, viz., the Isle of Wight and the lands of the Meonwara, *i.e.*, the hundreds of East Meon and Meonstoke in Hampshire, from the dominion of Cenwealh, and added them to the territory of the South Saxon king. The power of Cenwealh must have sunk very low for this dismemberment of his home province to have taken place, for the Jutish settlement on the mainland of Hampshire included not only the entire valley of the Meon, but stretched along the eastern shore of Southampton Water almost to the mouth of the Itchen. The South Saxon king thus became for a time possessed of a strip of territory adjoining the chief port of Wessex.

CHAPTER VII.

EARLY KINGS OF WESSEX.

THE conversion of the West Saxons to Christianity marks an epoch in their history. Cenwealh, who died in 672, was one of the last of the pagan kings of Wessex. Whether he quite abandoned all the old reverence for Woden and Thor is doubtful, but he appears to have re-adopted the Christian faith, and during his reign the new religion spread among the people of Hampshire. In 648 the minster, which in 643 he had commanded to be built at Winchester, was completed, and the Chronicle tells us that it was hallowed in the name of St. Peter. In 650 Birinus, the missionary bishop of the West Saxons, died, and Agilbert, a Frenchman, succeeded him. With the establishment of Christianity at Winchester, the ecclesiastical history of the county may be said to begin ; and it is significant that after this time we can trace little of the double kingship in the government of Wessex, such as prevailed at an earlier period. Henceforward the joint rule was that of king and bishop, and nowhere in England was this early combination of rule in Church and State better illustrated than in the relations between the successive bishops and kings of Wessex. This relationship took some time to grow, and disputes were frequent. Cenwealh quarrelled with Bishop Agilbert, drove him as a foreigner from the realm, and made Wini bishop.

After Cenwealh's death Sexburga, his queen, governed

the West Saxons for rather more than a year; but in 674
Escwin, who was descended from Ceolwulf, the son of
Cynric, succeeded to the kingdom. He became strong
enough to challenge the authority of Wulfhere, king of
Mercia, and to regain his Jutish province in Hampshire.
A battle between them was fought at a place called
Beadanhead in the Chronicle, and Wulfhere died the same
year.

Wulfhere, king of Mercia, was the acknowledged overlord of the South Saxons, and has left his mark on the
history of Hampshire in connection with the conversion of
the Jutes of the Isle of Wight and the Meon country,
whom he temporarily detached from the rest of this
county. The Jutes appear to have clung pertinaciously to
their ancient heathenism. They and the South Saxons, to
whose kingdom they had been annexed, were the last
English people who remained wholly pagan, notwithstanding the baptism of their king at the persuasion of
Wulfhere. The Mercian king was a great supporter of the
Church, and sent Wilfrid, who subsequently became Archbishop of York, to preach the gospel to these South Saxon
and Jutish pagans. Wilfrid appears to have succeeded in
planting Christianity among the Jutes of the Meon valley
as well as in Sussex, and the traditions of his mission have
survived in this valley and in the Isle of Wight, where
Brading Church is traditionally said to have been founded
by him, on the spot on which he first preached in the
island. It seems, however, to be doubtful whether he
visited the island himself, for the Chronicle says that it was
Eappa, the mass priest, who, by the command of Wilfrid,
first brought baptism to the people of the Isle of Wight.

In 676 Escwin, king of Wessex, died, and Centwine, son
of Cynegils, succeeded him. He enlarged the western
boundary of his kingdom in Somersetshire as far as the
Bristol Channel, by driving the Britons to the sea. In the
year of his accession, Hedda became Bishop of Winchester.
Centwine's reign was a short one, for in 685 a rival

claimant to the throne arose, Ceadwalla, whom Bede describes as a daring young man, of the royal race of the Gewissas, a descendant of Ceawlin, while Centwine was a descendant of the rival house of Cutha. Ceadwalla, who had been banished from his country, had a brother named Mull, and these two princes overcame Centwine, Ceadwalla becoming king. He recovered from Mercia the West Saxon provinces of Gloucestershire and Worcestershire, and united all the Gewissas under his rule. Mull, his brother, lost his life during an invasion of Kent. Ceadwalla upset the Mercian lordship over Sussex, and established his own authority instead. Then he turned his attention to the reconquest of the Isle of Wight, which had been separated from the West Saxon kingdom for about twenty-five years, since the time of Wulfhere in 661.

Notwithstanding the preaching of the priests sent by Wilfrid, the Jutes of the island remained pagans, the last of the worshippers of Woden and Thor among the English people. Ceadwalla's conquest of the island was accompanied by much slaughter. Bede says 'that the islanders were entirely given over to idolatry,' and it is certain that many of them were slain. Their prince, or under-king, was named Arwald, who had two brothers, royal youths, as Bede describes them. The savage nature of Ceadwalla at this time is illustrated by the touching story of these young princes. The king appears to have made a vow to give a fourth part of the land and the booty to the Lord, and this vow appears to have meant destruction to the pagan islanders. The two young princes escaped from the island, and came into the country of the Jutes on the mainland. Finally, they took refuge at Stoneham, where they were captured and ordered to be executed. This being known to a certain abbot and priest named Cynebert, the head of a very early monastic house at Reodford, now Redbridge, he came to the king, who was then lying in those parts, probably at Hampton, to be cured of the wounds he had received in the island, and interceded for them. The abbot begged that, if the youths must be killed, the king would allow him first to instruct them in the mysteries of the faith. This Ceadwalla granted, and the abbot having, as Bede says, ' taught them the word of truth and cleansed their souls by baptism, the executioner being at hand, they joyfully underwent the temporal death, through which they did not doubt they were to pass to the life of the soul which is everlasting.' The anniversary of these young princes thus pitilessly slain, in or near Southampton, was for many centuries subsequently commemorated by the Church on August 21, as the day of the Fratres Regis Arwaldi.

Two years later Ceadwalla resigned his crown and went on a pilgrimage to Rome. Bede says that he went there to be baptized, and, if so, we may conclude that he was not a Christian at the time of the slaughter of the Jutes of the Isle of Wight. What appears to be certain is that he died a pilgrim in Rome, shortly after his arrival there, and that Pope Sergius caused an epitaph commemorative of his pilgrimage to be written on his tomb.

He was succeeded as King of Wessex by one of his kinsmen, also a descendant of Ceawlin, named Ina, one of the most capable of the sovereigns who ever ruled over Hampshire. He had a long reign from the year 688 to 726. Ina widened the boundaries of his kingdom by subduing the Britons, or West Welsh, as far as Taunton. He was also acknowledged as their overlord by the kings of Sussex and Kent, and also by the city of London. It is probable also that the West Saxon power was advanced as far as Exeter in this reign, if not earlier, that the British people of Dorsetshire passed under Ina's rule, and that a new settlement of the Saxons was made there. This king was not only a successful warrior, but also an able administrator. The earliest code of West Saxon laws which has come down to us is that of Ina.* As his kingdom had

* Thorpe's ' Ancient Laws and Institutes,' I., p. 119, etc.

become enlarged, he divided it into two bishop shires, by
founding the see of Sherborne, in Dorsetshire. Hedda,
the Bishop of Winchester, died in 703, and was succeeded
by Daniel, in whose early days at Winchester the new
bishopric of Sherborne was established, and Adhelm placed
over it.

Ina successfully withstood an invasion of the Mercians
and defeated Ceolred, their king, in a battle at Wanborough. Then, after a reign of more than thirty years,
a rebellion broke out against him, led by some of the
ethelings, or princes of the royal blood, descended, like
him, from Cerdic, the founder of the royal race, but
sprung from the line of Cutha. One of the rebels, Cynewulf, was slain, and another, Ealdberht, was driven into
exile ; but the conspiracy went on, until at last it drove
Ina, in despair of being able to find peace in his old years,
to resign his crown. Notwithstanding his conquests, his
able administration, and his wise laws, the glory of his
reign was forgotten by the younger generation of the royal
line, who conspired against him. A legend says that on
one occasion, after he had feasted royally with the princes
in one of his country houses, as he rode away from it on
the next day, his queen urged him to turn back thither,
which at her request he did ; and although he had left it
only a few hours, he saw that insult had been cast on him
when he found the royal house stripped of its hangings
and vessels, and foul with the refuse and dung of the
cattle, which had been turned into it. On the bed where
he and his queen had rested the night before, a sow with
her farrow of pigs then reposed, and the queen turned to
him and said : ' See, my lord, how the fashion of this
world passeth away.'* Ina gave up his crown, retired to
Rome, and died there. This was in 728, when Ethelard
succeeded him as king, and, after suppressing a revolt
against his authority by one of his kinsmen of the royal
line named Oswald, a circumstance which appears to have

* Malm. Gest. Reg. (Hardy), I., 49, quoted by Green.

been in this century of common occurrence, he maintained his position for fourteen years.

He was succeeded by his kinsman Cuthred, who was king for sixteen years, and during his reign defeated an invasion of the Mercians and warred against the Welsh. He died in 754, and was succeeded by his kinsman, Sigebert, who reigned for only one year. The elective nature of the kingship of the West Saxons is apparent from the frequent succession of kinsmen to the throne during this and the preceding century, instead of the reigning king's son, which only appears to have occurred when he happened to be the fittest man to rule. After Sigebert had ruled the State for a year, the Witan, or national assembly, deprived him of the greater part of his kingdom on account of his unjust doings, and made his kinsman Cynewulf king of all the West Saxon territory, except the home province of Hampshire. This the Witan decreed should be left to Sigebert.

Whether the people of Hampshire concurred in this arrangement, owing to the greater popularity of the king in this county, or from some other reason, is not very clear, but it is certain that the partition did not please Cynewulf, who drove Sigebert out of Winchester into the forest of the Andredsweald, the great forest which stretched in an almost unbroken line from Kent into the middle of Hampshire. Sigebert found a refuge in this woodland, and lived there until he was stabbed by a swineherd at Privets-flood. This act, the Chronicle tells us, avenged the ealdorman Cumbra, who had probably been killed by Sigebert. The place must have been somewhere in or near the present parish of Privet, a village on the chalk downs about 580 feet above the level of the sea. From the place where Privet Church now stands, the ground falls to the east and also to the south. The chalk here is covered with clay containing large flints, and the surface water after heavy rains finds its way down the slopes into the dry upper valley of the Itchen, which stretches away eastward from Bramdean. This dry upper valley has a thick bed of gravel in the bottom, and the flood-water from the slopes around Privet is easily absorbed by the porous gravel, and passed underground down the valley slope to feed the Itchen springs near Cheriton. There can, therefore, be no difficulty in identifying the part of this old forest-land where the swineherd slew the fugitive king, as the lower part of Privet parish, where Privet-flood, or the flow of surface-water down the slopes, is collected in a flood and rapidly absorbed by the gravel.

Cynewulf reigned for thirty-one years and fought many battles against the Welsh, with a result generally favourable to the expansion of Wessex. Then he appears to have had a difficulty with some of the ethelings, as Ina had in his later years, and he purposed to expel one of them named Cyneheard, a brother of the former King Sigebert. The incident which led to the death of Cynewulf is one chiefly of Hampshire interest, and occurred near Winchester. It is one of those events that well illustrate the proverb which, in one form or another, is found in many languages, and is expressed in French by 'cherchez la femme.' Cynewulf found the lady he went to visit at Merdon, a place about four miles from Winchester, where the remains of a Celtic earthwork, with perhaps later intrenchments around it, still exists, and also the remains of buildings, and flint concrete work, some of it probably as old as the time of the Romans. The Chronicle tells us that Cyneheard the Etheling hearing that the king had gone to visit this woman, beset him there and surrounded the place on every side, before the men who were with the king discovered him. When the king perceived that he had enemies near, he went to the door and manfully defended himself, until he saw the etheling, and then he rushed out upon him and sorely wounded him, after which the men all continued fighting against the king until he was slain. Cynewulf's thanes, having heard the noise of the woman's cries, came to his assistance too late, but they refused the proffered bribes of the etheling, and all died fighting. The next day the other royal thanes came, and avenged his death by slaying the etheling and his party. The details given in the Chronicle of this tragic end of Cynewulf, of the fighting on the second day at the gates of the tun, and of the breaking through into the enclosure, leave, I think, no doubt that the scene of this tragedy was at Merdon, afterwards known as Merdon Castle, in the parish of Hursley, one of the castles which Henry de Blois, Bishop of Winchester, subsequently built.

This tragic death of Cynewulf, in which eighty-four men, royal thanes and others of position, perished with him, occurred in 786. He was buried at Winchester. Beorhtric, his son, succeeded to the crown, but his right appears to have been at once disputed by Egbert. Beorhtric, however, defeated him, and his rival went for refuge to the court of Offa, King of Mercia. Offa was at this time the most powerful of the English sovereigns, and had advanced his authority in Cynewulf's time by defeating him at Bensington, in Oxfordshire. Beorhtric for political purposes proposed an alliance with him, which was accepted, and he married Offa's daughter Eadburga, an event which had indirectly a very important subsequent influence on the history of Hampshire and of England, for Egbert was driven from Offa's court, and became an exile at the court of Charlemagne in France. In France and at the court of Charlemagne, he gained great experience in the arts of war and in the arts of politics, so that when he returned on the death of Beorhtric in 802, he had little difficulty in setting aside the claims of the princes of the line of Cutha, and in his own person finally recovered the West Saxon crown for the line of Ceawlin.

During this exile of Egbert Hampshire appears to have been much more under the direct rule of Offa than has hitherto been recognised. Offa described himself in charters as king of Mercia and of the nations round it. His coins have been found at Southampton, on the site of the Castle and in other parts of the town, and so these coins must have circulated in Hampshire. Charlemagne, who gave asylum to Egbert, espoused his quarrel by closing his ports against Offa's ships, and that king retaliated by closing his ports against the ships of Charlemagne. In this shutting out of trade and commerce Southampton and the other ports of Hampshire must have been much concerned. Beorhtric appears to have been merely Offa's vassal.

The accession of Egbert to the throne of Wessex marks the close of one period in the early history of Hampshire and the beginning of another, during which the position of the county, and especially the importance of Winchester, was greatly advanced. During the reigns of the twenty kings who preceded him, Hampshire was their home province, and the seat of their government as far as any part of the kingdom could be a seat of government. In the constant journeys and wars of these sovereigns, Winchester was, however, their home, as far back as the earliest records extend, and I have already stated my reasons for thinking that it must have become a centre of government soon after the West Saxon conquest.

At the court of Charlemagne, Egbert had learnt those imperial ideas, which he subsequently carried into effect in England, by establishing his authority over the whole country and making Winchester his capital city.

CHAPTER VIII.

LATER KINGS OF WESSEX.

EGBERT died in 837, at Winchester, where a chest is still pointed out in which his bones are said to be preserved. His successor was his son Ethelwulf, who was at heart an ecclesiastic, and had been admitted to minor orders in the minster at Winchester, but he became a very capable king and maintained the power which his father had won. He had the advantage of the advice and assistance of Swithun, the great Bishop of Winchester, one of the most sagacious men of this century. Ethelwulf defeated the Northmen at Ockley in Surrey, and for a few years this victory ensured peace. Subsequently, about the year 854, he made his great gift to the church of a tenth part of his lands. The deed was written at Winchester, and laid with much solemnity on the high altar of the minster, in the presence of Bishop Swithun and the West Saxon Witan. The original charter is in the British Museum, and it is to this charter that the origin of tithes has been usually ascribed, but Ethelwulf's great gift was in reality a gift of a tenth part of the land itself, and not a tenth of its produce. Soon after making this donation he made a journey to Rome in great state and was absent a year. Two years after his return, he died at Stanbridge near Romsey, where a Hampshire tradition still tells of his country house there. He was buried at Winchester.

Then, in quick succession, Ethelbald, Ethelbert, and

Ethelred, his three elder sons, followed each other as kings of Wessex.   In 866, the date of Ethelred's accession, the Chronicle tells us that 'a great heathen army came, and took up their quarters among the East Angles, and there they were horsed and the East Angles made peace with them.'   This establishment of the Northmen in the east after a few years brought serious consequences to Hampshire, for later on they made peace with the Mercians, and so much strengthened their position that when in 871 they invaded Wessex, they gained some advantages, and although defeated by Ethelred and his brother Alfred at the great battle of Ashdown, near Lambourn, in Berkshire, they were still strong enough to defeat the West Saxons at Basing, in Hampshire, fourteen days later.   This battle of Basing was a fight in which there was great slaughter on both sides. 'Many good men were slain,' the Chronicle tells us, and it appears to have disheartened the Saxons, for the Danes had possession of the place of carnage.   Traditions of the battle still survive in the neighbourhood of Basing.

Soon after this struggle Ethelred died, and his brother Alfred succeeded to the kingdom.   Nine smaller battles were fought during this year in Wessex between Alfred and the invaders.   It should be remembered that the Northmen had already established treaties with the East Angles and Mercians.   They had, in fact, been able to break up the Kingdom of England, which Egbert had consolidated. This, after their victories, and owing to the old antipathies between the states, was probably not very difficult, so that, when the Danish host was directed against Wessex, aided perhaps by some of their English allies, the war became not altogether different from that long series of wars, during the seventh and eighth centuries, between the several Saxon kingdoms.

For nearly eight years the struggle went on between the concentrated power of the Northmen and that of the kingdom of Wessex (which comprised all the country south of the Thames), led by Alfred, who encouraged his subjects in

efeat as well as in victory. Owing to his cheerfulness
nder reverses, he ultimately led his army on to a signal
ictory. At the peace of Wedmore, made in 878, between
im and Guthorm the Danish King, it was agreed to divide
England between them, the Danes retaining that which
ay east and north of a line from London to Chester, along
he Lea to its source and on to Bedford, and thence up
he Ouse to the line of the great Roman road. Alfred
hus retained Wessex, the subsidiary kingdoms south of
he Thames, and also a great part of Mercia.

Then he turned his attention to the internal administra-
ion of his dominions, and under him Winchester rose to
greater importance than it had hitherto attained.

The reigns of Alfred and his immediate successors, who
vere also strong rulers, have left their enduring marks on
he history of this county. In his time the building of
hips to oppose the Danish ships began. These were
probably built in some port on the Hampshire coast near
o Winchester. The Chronicle tells us that the king
ordered these ships to be built to oppose the esks, or
Danish vessels ; that they were very large for their time,
being 'full nigh twice as long as the others'; that ' some
had sixty oars, and some had more '; that they were both
swifter and steadier, and also higher, than those of the
Danes ; and 'that they were shapen neither like the
Frisian nor the Danish, but so as it seemed to him they
vould be most efficient.' From this we learn that the
king designed his new ships himself, and from this we
nay conclude that his shipbuilding operations must have
been carried on conveniently near for him to be able to
see them during their construction. One of his naval
yards was probably on the Itchen at Southampton, where
n succeeding centuries so many royal war-ships were
built.

Thus on the Hampshire coast, from which so many
famous ships have since been launched, began the building
of the first navy of England. The construction of war-

6

ships, when required from time to time, has been an industry which has never since left this county. South-ampton had for centuries a royal ship-yard and arsenal, in and from which vessels of war were built and fitted out ; and as its importance as a naval station declined, that of Portsmouth increased, until at the present time, a thousand years after King Alfred designed his ships ' so as it seemed to him they would be most efficient,' the newest designs and experiments in the construction of modern war-ships are still carried out on the Hampshire coast, and the greatest naval arsenal in the kingdom is located there.

In 897 the efficiency of Alfred's ships was put to the test during a battle with the Danes in the Solent, in which, after considerable losses on both sides, the invaders were defeated, and many of them captured and taken to the king at Winchester. Alfred commanded them to be hung, apparently as pirates who had ravaged the coast without the authority of the King of East Anglia, whose subjects they appear to have been, and who was at peace with Wessex.

Alfred was buried in Winchester, the city which he loved so well. His remains, at first interred in the Old Minster, were subsequently removed to the New Minster, and after-wards to Hyde Abbey. There for many centuries his tomb was greatly honoured, until the time of the Reformation, when the abbey was granted to Thomas Wriothesley, subse-quently Earl of Southampton. He pulled the buildings down, but the tombs were not disturbed. Finally, in the eighteenth century the dust of England's greatest king was scattered, when the magistrates of the county in 1787-88 built a bridewell on the abbey site, and took no care to preserve the remains of the illustrious dead buried there.

Alfred's will is of special Hampshire interest, for in it we read of his disposal of certain lands in this county nearly a thousand years ago. To his eldest son, afterwards King Edward, he left his land at Hurstbourn, subsequently ıown as Hurstbourn Tarrant, Sutton, probably that ıown later on as Bishop's Sutton, and Alton. To his ıunger son he left Meon, Twyford, and Southwick. To s eldest daughter Ethelfleda, the Lady of the Mercians, he ft Wellow; to Ethelgiva, Abbess of Shaftesbury, his iddle daughter, he left Clere and Candover; and to his ephew Ethelm he bequeathed Crondall.

On his death, in 901, his eldest son, Edward, was elected y the Witan, on which a revolt occurred in Hampshire, d by Ethelwold, the son of Alfred's brother, the former ling Ethelred, who from disappointment or some other ıuse seized the towns of Wimborne, near the borders f the county, and Twineham, now known as Christ-ıurch. The new king at once proceeded with his forces ʒainst his cousin, and encamped at Badbury, near Wim-ɔrne. Ethelwold barricaded himself in Wimborne, and eclared that he would there live or there die. Not-ithstanding this, when he saw that the affair was going ʒainst him, he stole away in the night and hurried off to orthumbria, where the Danes of that part of England, om political motives, chose him to be their king. East ınglia was at this time a Danish kingdom, as well as lorthumbria, and the allegiance their kings acknowledged ɔ the West Saxon sovereign at Winchester was not a very ıbstantial one. In the course of a few years, Ethelwold ıduced the East Angles and their king, Eohric, to invade lercia, and in 905, their combined forces advanced as far ɔuthwards as Cricklade. The West Saxon army under :dward, however, drove them back and followed them into :ast Anglia, where a decisive battle was fought, in which oth Ethelwold and Eohric were slain.

Then Edward strengthened his position by the construc-ion of burhs, or Saxon castles, as defences against future ıcursions. These burhs were fortified artificial earthworks nd mounds, thrown up at various places by the army with he king, while he remained at the several places it was onsidered necessary to fortify. Some of the Hampshire

6—2

burhs, such as those at Christchurch and Southampton, were perhaps built before this time, for Christchurch was probably a fortified place when Ethelwold seized it a few years before, and the burh on which the Norman castle at Southampton was subsequently built was probably in existence before the time of King Egbert, seeing that coins of King Offa of Mercia, who drove him out of Wessex, have been found on its site.

Early in the tenth century, an event of much ecclesiastical interest to Hampshire occurred. In 903 the New Minster at Winchester was consecrated, the great benefaction of King Edward in accordance with his father's wishes, and the bones of St. Judocus arrived there. The Old Minster had possessed since 861 the bones of St. Swithin, a wonder-working saint, and especially a Hampshire saint. It was consequently felt that some similar saintly relics were necessary to properly hallow the New Minster, and the bones of St. Judocus were opportunely brought thither by a number of refugees from Ponthieu in Picardy, flying from the ravages of the heathen Norsemen. Being desirous of preserving the relics of their own saint, St. Judocus, commonly known as St. Josse, from desecration, these homeless refugees, flying for their lives to the protection of King Edward, brought the bones of their saint with them. They were received with all honour in the New Minster, and a shrine, which attracted crowds of pilgrims, was built for them.

Edward re-established the direct authority of the king of Wessex over the whole of England. Among his minor annexations of special Hampshire interest was the final incorporation of the Jutes of the Isle of Wight into the kingdom of Wessex. They had been conquered before by Ceadwalla, but their submission had only been of a temporary kind. During the reign of Alfred the royal race of the Jutes of the island became extinct in the person of Albert or Ethelbert, their last king, after which the people of Wight placed themselves under the authority of King dward, and from this period no distinct mention of the utes of the island appears again in history.

As a consequence of the re-establishment of the power of Wessex over the whole of England, Winchester increased in nportance as the governing centre of the English kingdom. 'here was consequently an increasing traffic to and from ie city by the Itchen, amidst the chalk hills of Hampshire; nd this county, as the metropolitan county, occupied a re-eminent position among the English shires. This con- nued during the succeeding reign of Æthelstan, who ɔnsolidated his father's conquests by further victories in ie north. He did much in the enactment of new laws for ie better government of his kingdom. The payment of thes was rigidly enjoined. He re-enacted with modifica- ons his father's ordinances concerning bargains within the ɔwn gate, and legal proof in purchases. The market rivileges of some of the oldest towns in Hampshire are so ncient that no charters can be found or traced by which iey were established. Such markets as those of Basing- :oke and Andover existed from ancient prescriptive right, ased on immemorial custom, and this probably arose as arly as the time of Æthelstan's laws concerning bargains ithin the town gate and before witnesses. In consequence f the legal institutions, the earliest guilds arose. These ere fraternities for mutual assistance among traders or orkers.

Some of these early guilds survived in Hampshire for iany centuries, and traces of their names have in a few istances come down to the present day. Thus of the uild at Kingsclere we have a trace in the name of one of ie tithings called Guildable, which appears to have com- rised the land of the guild. During the reigns of Edmund, :dred, and Eadwig, who succeeded Æthelstan, Hampshire njoyed an era of peace. The wars of Edward and Æthel- :an had broken the power of the Danes, and the coast was ɔr the time freed from their ravages. This was the time f the early manhood of Dunstan, the most remarkable

Englishman of the tenth century. He was born of a noble West Saxon family, and after his early education introduced to the court of Æthelstan at Winchester, towards the end of his reign. His great talent soon attracted attention and aroused jealousy. After leaving the court, he came under the influence of Bishop Alphege, at Winchester, and under his guidance became a monk. King Edmund made him Abbot of Glastonbury, where, first of all the English abbots, he introduced the Benedictine rule, which was soon afterwards adopted at Winchester. He was banished from the kingdom during the reign of Eadwig, but returned to become the chief adviser of King Edgar.

Peace and prosperity prevailed in Hampshire during the reign of this king, sometimes called the Peaceable. In common with the rest of the kingdom, this time was marked by a reformation of the religious houses, under the vigorous administration of Dunstan, who became Archbishop of Canterbury. King Edgar spent much of his time in Hampshire, where he found leisure for hunting, and where he has left traditions of his debaucheries which have survived unto the present day. The rule of life among the West Saxon Kings was in the main a low one. Æthelstan the king was the son of King Edward when a prince or Etheling, by a shepherd's daughter. The troubles of Edwig's reign arose from his frivolity and unhappy marriage, and the loose life of Edgar left an inheritance of sorrow for his descendants, for the Danish troubles which came on Hampshire and the rest of England in the reign of Ethelred his son cannot be said to have been entirely unconnected with his father's domestic life.

After the lapse of centuries the ballad singers of the Middle Ages amused the bystanders at fairs, in Hampshire and other parts of the country, with stories of King Edgar's love intrigues at Andover. He married three times, and his eldest son Edward was the son of his first wife. His last marriage was with Elfrida, the daughter of the Ealdorman of Devonshire, and the romantic tale of his courtship

and alliance with her, and of its consequences, is one
which is especially connected with this county. Edgar had
heard of Elfrida's beauty, and he sent Ethelwold the Earl
or Ealdorman of Hampshire to visit the Earl of Devonshire, and woo the lady for him. It is well known how
Elfrida won the heart of the earl, who, concealing his
mission from the king, married her himself, and reported
to Edgar that she was a very ordinary person. The king,
however, announced his intention of visiting Ethelwold,
who thereupon begged his wife to attire herself unbecom-
ingly. Vain hope! for Elfrida, on finding she had been
deprived of a crown, spared no pains to fascinate the king,
and in this she succeeded. Shortly afterwards, while the
king and the earl were hunting together in the forest of
Harewood, on the south of Andover, Edgar slew Ethelwold,
by piercing him through the back, and his widow became
the wife of the murderer.

There is at the present day in Harewood Forest a place
called Dead Man's Plack, where a monument marks the
site of the tragedy, and where many a Hampshire rambler
reads the inscription which states how on this spot, ' About
the year of our Lord 965 Edgar, surnamed the Peaceable, in
the ardour of youth, love, and indignation, slew with his
own hand Earl Ethelwold, in resentment of the earl's
having basely betrayed his royal confidence, and per-
fidiously married his intended bride, the beauteous Elfrida,
daughter of Ordgar, Earl of Devonshire, afterwards wife of
King Edgar, and by him mother of King Ethelred II.,
which Queen Elfrida, after Edgar's death, murdered his
eldest son, King Edward the Martyr, and founded the
Nunnery of Wherwell.'

In curious contrast with King Edgar's other proceedings
at Andover, is that of the Witanagemôt he held there
about 962. The plague had broken out in his realm, and in
order to avert it, he and his Witan enjoined greater piety,
and a more careful payment of tithes and church shot.[*]

* ' Cartularium Saxonicum,' iii. 388.

Edgar had his good qualities, and among these was his zeal for good government. In his code of secular laws, the holding of burgh motes and shire motes three times a year is commanded, and some of the old burgh motes in this county probably had an origin quite as old as this king's reign.

In his laws a common pasture is mentioned as an adjunct to every township, and in this we find what is perhaps the earliest mention of such common lands, which every old manor in this county possessed until the period of their inclosure and partition.

Commerce must have greatly increased in England under his rule, for he found it necessary to establish a uniform monetary standard, and the general observance of the Winchester weights and measures.

In Edgar's time London grew and prospered ; but it did not yet supplant Winchester, the ancestral home of the West Saxon kings. He died in 975, and then, after the brief reign of his elder son Edward, came the tragedy of Corfe Castle and the remorse of Elfrida. The tale of her remorse lingers still among the legends of Wherwell, where on the banks of the upper part of the river Test she founded a nunnery, and spent the remaining part of her life in penance, close by the forest of Harewood, where her first husband was slain by her second.

CHAPTER IX.

THE DANISH CONQUEST, AND ITS RESULTS.

DURING the time of Ethelred, the son of Edgar and Elfrida, who began his reign in 978, the prosperity of Hampshire ceased and its miseries increased. The Chronicle tells us that Southampton was attacked by the Danes in 980, and the greater number of its inhabitants slain or carried off as slaves. Then followed constant fighting against these invaders, until the tax known as the Danegeld was imposed to buy them off. In 994 a large force of Danes and Northmen, under Swein of Denmark and Olaf of Norway, took possession of the Hampshire coast and wintered at Southampton. Ethelred opened negotiations with Olaf, who, having first received hostages for his safety, visited the king, and was conducted to him at Andover by Alphege, the venerable Bishop of Winchester. Ethelred gave the Norwegian king an honourable reception, and loaded him with presents. As a result of this visit he became converted to Christianity. In the meantime the army at Southampton was victualled from the realm of the West Saxons, and the Norse and Danish kings were paid sixteen thousand pounds in money. Olaf on his return home promised he would not again molest the kingdom, a promise he faithfully kept. This, however, did not bind Swein, the King of Denmark, who continued the war. In 998 the Danes took up their quarters in the Isle of Wight and obtained their supplies from the counties of South-

ampton and Sussex. In 1001 they again ravaged this
county, and Ethelred and his Witan then purchased peace
a second time, and a sum of twenty-four thousand pounds
was paid to the invaders, some of whom were also allowed
to settle in various parts of the country.

Then, in retaliation for a real or a supposed plot against
the life of the weak Ethelred, came the order for the
massacre of the Danes settled in England on St. Brice's
Day, November 13th, 1002 ; and then followed the vengeance of Swein, whose sister, the heroic Christian lady
Gunhild, was a victim under this order. In the spring of
1003, the Danish king devastated Devonshire and Wiltshire, and by the treachery of the West Saxon leader
Elfric, was allowed to regain the sea. In 1006 he came
with a great fleet to this part of England again, ravaging,
burning, and destroying wherever he went. The early
Saxon monasteries of Hampshire, such as those at Nursling
and Redbridge, were probably destroyed at this time.
The unhappy people of Hampshire suffered by the great
exactions of Ethelred, as well as from the ravages of the
Danes. Swein again wintered in the Isle of Wight, and
levied supplies from all Hampshire. At mid-winter his
troops marched through the county into Berkshire, past
the terror-stricken city of Winchester, 'lighting their war
beacons as they went.' They destroyed a band sent out
against them, and returned laden with booty. The miser-
able Ethelred, who had fled out of Wessex, again, with the
consent of his Witan, purchased peace, at the price of
thirty-six thousand pounds and rations for the Danish
army until payment was made.

Hampshire had suffered no desolation like this since the
days of Cerdic and Cynric, and this misery lasted for
several years longer, until, after again purchasing peace in
1012, the unhappy Ethelred in the winter of 1013 became
a fugitive at Southampton, whence he passed over to the
Isle of Wight, and escaped to Normandy. In 1214 Swein
died, and Ethelred was recalled ; but before the end of the

next year, 1215, Cnut, the son of Swein, made himself master of Wessex. In 1216 Ethelred died in London, and the citizens, with such leading men as still were with the king, chose Edmund his son for their king. Cnut at this time was at Southampton, where an assembly of the Witan of Wessex was held, by which he was chosen to be their king. Then Edmund came with his army into Hampshire, and a battle was fought between the forces of the two kings near Andover without a decisive result. Battle followed battle in different parts of Wessex, and the brave Edmund had to fight against the treachery of the ealdorman Edric, who led the men of Hampshire, and betrayed him while professing to be his friend.

Whether Edmund and Cnut fought a single-handed combat, as some Chronicles mention, may be uncertain ; but it is certain that they agreed to divide England between them, as Alfred and Guthorm had agreed more than a hundred years before, that very shortly afterwards Edmund was murdered, and that both Edric and his son were accused of this crime.

On the death of Edmund, Cnut summoned a Witan at London, and he was there again elected king. He reserved Wessex for his own immediate government, and under his rule, when in England, Winchester became the chief seat of administration for his whole empire, which comprised Denmark, as well as England, and subsequently Norway.

For nearly twenty years Hampshire enjoyed the blessings of peace under a strong government, during which there can be no doubt that both Winchester and South-ampton revived and greatly increased in prosperity. Cnut passed a considerable part of his time in these towns, and it was on the beach at Southampton, while surrounded by many of his chief men, that that scene is traditionally said to have occurred in which he reproved the flattery of some of his courtiers. Traditions of his residence still survive at Southampton, where the remains of an ancient building may be seen, of the Norman style of architecture, in Porter's

Lane, formerly facing the sea on the south, called Cnut's Palace. This was described nearly a century ago by Sir Henry Englefield, when it was much more perfect.* Cnut re-enacted the laws of Edgar concerning the Danes dwelling in England, and was assiduous, also, in his care that justice should be done to his English subjects. His laws relating to the royal forests and chases are the earliest code of Forest Law we possess, although it is probable that these laws were commonly applied to the forests before his time· The south-west part of Hampshire, which subsequently became known as the New Forest, was not at that time afforested, and consequently not subject to these laws ; but this county, in Cnut's time, had its more ancient forests. The old heathenism, which had found many a lurking-place in the popular belief of the Anglo-Saxons, and which had probably increased by the settlement of the Danes, was strictly prohibited.

Cnut's foreign possessions, and his international relations with other European countries, must have greatly benefited the maritime trade of Southampton.

He died in 1035, and his remains were interred in the Old Minster at Winchester—the burial-place of the West Saxon kings, above the high altar of which it is said he hung up his crown during the later years of his life.

Hardacnut, his son by Emma of Normandy, the widow of Ethelred, whom he intended to succeed him, was in Denmark at the time of his father's death, and his half-brother Harold, an elder son, was elected king by the chief men of the whole country lying to the north of the Thames. Harold immediately sent an armed force to Winchester to seize on the treasures left by his father in the possession of Queen Emma. Some agreement was, however, subsequently arrived at by the Witan held at Oxford, and Emma was allowed to reside at Winchester, as regent of Wessex, during the absence of her own son. As Hardacnut, from some cause or other, still tarried in Denmark, Queen

* See 'Archæologia,' vol. xiv. and plate.

Emma turned her sympathy towards her elder sons—the children of King Ethelred—then residing at the court of the Duke of Normandy, whom she urged to come over and regain their lost inheritance. Then occurred a Norman invasion of Hampshire under the Etheling, Edward, afterwards Edward the Confessor. He embarked at Barfleur with a well-appointed body of troops in forty ships, and landed at Southampton, whence he hastened to meet his mother at Winchester. He met with a cold reception from the people, and consequently returned to Southampton ; but his troops began to plunder as if they had been in an enemy's country, which roused the people of Southern Hampshire against them, so that he abandoned his hope of gaining his father's kingdom, and returned to Normandy.

When Harold suddenly died, in 1040, Hardacnut succeeded him, and the Danish empire was re-established under him for two years. He appears to have been fond of feasting, and during one of these rejoicings at Winchester, we are told that four royal banquets were daily spread in the great hall, that all might sit and feast. He also died suddenly, in the midst of another feast at Lambeth. His body was laid by that of his father, in the Old Minster at Winchester ; and the Chronicle tells us that his mother gave to the New Minster, for the good of his soul, the head of St. Valentine the Martyr.

Then came the restoration of the Anglo-Saxon royal line under Edward, known as the Confessor. Although the Danish rule lasted only twenty-six years, it left some permanent influence on Hampshire history, traces of which have survived unto the present day. Either in the time of Cnut, or earlier, some of the Danes were allowed to settle in various parts of the county, and land appears to have been allotted to them on the ancient crown demesnes. We find traces of these settlements in the hamlets still called ' thorps.' A good example occurs at Basingstoke, which was a royal manor, where we find a suburb called Easthorpe. On the royal manor of Kingsclere we find Edmundsthorp, which may have first become a settlement before the death of King Edmund. On the royal manor of Hurstbourn Tarrant we find a hamlet called Ibthorpe, where the inhabitants possess the unusual privilege of being lords of their own manor. Near Winchester is Milnthorpe, near Christchurch is Throop, near Crondall is Swanthorpe— perhaps originally Sweinthorpe—and in what was part of the ancient forest of Odiham is Southrope.

In the Domesday Survey some free tenants, known as Radchenistri, are recorded at Christchurch and Ringwood. This name is derived from the Norse,* and its occurrence points to a settlement of Northmen at these places.

Among other place-names in Hampshire which probably are of Danish origin, is Swanwick, on the river Hamble— perhaps originally Sweinwyk. Its situation is just such as the Danes chose for mooring their ships while they plundered the country; and beneath the tidal mud at Swanwick there still lies the keel of an ancient Danish galley, parts of which were removed a few years ago, and specimens of which, illustrating the Danish method of caulking and riveting the timber in ships, are shown in the museum of the Hartley Institution. Near Bramshaw is Piperswait, a name probably derived from ' thwait' (Norse), a forest-clearing. On the east side of the Itchen, opposite to Southampton, is Woolston, mentioned in Domesday Book under the name of Olvestune, perhaps originally Olafston. It is not unlikely that this was the place where King Olaf's army wintered while at Southampton in 994. A creek there is still known as Jurd's Lake, and the family name of Jurd —derived probably from the Norse ' jörd,' ' earth,' perhaps denoting the worshippers of Hertha, or mother earth† —still survives there.

We find other Danish traces along the Hampshire coast, in the surviving place-names of the Danish word ' or,' ' ore,' a strand: such as Cracknore, Needsore, Rownore, and Stansore.

* Gomme, ' Folk Moots,' p. 299, quoting Sir H. Ellis.
† Ferguson, ' Teutonic Name System.'

During the first ten years of the reign of Edward the Confessor, his mother, Queen Emma, lived on, and remained an important personage in Hampshire history. She resided at Winchester, where she maintained a court of her own. She, the wife and mother of so many kings, was one of the most remarkable women ever connected with this county, and her influence, which had been greater during the reign of Cnut than during the time of her first husband Ethelred, waned, but did not cease during the reigns of Cnut's sons. Edward, the son of Ethelred, who succeeded in 1042, was her eldest son, but there was not much love between them, for she had long centred her affections on her children by Cnut. She had amassed a great treasure, which Harold, her stepson, had first seized, but apparently restored, and the queen, with her hoard near her, lived at Winchester.

Edward was crowned king in that city at Easter, 1043, with great pomp, by the Archbishops of Canterbury and York, in the presence of a brilliant assemblage, which included embassies from France and Germany. Some months later, before the year was over, he cast longing eyes on his mother's hoard. The plot against it was hatched at Gloucester, where the king was advised suddenly to ride over to Winchester with the three great earls, Leofric, Godwin, and Siward, and their followers, and seize this treasure. No doubt Edward was short of cash at the beginning of his reign, and money was wanted. The Chronicle tells us that they came unawares on the lady, and 'bereaved her of the countless treasure which she possessed, because before that she had been very hard with the king, her son, inasmuch as she had done less for him than he desired before he was king, and also since, and they suffered her after that to remain at Winchester.' The story of Emma, her marriages, her Saxon and Danish sons, her hoard, her Court at Winchester, and her domestic life, lingered long among the folk stories of Hampshire, until in the fourteenth century it appears to have become amplified, by those details which tell us of that suspicion on her honour and that of Bishop Alwyn, to purge herself of which she undertook the ordeal of the red hot ploughshares. As no chronicler earlier than three centuries after the queen's time mentions this story, it must be regarded only as one of the romantic legends of this county.

The most powerful man in England during the early years of Edward the Confessor's reign was Godwin, a warm friend of Queen Emma, who had risen from a comparatively low position to be earl of the West Saxons. Hampshire was under his immediate administration, and in and close to this county we can identify some of his estates, such as Chalton, near Petersfield, and Bosham, on the Sussex border.

Edward did not live much in Hampshire. His mother was there, and he kept away from her. Godwin, whose daughter he married, ruled the county as part of his earldom, and the king consequently only went there occasionally. He does not appear to have had any great affection for Winchester, the ancestral home of his race, which had once received him so coldly, and had rejected his early claims. During this reign we may note the beginning of two changes, which had much effect on the subsequent history of Hampshire—viz., the growth of Norman influence in England, and the gradual removal of the seat of government from Winchester to Westminster. The intercourse with Normandy was the commencement of that growth in the trade and commerce of the port of Southampton, which became so marked in subsequent reigns; and the fondness of Edward for Westminster deprived Winchester for a time of its position as the governing centre, a position which it did not entirely regain under the Norman kings. Edward observed as regularly as he could the custom of wearing his crown, and holding his court at three places in the kingdom—at Gloucester at Christmas, at Winchester at Easter, and at Westminster at Whitsuntide, which was continued by the Norman kings. His piety led him to become the founder

)f a great abbey, like his ancestor Alfred. This was built, 1owever, not on the banks of the Itchen, but on the Thames at Westminster.

Queen Emma was despoiled of her treasure in the first rear of Edward's reign. Whether she then lost all her :states is uncertain ; but we know that after the loss of 1er wealth she lived on for nine years at Winchester, and vas known as the Old Lady, the name ' lady ' being at that ime the highest title of dignity. Her manors in Hamp-:hire, which passed into the possession of the Church,)robably by her own gift, were Bransbury, Bergefield, ?yfield, Houghton, Michelmersh, and Hayling, and the ransfer of these estates was in subsequent centuries)elieved to have been made as a thank-offering for her rindication by the ordeal of the ploughshares.

During her later years at Winchester, from 1047 to 1052, she appears to have found a friend in Stigand, iubsequently Archbishop of Canterbury, who became 3ishop of Winchester in 1047. The circumstances of her ife at this time were very peculiar. Emma the Old Lady, ;rand-aunt of William, the young Duke of Normandy, ind mother of King Edward, who was an Englishman only)y name and birth, but a Norman by long residence, lived n the old city of the West Saxons, more or less estranged 'rom her son the king. He was at the same time gradually iurrounding himself with Norman courtiers, and Norman)ishops whom he placed over English sees, while his nother found comfort in her last years in the friendship)f Stigand, the representative of the English party among :he bishops of his time. Struggling against the growth of :he Norman influence was Godwin, the West Saxon earl, ind his son Harold. The king had married Eadgyth, the daughter of Godwin, a marriage concerning which much ;ossip subsequently arose.* It was an alliance dictated no doubt by political considerations on the part of the king, as well as on the part of the earl ; but it failed in its purpose,

* Freeman, ' Norman Conquest,' vol. ii., p. 46, and Appendix B.

for nine years after Edward's accession the Norman influence became too strong for even the great earl to withstand, and Godwin and his sons were banished.

The weak character of Edward, in some respects so like
that of his father Ethelred, is shown by what followed ; for
in accordance with the desire of the Normans by whom he
was surrounded, who dreaded lest the presence of the queen
would be detrimental to their schemes, after her father and
brothers had been exiled, he consented to send even the
Lady Eadgyth away. He allowed his wife to be deprived
of all her goods, but saved her only from personal disgrace,
and she was sent with a suitable retinue to the Abbey of
Wherwell, that royal nunnery on the Test which Elfrida,
the grandmother of her husband, Edward, had founded in
penance for her sins. She was there given into the safe
keeping of the abbess, a sister of the king, and the young
wife of the elderly Edward appears there to have received
such consolation as her elderly sister-in-law could give her.
In her retirement, in the beautiful valley of the upper Test,
she had time to reflect on the vanity of human greatness,
and if she took any interest in natural objects, she could
not have failed to have observed many things at Wherwell
which we may see there at the present day. Hampshire
had at that time two queens in retirement, the Old Lady at
Winchester, and the Young Lady at Wherwell.

Then occurred the visit which William, the young Duke
of Normandy, paid to his relative King Edward in England,
and then followed the awakening of the nation. The re-
action against the Norman bishops and courtiers set in,
during which Godwin and Harold returned, and a general
exodus of the Norman knights and priests took place. The
Lady Eadgyth was brought from Wherwell with much
pomp and restored ; but Godwin soon afterwards died at
Winchester, during the rejoicings at the Easter festival in
1053. Then Harold became Earl of the West Saxons, and
the ruling man in England. His estates in Hampshire
comprised the large manor and forest of Odiham, and the
manors of Quarley and Nether Wallop.

CHAPTER X.

THE EARLY NORMAN PERIOD.

On the death of King Edward, Harold, who had long been the virtual ruler of England, was chosen king. His brother Tostig, who had already given him trouble elsewhere, then came with as large a fleet of ships as he could procure to the Isle of Wight, where he had extensive estates. There he made his headquarters in the summer of 1066, during which time he obtained his supplies from the island and perhaps from his manors of Ringwood and Holdenhurst. Subsequently, in alliance with the King of Norway, he attacked Yorkshire, and then followed their defeat by Harold, in a campaign which detained him in the North while he should have been in the South making more effective preparations against the coming of the Norman duke. The leading people in Hampshire at this time were divided in opinion. The folk in the Isle of Wight do not appear to have been unfriendly to Tostig while he was there. Consequently they had no great love for Harold. In any case, they do not appear to have sent help to the king against the Normans, a neutrality by which they subsequently benefited.

It is interesting to note the opposite views taken by the monks of the Old and New Minsters at Winchester during this crisis in the history of the country. The New Minster was governed by the Abbot Elfwig, an uncle of Harold. He and his monks not only supported the cause of his nephew, but themselves took up arms and joined the king in the field. The Old Minster, on the contrary, remained neutral, and gave the king no assistance. This old monastery of St. Swithun had long been accustomed to Norman ideas. Queen Emma had for a long time before her death been closely connected with it, and had made it great presents. There had long been a rivalry between the two great abbeys, and after the Conquest the one suffered no loss, but rather increased in importance, while the other was despoiled by the Conqueror of twenty thousand acres of land. Abbot Elfwig and his monks died fighting against the Normans on the field of Hastings.

When it was reported to William that the bodies of the abbot and monks of the New Minster had been found among the dead, he is recorded to have said that 'the abbot was worth a barony, and each monk a manor,' an intimation of the confiscation which he afterwards carried out.

The manors of Hampshire which were held by Harold before he became king, and the royal demesnes which passed into his possession on the death of King Edward, were no doubt required to furnish men for the English army at Hastings, and there can be little doubt that men from Odiham, Quarley, and Wallop were there, and also that a more numerous contingent of Hampshire men were there from the royal demesnes of Andover, Basingstoke, Kingsclere, Broughton, Alton, Meonstoke, Hurstbourn Eling, Sombourn, Selbourn, and many other places. Stigand, who was Bishop of Winchester as well as Archbishop of Canterbury, was a great supporter of Harold, and his thanes probably rallied round the English standard.

We know that Hampshire suffered less from the Norman Conquest than almost any other county, and from this we may perhaps conclude that Harold had comparatively little support from the thanes of this county, in addition to such a personal following as he could command. After his coronation as king, all the royal demesnes of course passed into the Conqueror's possession as part of his personal revenue. These royal possessions, in addition to the manors above mentioned, included the city of Winchester, the town and port of Southampton, the revenues arising from the hundreds of the county, except those held by the abbeys, and the ancient forests of Hampshire. We have no knowledge to what extent, if any, Winchester and Southampton assisted Harold, but it is probable that these towns already contained a Norman element among their people, and that they watched the course of events. There is but one manor in Hampshire concerning which the Domesday record tells us that its former tenants were killed in the battle of Hastings, and that is the manor of Tytherley.

Soon after his victory William sent to Winchester to demand tribute of the city, whereupon the leading men consulted the Lady Eadgyth, who since the death of King Edward had occupied the same position in the city as was formerly filled by the Lady Emma. She concurred with them in sending tribute to William in token of their submission, and the Conqueror's messengers 'carried back the gifts of the lady and those of the chief men also.'*

Before long William himself came to the ancient capital, and made it his head-quarters. The old city, which had to some extent been neglected by King Edward, began to rise again in importance, for it was conveniently near to Normandy, and there was necessarily much traffic between it and William's great duchy. The king was often at Winchester, and in 1070 held a great council there, when, according to the ancient custom, he wore his crown, and was confirmed in his kingship with much pomp in the Old Minster by three papal legates, who recrowned him on behalf of the Pope.

During the first half of the Conqueror's reign some remarkable personages lived at Winchester. First, there was the widowed queen, who was allowed to reside in the royal city in suitable state until her death in the winter of

* 'Guy of Amiens': poem.

1075, when the king caused her body to be taken to
Westminster with great pomp, and laid in the abbey there
by that of her lord, King Edward. Next, there was
Stigand, who between 1066 and 1072 was for the most
part a hôstage in Normandy or a fugitive; but in the latter
year he fell again into William's hands at Ely, and was
brought a prisoner to Winchester and kept under guard
there until his death in the same year. Among the con-
fiscations of Church land which William made in Hampshire was one, that of East Meon, which belonged to
Stigand as Bishop of Winchester, by which the king
appears to have intended to mark his displeasure at the
course the bishop took against him. This property was
an extensive domain, comprising the hundred as well as
the manor, and it was not again restored to the Church
until the time of King John.

Another state prisoner at Winchester for several years
was Earl Waltheof, who, we are told, 'was one of the
most ancient and wealthy of the princes of England, in
stature and form as fair as a second Absalom.' His earldom under King Edward had comprised the counties of
Northampton and Huntingdon. He was a very popular
Englishman, but. somewhat weak-minded. During an
invasion of Yorkshire in 1069 by the Danes, he joined
them and the men of Northumbria in expelling the
Normans from the city of York, for which hostility he
was subsequently pardoned.

In the year 1075 he took part in another conspiracy,
and, as a result, had to flee the kingdom. He asked
forgiveness of William, and offered a ransom. The
Chronicle tells us 'the king let him off lightly until he
came to England, when he had him seized' and conveyed
a prisoner to Winchester. There he became, as William
thought, dangerous to his government, for the people
considered him to be the last representative of the old
English rulers, and so the king resolved on his execution.
For fear lest a popular tumult should arise, however, even

in Winchester, this execution was carried out suddenly early on a May morning in 1080, when the earl was led out of the city over St. Swithun's Bridge on to St. Giles's Hill, and there beheaded before the citizens were awake.

Another remarkable man who came on the scene at Winchester during the early years of William's reign was his kinsman Walkelin, who was appointed bishop. He was the first builder of the cathedral which exists at the present day, and the massive transepts and the timber in the roof of the nave remain in much the same condition as he left them.

Like his kinsman Edward the Confessor, William was very fond of hunting. Eastward of Winchester was Bere Forest, and westward of it was West Bere, Parnholt, and Buckholt; but these ancient royal forests were not exactly to his mind. It is probable that they did not contain enough open glades, and that the trees were too thick to make these woodlands well adapted for the pleasures of the chase.

In any case, he resolved that a greater Hampshire forest than any one already under forest-law should be formed, and between the years 1070 and 1081 the afforestation of the south-western part of the county, the district which bore the ancient name of Ytene, was carried out, and thenceforward became known as the New Forest.

A few years later the king ordered his great survey to be made, and commissioners were sent throughout the kingdom to inquire what land there was in each shire, what lands and cattle the king himself owned therein, what was due yearly to him for it, what lands his bishops, abbots, and earls held, and what his other tenants held of lands or stock, and their annual value.

The returns which were made by the several sets of commissioners were sent to Winchester, where the original rolls were copied out into the great Domesday Book. These returns were completed in the summer of 1086, perhaps in the spring of that year, when the king wore his

crown and held his court at Easter at Winchester. The copy-
ing of the original rolls into a book was perhaps ordered
at this time. In any case, the Domesday Book was made,
and in August, 1086, William rode along the Roman road
over Teg Down, past Farley and Ashley, and so on across
the Test near Horsebridge, and through Buckholt Forest
to Salisbury Plain, where he met all the landholders of
substance in the kingdom, who all submitted to him,
became his men, and swore him oaths of allegiance. At
the western border of the county, close to the Roman road,
is a place known as Norman Court, recorded in Domesday Book under the name of Chinges-camp, where a
Hampshire tradition says that William encamped on this
memorable occasion.

The account which the Domesday Survey gives of this
county enables us to realize its condition in the eleventh
century far better than would otherwise be possible. The
survey is fairly complete as regards Hampshire and the
Isle of Wight, the most notable omission being Winchester.
There is no mention of Portsmouth, Newport, or Petersfield,
because these places are of later origin. The most important landowners were the king, who held about seventy
manors ; the Bishop of Winchester, who held twenty-four
manors ; St. Swithun's Priory, Winchester, also known as the
Old Minster, which held thirty manors ; St. Peter's Abbey,
the New Minster, called also Hyde Abbey, which held
eighteen manors ; St. Mary's Abbey, Winchester, which
held six manors ; Romsey Abbey, which held five manors ;
Wherwell Abbey, which held six manors ; Christchurch
Priory, which held three manors ; Roger, Earl of Mont-
gomery, who held twelve manors ; Hugh de Port, the chief
Hampshire baron, who held fifty manors ; Robert, the son
of Girold, who held ten manors ; Ralph de Mortimer, who
held thirteen manors ; William Malduith, who held seven
manors ; Bernard Pancevolt, who held five manors ; Gilbert
de Bretville, who held five manors ; and Waleran, the
huntsman, who held six manors.

The other abbeys which held one or more Hampshire manors at the time of the survey were St. Peter's, Gloucester, St. Peter's, Westminster, the abbeys of Chertsey, Glastonbury, also Grestain and Jumieges, in Normandy.

Among other ecclesiastical landholders was the Archbishop of York, who held Mottisfont, with certain revenues arising from its church and six subordinate chapels, the Bishop of Exeter, who held the manor of Farringdon, and Odo, Bishop of Bayeux, the half-brother of the Conqueror. His other half-brother, Robert, Count of Mortain, held a manor in Sombourn Hundred, while Count Alan of Brittany, who led the Bretons and Poitevins in the battle of Hastings, held Crofton and Funtley. Count Hugo of Avranches, first Earl Palatine of Chester, held Bighton, and Count Eustace held the important manor of Sutton, afterwards known as Bishop's Sutton.

The Hampshire survey tells us of the manors in the county which were held by huntsmen. The most important of these appears to have been Waleran, in addition to whom manors or lands were also held by Ulviet and his son Cola, by Croc and his son Rainald, by Terbert, Edwin, and Uluric, who were all huntsmen, and these tenures show how great was the care bestowed on the royal sport of hunting in this county, so many chief huntsmen being men of substance in it. The royal sport of falconry also was not unrewarded, for Osborn the falconer held the manor of Goreley, apparently as part of his office, and Godwin, another falconer, held half a hide of land at Steventon.

A considerable number of officials in the royal household were provided with manors or lands in Hampshire, such as Herbert and Hunfrid the chamberlains, Henry the treasurer, Nigel the physician, and Durand the barber. The physician held the manor of Brockeseve, and also had four houses at Southampton, and the barber, or barber surgeon, held a hide of land in the hundred of Titchfield, tenures which show that these professions were regarded as honourable occupations as early as the time of the Domesday Survey.

A large number of thanes held lands directly of the king, both in Hampshire and in the Isle of Wight. In the island, the king's thanes were very numerous, a circumstance which shows that the confiscation of land could not have been great there. The names of most of the thanes are Saxon names, both in the island and on the mainland, from which we may perhaps conclude that the manors and lands they and their predecessors had held of King Edward they continued to hold of King William, and apparently by similar obligations, for thane service was a much lighter tenure than feudal service, the thane being only liable for service in the field in the case of war, for the repair of local fortifications, and the repair of bridges, these three obligations being the only services attached to the land held by allodial tenure in Saxon time.

The number of servile tenants enumerated was not quite 9,000. In addition, about 1,620 slaves or serfs are recorded. These latter were bondmen, and the proportion of these slaves was nearly a fifth of the whole servile population. The villeins were agriculturists who were attached to the manors, and who, in consideration for the land which they held and farmed in common, had to perform a certain amount of work with their teams of oxen for their lords. The borderers were cottagers who, for a share in the produce of the land held in common with the villeins, had to give a certain amount of manual labour to the lord.

The manors had a large area of common land, which these servile tenants farmed for their own subsistence, and which in subsequent centuries became gradually changed into copyhold land, the villeins or small farmers paying a quit rent, instead of doing so much ploughing and other work on their lord's land. This change had already begun in the Isle of Wight at the time of the survey, for at Cheverton mention is made of villeins paying a rent, and at Bowcomb mention is also made of borderers paying a rent for their cottages. As time rolled on some of the villeins' land became held by a higher class of tenants who were not villeins, but paid a rent to the lord of the manor at his court, their names and the amount due from each being recorded on the court-roll. Such tenants also became known as copyholders, and the Domesday Survey of Hampshire shows us that this change had already begun in this county, for at Whitchurch and Fareham certain tenants are mentioned as holding villeins' land. The whole of the land at Millbrook and at Alverstoke was held by villeins, who paid a rent to the bishop.*

The number of churches mentioned as existing in Hampshire at the date of the survey is 124, and in the Isle of Wight 9, making together 133 for this county. Several others, which are not mentioned under the names of the manors in which they are at present situated, such as those of Tichborne and Hambledon, must have been in existence at that time, for they contain unmistakable remains of Saxon architecture. No less than 331 mills are recorded in Domesday Book as then existing in Hampshire and the Isle of Wight, and the information concerning some of them is peculiar, for at Bedhampton, Boarhunt, Winkton, and Stratfieldsaye, there were mills for the use of the manor court, so that the villeins, by local custom, were not obliged to grind their corn at their lord's mill.

Fisheries are recorded at twenty-four places, and at Middleton, Holdenhurst, Porchester, and Periton, the tenants who formed part of the court had a right to catch fish.

The manufacture of salt was largely carried on on the coast of Hampshire and the Isle of Wight at the time of the survey, for twenty-seven salterns are mentioned as then existing.

An interesting entry occurs of a 'ferraria,' or iron works, at Stratfield, at which iron appears to have been extracted from the native ironstone which occurs in the Tertiary beds, and which was subsequently worked in the south of of the county.

* See paper by the author on 'Traces of Old Agricultural Communities in Hampshire,' in the *Antiquary*, February, 1888.

Markets are mentioned as existing at Basingstoke and Titchfield, and Neatham, and toll-places are recorded at Clere, Bowcombe, and Titchfield.

The clergy held land as part of their benefices in sixteen places in Hampshire, and at Wallop we are told that the Church had half the tithes of the manor, the whole of the church shot, forty-six pence for the villeins' tithes, and half of the lands.

An early record, in this county, of the enclosures known as parks, occurs in the Domesday Book, where parks are mentioned at Soberton and Watchingwell.

During the reign of William Rufus several prominent events of national importance occurred in Hampshire. It was to Winchester that Rufus hurried from the chamber in the priory of St. Gervase, where his father was dying. He landed at Southampton, and went on to the ancient West Saxon capital, where the first act of his reign was to thrust again into prison there the two Saxon earls, Morkere and Wulfnoth, whom his father had set free a few days before, after a captivity in Normandy. He went on to Westminster, and, after being crowned there, returned to Winchester to take possession of the treasure his father had amassed in that city, which the chronicler tells us consisted of 'gold and silver, vessels of plate, palls, gems, and many other valuables that are hard to be numbered.' 'He did as his father, before he died, commanded him, and distributed treasures amongst all the monasteries in England for the sake of his father's soul.'

In 1088 he held a Witana-gemôt at Winchester at Easter, according to ancient custom. Soon after this, Randolf Flambart, his chief minister and his willing tool in the heavy exactions he levied, appeared on the political stage. Flambart was connected with this county. At the time of the great survey he appears to have held lands at Bile and Beceslei, in the New Forest, and his estates had been diminished by part of his land being afforested by the Conqueror. Flambart was a priest, and became Dean or

Prior of Christchurch or Twynham, and subsequently Bishop of Durham. Rufus rigorously established the feudal system which his father had introduced in a milder way, and many a Hampshire thane who had hitherto been free from its exactions must have felt the burden of its services in this reign, burdens from which the land was not again entirely freed until feudal tenure was swept away in the seventeenth century. During the time of Rufus the forest law was made more severe, and any man who slew a hart had to pay for this crime with his life. In Hampshire, where so much ancient forest-land still existed, and where almost the whole of the south-west of the county had been newly afforested, this more rigorous code of forest law must have been especially oppressive.

Under Flambart's administration many of the Church lands were altered in their tenure and reduced to fiefs, with feudal obligations, and of this we find examples in Hampshire centuries later.

The most notable assembly which was held in this county during the reign of William Rufus was the great council which met at Winchester on October 14, 1097, on the thirty-first anniversary of the battle of Hastings.

The long dispute between Archbishop Anselm and the king culminated at this council, where he and Rufus met for the last time. For several days the discussions and conferences between the king and his nobles, on one side, and Anselm and the bishops on the other, went on, until that final interview between the archbishop and the king, at the end of which, although they could not agree, the archbishop desired, if the king would receive it, to give him his blessing before he left, and we read that the king bowed his head and Anselm made the sign of the cross over it.

The short reign of Rufus began in Hampshire with an act of tyranny against the Saxon earls who had been released from their bonds by the dying Conqueror, an act in which he heeded not his father's dying wish, and his reign also came to an end in this county by the fatal arrow

at Malwood, in the New Forest. Then followed the
abandonment of his corpse in the forest, and its conveyance to Winchester by Purkis the charcoal-burner,
after all the nobles and knights had hastened after Prince
Henry to pay their court to the rising sun, while Walter
Tyrell was riding for his own life in an opposite direction.*
Prince Henry rode straight to Winchester, and demanded
the keys of the treasury, but night came on before he got
them. The news travelled fast. Rufus was slain on
August 2, 1100, and by the next morning a crowd of
Hampshire people, of various ranks and orders, came
trooping into the city, drawn thither by a feeling of
wonder and a desire to know what was coming next.
First they saw coming over Compton Down the two-
wheeled forest-cart, not much unlike the rough New
Forest carts of to-day, on which lay the stiffened corpse of
the late king. They saw the rude funeral cortége pass on,
until it came to the Old Minster, where no bell was rung,
no Mass was said, and no offerings for his soul were made,
but the body was silently buried under the central tower
of the great church. Then all those who were assembled
at Winchester, and were eligible to attend the Witan
which was immediately held, chose Prince Henry to
be king.

* The local traditions connected with the death of Rufus are
supported by stronger circumstantial evidence than those historians
are aware of who have not studied them on the spot and who ignore
them. Avon Tyrell, where Walter Tyrell is said to have crossed the
river Avon, was a manor held by the Tyrell family in the fourteenth
century.

CHAPTER XI.

LATER NORMAN AND ANGEVIN RULE.

ONE of the earliest acts of Henry I., connected directly with this county, after his coronation at Westminster, was his courtship of Maud, the daughter of Malcolm, King of Scotland, a princess descended from the royal Saxon line. He resolved to strengthen his position by an alliance with her. She was living at Romsey under the care of her aunt Christina, the abbess of the nunnery there, and afterwards became known as good Queen Maud, a founder and bene-factor of abbeys and churches, a builder of bridges, and author of other beneficial works.

During the earlier years of his reign Henry resided much at Winchester, where his son was born. It was on this occasion, while he was absent in Sussex, that his brother Robert, who had landed at Porchester, moved with his army towards Winchester ; but on hearing that the queen was lying there in childbed, he from motives of chivalry turned eastward, and directed his march towards London. Henry, hearing of his landing, also moved towards Win-chester through Midhurst, and the two armies almost met, being separated only by the wood around the upper Meon valley. The king, hearing that his brother was on the other side of the wood, arranged an amicable meeting, which took place at Westbury,* near West Meon, and a treaty between them was made there.

· * See *Notes and Queries*, January 3, 1880 ; and the *Athenæum*, December 19, 1885.

Henry held his Easter court at Winchester, according to the ancient custom, in the years 1100, 1101, 1102, 1103, 1104, and 1108. Subsequently his French wars kept him much in Normandy, but in 1116 he spent the Easter season at the royal manor of Odiham. He again held his court at Winchester in 1123, and two years later that city was the scene of a strange assembly at Christmas. The king's incessant wars had caused the taxation to be great, and the minters debased the coinage. The complaints of this were loud and long, until in 1125 the whole of the moneyers in the kingdom were summoned to Winchester, and all whose metal was found bad lost their right hands, all of which we are told 'was done within the twelve days, and with much justice, because they had ruined this land, with the great quantity of bad metal which they all bought.'

A very remarkable man made his first appearance in Hampshire in a prominent position in the latter years of the reign of Henry I. This was Henry de Blois, the king's nephew, and the brother of Stephen, afterwards king. His uncle made him Bishop of Winchester in 1129. When King Henry died six years later, and the bishop's brother Stephen had been elected king in London, the troubles of this, as well as of other counties, began anew. Stephen hastened from London to Winchester, and, as so many other new kings had done before him, he hurried to the treasury in the palace, for, as the Chronicle says, 'mickle had Henry, king, gathered of gold and silver.' With some trouble he won over the keepers of the hoard, Roger of Salisbury, and William Pont de l'Arche, and so got the keys of the treasure house. Stephen perhaps reckoned on the adhesion of his brother Henry, but in the troubles which followed he proved himself to be a variable adherent. Hampshire, like the rest of England, was divided in the struggle which ensued. The Empress Maud, daughter of Henry I., soon appeared on the scene, and Henry de Blois at first supported her party against his brother. Then, the Chronicle says, 'every rich man built his castle, and they filled the ınd full of castles, and when the castles were finished they lled them with devils and evil men.' Neither king nor mpress was lord of those who followed them ; all fought r their own hand.

The bishop was one of these castle-builders. He trengthened the ancient royal palace of Wolvesey with a reat tower and additional walls, and it grew into a great ʌrtress, at the eastern part of Winchester, where the ʌmains of his work may still be seen. He also built or trengthened the castle of Merdon on the site of the old ʃritish fortress near Hursley, and having got himself ppointed the Pope's legate, he summoned a council at Vinchester, and went so far as to cite the king before it, to nswer for his action against the bishops. The bishop ʌroduced a papal brief, in virtue of which, as legate, he ʌresided over the assembly, and after some delay the arch-ishop was obliged to allow him this precedence.

Then followed the civil war between Stephen and the mpress, supported by her half-brother, Robert, Earl of ʃloucester, who also held some estates in the eastern part f Hampshire. Stephen was taken prisoner at Lincoln, nd sent under guard to the earl's castle at Bristol. Then he empress arrived in Winchester. She, with Earl Robert, ʌas escorted by the bishop to the Old Minster or Cathedral, nd, after a solemn service there, went to the castle on the ising ground to the west of the city. London, however, ided with Stephen, and the empress, having visited that ity, failed to win the citizens over, as she treated them too ʌaughtily. Bishop Henry de Blois also did not meet with ʌll the consideration he expected, and consequently he hanged sides, and endeavoured to hold Winchester for ʃtephen. Then Hampshire became the chief scene of the ivil war which ensued, during which Andover was burnt, ınd much fighting went on in the county and in the streets ʌf Winchester, between the king's party, led by the bishop rom his castle at Wolvesey, and the party of the empress, ed by Earl Robert, who held the royal castle at the

8

opposite side of the city. A great part of the city was burnt, and ultimately Robert and the empress had to retreat. He delayed the pursuers at the passage of the Test, while Maud was thereby enabled to escape towards Bristol, but he waited too long for his own safety, and was taken prisoner somewhere near Stockbridge.

Then subsequently followed the exchange of the king as a prisoner for Earl Robert, and ultimately peace came, under the agreement by which Stephen remained in possession of the kingdom ; but the empress's son, Henry, was declared his successor.

Henry had not long to wait, for Stephen died in 1154, and England had again a strong king. The accession of Henry Plantagenet destroyed the power, and for a time, the influence of Bishop Henry de Blois. He enjoyed an immense revenue, but in the new order of things he found his power gone, and having secretly sent his treasure across the Channel, he left his see in 1155, and did not return until 1159, after which he lived until 1171 in peace at Winchester. After his flight, Henry II. demolished his castles of Wolvesey and Merdon. Wolvesey was subsequently patched up as an episcopal residence, but its ruined walls have for more than seven centuries told the tale of Henry's vengeance, and the scanty remains of masonry among the huge grassy mounds of Merdon are all that is left to tell the story of that episcopal fortress.

The reign of Henry II., commonly called Henry Fitz-Empress, like that of his grandfather, began in Hampshire. He landed at Southampton a few weeks after King Stephen's death, and went on directly to Winchester, like his predecessors, but, unlike them, owing to the troubles of Stephen's time, he found no great treasure there. He held a great council at that city in September of the next year, 1155, at which some important business was transacted ; and among the charters he granted at this time was that of the Knights Hospitaller, which he gave 'for

:he health of himself, of his mother the empress, of his
queen, and of their children.' He was at Winchester many
:imes during his reign, but usually for short periods. He
:ravelled much through his wide dominions, and the ports
of Southampton and Portsmouth were the places from
which he usually embarked and disembarked in his
voyages across the Channel. The accounts of the receiver
of the royal dues, called the Fermor of Southampton,
contain many entries relating to the cost of providing
ships for the conveyance of the king and his retinue to or
from Normandy, and it is probable that it was at this time
that the royal waterside house at Southampton, a part of
which still remains, was used as a convenient lodging-
place for a night or two at a time, in connection with these
voyages. He landed or embarked at Southampton eight
:imes, and at Portsmouth ten times, in the course of his
reign. When he landed at Southampton in 1163, he was
met there by Archbishop Becket and Prince Henry, the
king's son, who was then his pupil. Eleven years later, on
his arrival at Southampton on July 8, 1174, he was on his
way to Canterbury to do penance at the tomb of the same
Archbishop Becket. He travelled on this occasion through
Winchester to London without delay, and then proceeded
to Canterbury by that pilgrim's road along which, in later
centuries, so many other pilgrims travelled. It was on this
occasion of his arrival in July, 1174, that he brought the
queen a prisoner to England.

One of his most remarkable embarkations was that
from Portsmouth a month later, on August 8, 1174, when
he took with him to Normandy as a prisoner William the
Lion, King of Scotland. The capture of this king at
Alnwick a short time previously, during his invasion of
Northumberland, is not unconnected with Hampshire
history. Two years before this event, the chief Hampshire
baron, Adam de Port, the lord of Basing and of many
manors in this county, was outlawed for an attempt on the
life of the king. The cause of this attempt, so far as I am

aware, is unknown ; perhaps it arose through the murder of the archbishop. Adam de Port took refuge in Scotland, and was honourably received by the Scottish king. He joined him in his invasion of the North of England. A force of English knights and men-at-arms, hearing of this invasion, hastily assembled, and hurried northwards into Northumberland in misty weather. In the meantime, the Scottish king, meeting with no resistance, sent his army to plunder the country, while he sat down before Alnwick Castle with only sixty knights. As the English force advanced through the mist, they saw the friendly castle of Alnwick rise before them, and were much surprised to find the Scottish king besieging the place with only sixty followers. These were surrounded, and after a fight the king and his small band were all captured, except two persons, one of whom was Adam de Port, the outlawed Hampshire baron, who cut his way out through the English force and again escaped to Scotland. Subsequently he was pardoned and his estates restored.

Henry II. held his Easter court at Winchester, according to the ancient custom of the West Saxon kings, in 1176, and in August of that year he also held a great council there. He was in Hampshire for many weeks in the summer of 1177, a boisterous season, during which he was detained in England partly by the rough weather and partly by an illness which obliged him to go to Winchester and lie up for about a month. Shortly before his embarkation for Normandy in 1182, he held a council at Bishop's Waltham, and on this occasion he made his will.

After landing at Southampton in 1186, he paid a visit to the Bishop of Winchester at Marwell, about seven miles northwards of Southampton, where Henry de Blois had founded a collegiate chantry for priests. Here the bishop entertained the king, and here may be seen at the present day some remains of the episcopal establishment, the sites of the disused fish-ponds, the foundations and some walls of the buildings, and the ruins of the chapel, now a cowshed.

The death of Henry II. occurred in Normandy, and the first official act of his son Richard, as King of England, was to order the liberation of his mother, Queen Eleanor, who had been a state prisoner in England for about sixteen years. He appointed her regent in his absence, and until his arrival she maintained a court of her own. At her invitation, the earls, prelates, and barons assembled at Winchester in August, 1189, to receive their new sovereign, and at this meeting the date of the king's coronation was fixed to take place at Westminster on September 3. That event was a brilliant assembly, and at the feast which followed the citizens of London served in the royal cellars, and the citizens of Winchester in the royal kitchen. Richard soon left for his continental dominions, and did not return until after his wars in Palestine and his captivity in Germany. The shipmasters of Southampton had an opportunity of showing their skill as navigators in the Palestine expedition, as many of their ships and galleys were employed in conveying troops and provisions. After the expedition was over, and Richard's long captivity at an end, it was in the galley of a Southampton shipmaster, named Alan Trenchemere, that he embarked at Antwerp in February, 1194, on his return to England. Then, after he had reduced the castles in the midland counties, which were held against him in the interest of his brother John, he moved southwards towards Winchester, it having been decided that he should be crowned a second time there. He entered Hampshire in the middle of April, and lodged at Freemantle, on the royal manor of Kingsclere. The next day he moved on to Winchester Castle, and the day following left the castle and took up his quarters in St. Swithun's Priory. On April 17, in the midst of a distinguished assembly and a vast multitude of people, chiefly Hampshire folk, he was crowned in the cathedral by the Archbishop of Canterbury. All the chief men in the kingdom were present on this occasion, as well as William, King of

Scotland. The Archbishop of York, however, the king's half-brother, the son of Fair Rosamond, although he was in Winchester, did not attend the coronation, because the king had commanded him not to insist on his claim to have his cross carried before him, an official act to which in the southern province the Archbishop of Canterbury would not consent. At this coronation feast the citizens of London appeared, made a payment of 200 marks to the king, and claimed to serve in the royal cellars. The citizens of Winchester withstood this claim, but their objection was overruled, they, as before at Westminster, being allowed to serve in the kitchen. This civic dispute concerning ancient privileges, the honour of which Winchester formerly had all to itself, shows how London had grown in importance, while Winchester had already begun relatively to decline.

A few days later King Richard left Winchester and moved towards Portsmouth, where an army was already assembling to cross over to Normandy. He probably journeyed along the old Roman road over the downs to the south of the city, and he certainly stopped at Bishop's Waltham. There he held his last council on English soil, and on this occasion Geoffry, Archbishop of York, caused his cross to be carried before him as he went to the assembly, which much offended the Archbishop of Canterbury ; so that, by advice of the king, the subject was referred to the Pope for his decision. The ruins of the great episcopal palace at Waltham has many memories, and this archiepiscopal dispute during the meeting of the last English council of King Richard is one of them. The king went on to Portsmouth, and, while his ships were loading, turned aside to Rowland's Castle to have a day's hunting in the forest of Stanstead, but a quarrel arose between those ill-assorted comrades in arms, the Brabanters and the Welsh, and they had a hostile meeting on their own account, at which some were slain on both sides. Richard could not afford to lose his troops in this way, so he hastily returned and quelled the disturbance. After waiting some ten days on account of the boisterous weather, he finally set sail with about 100 large ships, and England saw him no more.

A noted man in Hampshire at this time was William Briwere, who was a trusty councillor of Richard, as he, or his father of the same name, had been of Henry I. and Henry II.

William Briwere was one of the commissioners sent by Richard in 1193 to make peace with the King of France. His chief place in Hampshire was King's Somborne, where he resided when in the county. This royal manor he held of the king, and in the church there is a worn monumental effigy, which is traditionally said to be that of this trusty servant of the early Plantagenet kings.

It was during the reign of Richard that English people took part in a crusade led by their own king. Part of the fleet for this expedition assembled in Southampton Water, and the sheriff of the county was ordered to supply 800 hogs, presumably in sides of bacon, and also 10,000 horse-shoes with double sets of nails, for the cavalry with which the king gained such renown in Palestine.

The port of Southampton being much concerned with the traffic to and from the continental dominions of the Norman and Angevin kings, was concerned also in the crusading expeditions. In 1147, a contingent of ships sailed from this port, and joined others from London and Bristol, to assist Alphonso, King of Portugal, against the Moors, and it was in that year that Lisbon was taken from them. In the reign of Henry II., voyages were also made to Palestine. Hampshire still retains some traces of this crusading age. The first reputed Mayor of Southampton entered on the list preserved in the municipal records is Benedict Ace, Acon, or Azon—a name probably derived from some trading connection he had with Acre, the chief port of Palestine. In some Hampshire churches, such as Winchfield and Nateley Scures, there are examples of Norman arches so modified in form as almost to resemble arches of the Saracenic style, which it is reasonable to suppose was caused by the influence of Saracenic art. The first charter to the town of Portsmouth was granted by Richard I. in 1193, and the arms of that borough, whether as old as this time or not, contain a crescent moon, an emblem suggestive of the eastern wars of that king. In the name of the river Medina, which flows from Newport, the chief town in the Isle of Wight, we may perhaps trace an imported Saracenic name; for Medina is derived from the Arabic, denoting a chief city, and it appears from the charter of Isabella de Fortibus, the Lady of the island in the thirteenth century, to have been also the name of the town, which is there mentioned as the 'novo burgho de Medina.'

In some of the Hampshire churches we meet with other traces of the crusades in the effigies and other monumental remains of knights who took part in them, or of those knights who were members of the military religious orders —the Templars and the Hospitallers.

John, Count of Mortain, and Earl of Gloucester in right of his first wife Hawissa, daughter and heiress of William, Earl of Gloucester, and grand-daughter of Earl Robert, was connected with this county through the important manor of Mapledurham, which formed part of the honour of Gloucester. The origin of Petersfield, and its rise into the position of a market town, must be ascribed to charters granted by the Earl of Gloucester and his daughter, and to another charter granted by the Count of Mortain, afterwards King John, which is still preserved in the town chest at that place.

John, both before and after he became king, appears to have been very fond of hunting, and, considering how much he travelled from place to place, he spent a considerable part of his time in the Hampshire forests. Traditions of his hunting expeditions survive at Southampton, at

Freemantle near Kingsclere, at Odiham, and at Worldham near Alton.

His favourite hunting seat was Freemantle, which he visited, while he was king, on thirty-seven separate occasions. He was at Odiham on twenty-four occasions during his reign. In his progresses through Hampshire he appears to have secured a few days' sport whenever he could. He travelled rather frequently from Winchester to Clarendon, near Salisbury, and on these journeys he usually turned aside and stopped for a day or more at Ashley. There appears to have been a hunting-box of some sort on that manor, which was later on held of the crown, with the custody of the forest of Bere. John came to Winchester on fifty-one separate occasions while he was king, and he appears to have remained there as long as his business elsewhere would allow him. His son Henry, who succeeded him, was born there in 1207.

On May 19th, 1215, John's Itinerary shows that he paid a visit to the site of the old Roman city of Silchester. We should be glad if we could learn in what condition, at that time, he found the ruins of that interesting place. He was then on his way to Odiham. The barons were pressing him, and he was no doubt considering what he should do. His inspection of the ruins of Silchester may have caused him to reflect on the decay of human greatness. He left Odiham on June 9th, and the Great Charter was signed at Runnemede, on the 15th of the same month.

During the first years of his reign he spent much of his time abroad, fighting for his Norman dukedom. He embarked and disembarked at Portsmouth on several occasions during these years, and when the fortune of war had gone against him, it was at Portsmouth he arrived, in December, 1203, having lost Normandy.

He was, however, still lord of Gascony; Bordeaux, and most of the country from the Loire to the Pyrenees still owned him, and he was represented in these provinces by his seneschal. When he resolved, in the summer of 1206, to try again to recover his lost dukedom, he assembled a fleet in the Solent and embarked at Yarmouth in the Isle of Wight. This expedition sailed direct to the friendly port of La Rochelle, and was the first of the English expeditions to France, after the loss of Normandy. A similar expedition left the Solent for the same destination, in the winter of 1214. The loss of Normandy increased the commercial traffic between Southampton and Bordeaux, for, after Rouen was lost, Bordeaux continued to be the centre of English influence in France for more than 200 years.

We have now traced consecutively the course of events in the history of this county down to the time of the Great Charter. Many kings and other high personages have passed before us across the Hampshire stage. They have had their entrances and their exits in succession, all too quickly. Enough has, however, been said about them to show that Hampshire, during these earlier centuries of English history, was the scene of many events of national importance.

The history of this county must now be viewed from other aspects. The doings of kings, earls, bishops, and barons, and the assembly of armies and councils, do not make the history of the people, and we must now view the history of Hampshire from its more local aspects. The chief events of national interest, after the date of the Great Charter, which form part of the history of this county, will be alluded to in the following chapters—some of them under the localities in which they occurred.

CHAPTER XII.

MONASTIC LIFE.

THE earliest religious house in Hampshire of which any record has come down to us is that one which, as early as the beginning of the tenth century, became known as the Old Minster at Winchester. A tradition which was current in the Saxon period states that an earlier abbey founded in Romano-British time, the brethren of which were known as the Monks of St. Mark, existed in Winchester, presumably on the site of the Old Minster. Whether this was so or not, it is certain that Roman buildings of some sort stood on this site, for many Roman remains have been found close to the present cathedral, and a mass of very hard flint concrete similar to Roman work, and different from anything else in the basement, still exists in the crypt of the cathedral. The tradition says that this monastery was destroyed early in the sixth century.

The Old Minster of later Saxon time arose from the munificent bequest of King Cynegils in 646, who gave to it the whole of the land round the city, at that time all known as parts of Chilcombe, and including the present parishes of Chilcombe, Winnal, Morestead, Compton, Wyke, Littleton, and Sparsholt. At the time of the Domesday Survey this great manor had nine churches in various parts of it. The Old Minster was under the Benedictine rule for about 200 years. In 868 the Benedictine monks were replaced by secular canons, and these were

expelled by Bishop Athelwold, and the Benedictines re-
instated in 963.*

The next monasteries established in this county were
those of Redbridge, which was founded about 680, and
Nursling, which was in existence before 710. These disappeared entirely in later Saxon time, and were in all probability destroyed by the Danes. Out of the monastery of
Nursling came the missionary Winfrid, or St. Boniface, the
great missionary of Germany, whose name is far better
known in that country than in Devonshire, where he was
born, or in Hampshire, where he received his education
and training.

The New Minster at Winchester was founded by Edward
the Elder in 901, and his gift of land to it rivalled the
earlier gift of Cynegils to the older foundation. This land
included the great manor of Micheldever, which comprised
a hundred hides, and was about as large as that of Chilcombe, given to the Old Minster 250 years earlier. The
New Minster was also a community of secular canons until
963. These canons were generally men of noble families,
often of royal blood, who were desirous of devoting themselves to a religious life. In the course of time that life
became a very loose one, for the canons married wives, and
some had more than one. They commonly lived in the
country away from the abbey, and performed their religious
services, as far as they were performed, by deputies.
These abuses of a system of conventual life, which was no
doubt at first free from reproach, went on until the time of
Dunstan, the great monastic reformer, when Bishop Athelwold, with his support, drove the canons out, and established the monks of the regular Benedictine order in their
places. A group of abbeys, founded by the son and widow
of King Alfred, arose in Hampshire ; for, in addition to the
New Minster, Edward the Elder founded the abbey of
Romsey, and the Lady Eanswith, the queen of Alfred,
founded St. Mary's Abbey for nuns at Winchester. It is

* 'Fasti Monastici Ævi Saxonici,' by W. de Gray Birch, pp. 1-11.

ncertain whether the abbey at Romsey was originally stablished for monks or nuns, but it became a female ommunity living according to the Benedictine rule in 967.

Wherwell, another royal foundation, arose in this ounty in the tenth century, and was established by the .ady Elfrida, queen of King Ethelred, about 986, in ontrition for her sins. Another monastery, known as that f Sapalanda,* is ascertained by charters to have existed efore the time of the Norman Conquest, but its locality is nknown, and as no traces of it are left, it was probably lestroyed, like the houses at Redbridge and Nursling, luring the later ravages of the Danes and Norsemen.

Subsequently Edward the Confessor founded at Twyn-iam, near the mouth of the Avon, the priory for secular anons which was afterwards closely connected with the listory of the south-west corner of the county, and became :nown as Christchurch.

One other religious house, that of St. Brinstan's Hospital .t Winchester,† completes the number of Saxon founda-ions in Hampshire. This was in existence before 935, .nd was the earliest hospital in the county ; but its life was hort, at any rate under this name, for it does not occur in he records of the city in later centuries.

A marked change occurred in the monastic history of Iampshire during the Norman and Angevin period. The Vorman kings and nobles cared little for the West Saxon eligious houses. Their sympathies were with the great ibbeys of their native land, and many of their religious)enefactors in this county were subsidiary priories, estab-ished, indeed, in Hampshire, and supported by the produce)f Hampshire lands, but vested in the abbeys of Nor-nandy, to which the surplus revenues of these priories vent after the cost of their primary purposes had been lefrayed. From the piety of these kings and nobles there hus arose in this county twelve houses, or cells, which vere all attached to foreign abbeys, and which, after the

* 'Fasti Monastici Ævi Saxonici.'   † *Ibid.*

English kings had lost Normandy, became known as the alien priories.

One of the best examples of these is that of Sherborne, near Basingstoke, which was founded by Henry de Port, a baron of the Exchequer, in the time of Henry I. He was the son of Hugh de Port, a follower of the Conqueror, who held so many Hampshire manors at the time of the Great Survey. The purpose for which Sherborne Priory was founded was similar to that for which other priories of the same kind were established. Hugh de Port held this manor of Odo, Bishop of Bayeux, the half-brother of the Conqueror, the prelate to whom we are indebted for the Bayeux tapestry, which depicts the scenes of the Norman conquest. Henry de Port states in his charter that he gives the lands at tithes at Sherborne to God and to St. Vigor of Cerisy (a great abbey in the diocese of Bayeux), ' for the soul of my lord King Henry, for the soul of William the king's son, for the souls of my father and mother, also for the souls of myself, and my wife and children, and of all the people of Shirebourn.' Here the De Port family made their mausoleum, and here the community prayed for the souls of the founder and his successors, who were also its benefactors, and at Sherborne a part of their noble church still remains.

It was for similar purposes that William FitzOsborne founded the priory of Hayling, and attached it to the abbey of Jumieges, and that the priory of Andover was founded by the Conqueror himself, and attached to the abbey of St. Sauveur le Vicomte. The priory of Stratfieldsaye was established by Nicholas de Stuteville, and attached to the abbey of Vallemont. Similarly Hamble Priory was attached to the abbey of Tyrone, Selborne to St. Vigor of Cerisy, Andswell to Tyrone, Applederwell to St. Mary de Montisberg, Carisbrooke to Lira, Ellingham to St. Saveur le Vicomte, and St. Cross in the Isle of Wight to Tyrone. St. Helens was also attached to some Norman abbey.

The other religious houses which were established in Hampshire during the Norman and Angevin period were independent communities. Of these, the priory of St. Deny's, founded in 1124, and the priory founded within the enclosure of Porchester Castle in 1133, and subsequently removed to Southwick, were established by Henry I. That unhappy monarch, during his later years, had to mourn the death of his son, Prince William, who was lost at sea in 1120, and his wife, the good Queen Maud, who died in 1118, and the establishment of these priories had for their object the spiritual benefit of himself and his relatives. His charter, founding the priory of St. Deny's, shows that the sorrow-stricken king designed the Augustine canons of that house to offer perpetual prayers for these, for he says that he makes his gift to the priory for the salvation of his soul, for the redemption of the soul of his father, and of his mother, also of Matilda the queen his wife, and of William their son. In his charter establishing the Augustine priory at Porchester, he remembers also his brother Rufus, for he says that it is founded for the souls of his father, of William his brother, of his mother, and of his ancestors and his successors.

At that time the Lord of the Isle of Wight was Baldwin de Redvers, Earl of Devon, whose great fief on the mainland extended as far eastward as the river Avon in Hampshire. He founded, in 1132, the abbey of Quarr, the chief monastic house in the island, and one of the earliest Cistercian houses in England. The charter by which he established it appears from internal evidence to have been executed in Normandy. He gave the manor of Arreton, in the Isle of Wight, and other possessions, to Godfrey, the Abbot of Savigny, in Normandy, for the building of this abbey at Quarr, and its first inmates were monks from Savigny. Earl Baldwin also founded the priory of Braemore, on the Avon, near Fordingbridge, at the eastern border of his earldom, and there his descendant, the famous Isabella de Fortibus, was subsequently buried.

The priory of Hartley Wintney, a small Cistercian nunnery in the North of Hampshire, also appears to have been established before the end of the twelfth century.

In the·beginning of the reign of King John, another Augustine priory arose at Mottisfont, through the benevolence of William Briwere, the chief Hampshire baron at that time.* He was made sheriff of the county in 1207, and lived at King's Somborne, a few miles away. He had a brother, who was probably a hermit of some sort, for he got the name of Peter de Rivallis, and was popularly called 'the holy man in the wall.' Apparently he lived in a mural cell somewhere in the neighbourhood, and was held in great reverence as a worker of miracles. However this may have been, he had saved a large sum of money, and this he gave to enrich the priory at Mottisfont his brother had founded.

The great Cistercian abbey of Beaulieu, founded in the New Forest by King John, also began its existence about this time. Its abbot was one of the commissioners to whom the king entrusted the duty of conveying the queen and his children, Richard and Joan, to him in France in 1214, and to whom also he entrusted the care of his son John. King John visited Beaulieu on four occasions between 1206 and 1213.

Another abbey, that of Titchfield, the canons of which were of the Præmonstratensian order, was founded in 1231 by Henry III., who dedicated his gift to God, and the church of St. Mary of Titchfield, for the salvation of his soul, for the souls of his ancestors, and for the souls of his heirs and successors.

For a similar purpose, eight years later, Henry III. founded the Cistercian abbey of Netley, at the place then

* Maddox, 'Hist. Exchequer.'

:alled Edwardstowe. The first monks of Netley came rom Beaulieu. This was the last monastery established in Hampshire, and its remains are at the present time the nost interesting ruins in the county.

There were also the Dominican, Franciscan, and Carnelite Friars, the hermits, the recluses, the Knights Templar, and the Knights Hospitaller. There were likevise the hospitals for the relief of the poor, infirm, and iick, and for the reception of distressed travellers, and other 1ospitals for lepers. These were all managed by commu-lities of brethren and sisters living under some religious ·ule, generally that of St. Augustine.

The coming of the friars, and the religious reformation which resulted from their itinerant preaching, led to the :stablishment in Hampshire of three friaries in Win-:hester and one in Southampton. In Winchester a :onvent for Dominican, or Black, Friars was established in [230 ; for the Carmelite, or White, Friars in 1278 ; and for :he Franciscan, or Grey, Friars also in the time of Henry III. The Franciscan friary at Southampton also :ame into existence about the same time. The friars were iocial and sanitary reformers as well as preachers, and at Southampton they left proof that they were no theorists, out practical men. The sanitary condition of the towns n the thirteenth century was deplorable. Dirt and filth :eigned supreme in the streets, there was no effective drainage of houses, and no good water supply. At Southampton the Franciscan friars, aided by the Warden of St. Julian's Hospital, brought a supply of pure water nto the town from a spring more than a mile away. They supplied this water to the town conduits, and for more than ive centuries the people of Southampton were benefited oy their enterprise and industry.

Some of the great Norman abbeys had important estates in Hampshire. The Conqueror's favourite abbey of Bec held the manors of Anne de Bec now called Monxton, Combe, and Quarley, in the north-west of the

county, through the alien priory of Okeburn. The abbey
of Jumieges held a great part of Hayling Island, that of
Greistain held the manor of Penton, and that of Lira held
six churches in the Isle of Wight and one in Southampton.
. With the reign of Henry III., the foundation of abbeys
and priories in this county came to an end, for the Statutes
of Mortmain, passed soon afterwards, made it illegal to
bequeath land for the establishment of any more. The
religious houses exerted a great influence on the medieval
life of Hampshire, and have left permanent marks of that
influence. Some of the names of parishes, manors, and
farms at the present day, have been derived from the
former connection of these lands with the abbeys and
priories. Abbots Ann, Abbots Worthy, and Abbotston
belonged to the Abbot of Hyde, Hurstbourn Priors, to the
Prior of St. Swithun, Prior's Dean to the Prior of Southwick, Itchen Abbas to the Abbess of St. Mary's, Winchester, and Monk Sherborne to the Benedictine priory at
that place. Many local customs which have survived on
the old monastic manors arose through their connection
with these religious houses. The greatest of these houses
in Hampshire were the priory of St. Swithun and the
abbey of Hyde, at Winchester, the Old and New Minsters,
which owed their wealth to the munificence of the West
Saxon kings.

The Benedictines have left their permanent marks in the
great churches which have come down to us, the cathedral
at Winchester, and the abbey church at Romsey. The
church of the Augustine priory, at Christchurch, has also
happily been spared. No Cistercian church has been preserved in Hampshire. The sites of the noble churches at
Quarr, Beaulieu, and Netley are now overgrown with grass,
but the outline and foundations of that at Beaulieu and the
remains of the abbey church at Netley tell the story of
their former magnificence. The permanent mark which
the Cistercians have left is of another kind. We may read
the story of their industry on the surface of the lands which

hey brought into cultivation on their great estate at Beau-
ieu, where the remains of the great barn—one of the largest
n England—in which the produce of some of these lands
vas stored, may still be seen at St. Leonard's Grange.
They also greatly increased the cultivated area on the
:states which belonged to Quarr and Netley, and succeed-
ng generations of men have reaped the benefit of that
abour.

The Benedictine and Cistercian monks and nuns, and the
Augustine canons, whose houses were situated in Hamp-
;hire, do not represent the whole of the monasteries and
·eligious orders which were connected with this county.
There were also the foreign abbeys which held possessions
n it, and abbeys and priories in other parts of England
vhich also owned Hampshire manors or lands. For
:xample ; Westminster Abbey held the manor of Eversley,
hat of Chertsey held the manors of Winchfield and Elve-
ham, and St. Peter's, at Gloucester, held Linkenholt ;
Milton Abbey, in Dorsetshire, held the manor of Watch-
ngwell, Newark Priory held land at Ropley, Waverley
Abbey held a grange at Boviatt, the prioress of Amesbury
ield Nether Wallop, and the Abbess of Tarent, in Dorset,
ield the manor of Hurstbourn Tarrant, given to her house
oy Henry III.

The influence of the monastic system on the history of
:his county was very great. That influence was both eccle-
;iastical and secular, and may be seen even at the present
:ime in such places as Romsey and Christchurch, which
became market towns under this influence, and at Beaulieu
ind Wherwell, which grew into large villages, possessed of
exceptional privileges in regard to markets, fairs, local
government, and the administration of justice, under the
fostering care of the abbeys. These abbeys possessed
:harters giving their tenants certain liberties, which the
neighbouring places did not possess. Although the monks
ind nuns have departed from Beaulieu and Wherwell for

more than three and a half centuries, the fairs at these places, which were granted to the abbeys by royal charters, still survive. The privileges which the religious houses possessed in regard to fisheries, common pasturage, and forest rights, passed at the dissolution to those who became their legal successors, and thus many an old custom on the monastic estates has survived until the present time.

The larger abbeys and priories all possessed the right of holding their own courts-leet, independently of the hundred-courts held under the jurisdiction of the sheriff, at which their tenants would otherwise have been obliged to render suit, and an abbey or priory which had this right on its home estate generally had the same powers on its outlying manors. Such houses also usually had the privilege of capturing offenders who had committed any crime on their estates, and of bringing them to justice.

They had also the power of free gallows, on which the convicted felons were hanged ; and as there were so many abbeys and priories in the county, the gallows were numerous. They had also the privilege of the assize of bread and ale, so that instead of being subject to the inquisitorial functions of the hundred-courts, the courts-leet of the abbey manors could appoint their own officials, such as the ale-taster, to see that the bread was of good weight, and the ale ' fit for man's body.'

This local system of government and administration of justice on the estates of the great abbeys and priories independently of the hundred - courts, occasionally caused disputes to arise. Thus, in 1280, a complaint was made against the Prior of Merton, who held land in Hampshire, that his villeins at Heggefield did not render their due suit at the Holeshete hundred-court. In answer to this he produced a charter of Richard I., confirmed by Henry III., which proved their immunity.

Many Hampshire villages, such as Micheldever, were the centres of rural life on the monastic manors, and although they were not near the abbeys to which they belonged, they were the places where the courts were held. Such great estates were, as in the case of Micheldever, separate hundreds; but the hundred was under the jurisdiction of the abbot, and not of the sheriff of the county. Similarly, the Abbess of Wherwell, through her steward, had jurisdiction over the manors which formed the hundred of Wherwell.

The customary services which the tenants on the abbey or priory manors had to perform were different in different places—in some cases more burdensome than in others. When the religious houses acquired their estates, they acquired the right to such local customary services as had been usual on the manors. Thus in the case of St. Deny's Priory, the men of Portswood performed for the priory the same customary work they had previously performed for the king, and this appears to have been somewhat heavy. From June 24 to August 1, they cleaned half an acre of ground daily; in the month of August they reaped half an acre daily, and each one had a sheaf; they stored the harvest in the barns. After harvest they collected clay for repairing the houses till Michaelmas; afterwards they gathered apples and made cider. At Martinmas they paid their Church dues and custom for the rights of pannage; then they trenched the land and made up the fences. In the spring and early summer they cut the meadows, carried the hay, sheared the sheep, measured out the folds, and repaired the king's weir. These numerous services were distributed among the tenants, and in return these tenants, both villeins and borderers, had their homesteads and cottages, their common fields and pastures, which they cultivated for their own use.

A class of religious fraternities which differed considerably from the regular conventual establishments was that of the colleges of priests, of which there were some in this county. These small colleges of secular priests were not uncommon in the Middle Ages. At Winchester there was the College of the Holy Trinity, founded in 1318, for a warden and several priests, near St. Mary's Abbey, the

Fraternity of St. Peter, consisting of a prior and brethren attached to the church of St. Maurice, the College of St. Elizabeth of Hungary, consisting of a provost, six chaplains, six clerks, and six choristers, and the College of St. Mary Kalendar, an educational fraternity learned in the calendar, with a very fine church on the north of the High Street.

At Marwell there was a college for four priests, and at Barton, in the Isle of Wight, a similar college or oratory, presided over by an arch-presbyter. The site of the Barton oratory, with the land around it, is now included in the royal estate of Osborne.

At Lymerston, in the Isle of Wight, there was a community of chaplains living under the rule of St. Augustine, and at St. Mary's, Southampton, there was a chanter, or warden, and chaplains associated together as a small religious community.

There were also the fraternity known as the Guild of the Holy Ghost at Basingstoke, which was an educational community, and its ancient possessions and functions were subsequently passed on to the Grammar School in that town. The ruin which remains of its buildings near the railway-station is familiar to travellers on the South-Western Railway.

In the early part of the sixteenth century there was also a Brotherhood at Alresford, which is mentioned in 1527 in the will of John Lomer of Lomer.

The hermits and recluses, who lived solitary lives, must also be included among the religious orders. The popular ideas concerning the hermits is very different from the true one. A hermitage was practically a monastery, with one inmate. In his cell the hermit lived his solitary life, but it was not a useless one. He was inducted into his hermitage by a religious service, and afterwards he lived and died there. He must in some cases have had a servant or lay brother, who ministered to his wants and otherwise assisted him. The hermit had some means of support. A good example of a Hampshire hermitage is that one which existed at a spot now known as Chapel, in the parish of St. Mary, Southampton. When it was first established is unknown, but it is certain that Henry VII. recognised the usefulness of the hermit who lived there in his time, named William Gefferey, by granting to him, conjointly with the mayor, aldermen, sheriff, bailiffs, and burgesses of Southampton, the privilege of holding an annual fair and market on the feast of the Holy Trinity and three following days. This fair was held around the hermitage, and the profits arising therefrom belonged partly to the hermit and partly to the town. Some remains of this hermitage, which was situated close to the Itchen, lately existed at Chapel Wharf. From other cases, in which it is known that hermits located at ferries discharged the useful functions of providing a light, and often a boat, for travellers, it is reasonable to suppose that William Gefferey, the hermit of the chapel of the Holy Trinity, opposite to the old ferry at Itchen, performed similar functions there.

Another noted hermitage was that which existed on St. Catherine's Hill, at Chale, in the Isle of Wight. There is a record of the admission of Walter de Langstrell to this hermitage in October, 1312, and an engraving of the tower in which this hermit performed the useful function of a lighthouse-keeper has come down to us. There were no Elder Brethren of Trinity House in those days to place lights round the coast.

The hermits on St. Catherine's Hill were the only lighthouse-keepers in the Isle of Wight in the Middle Ages as far as is known, and it is impossible not to admire the self-sacrifice which led them to devote their lives to this useful work. Everyone must respect the devotion of the hermit, who kept his light burning on this hill in all weathers, and while he attended to his beacon-fire or lamps on tempestuous nights, mingled his nocturnal prayers for the safety of mariners with the howling of the storm.

Another hermitage at Stratfieldsaye was endowed with certain lands near it in Hampshire and Berkshire in the

reign of Edward III.,* and the purpose of such an establishment in this place was, apparently, that the hermit
should direct travellers on their way through that part of
the forest of Eversley.

There are traces of other Hampshire hermitages in the
old forests of the county, at Hambledon and at Colemore.
Near Havant there was a hermitage, whose occupant
apparently performed the duty of guiding travellers across
the dangerous wadeway which led into Hayling Island;
and near Emsworth, on the Sussex border, there was
another where the hermit showed the way, or ford, which
led the traveller safely into Thorney Island.

* Inq. p. m. 17 Edw. III.

CHAPTER XIII.

OTHER PHASES OF MEDIEVAL RELIGIOUS LIFE.

THE military religious orders were well represented in Hampshire. The Templars, or Knights Templar, who were first introduced into England in the reign of Stephen, and whose headquarters in this country were at the Temple, close to the city of London, had a preceptory in Hampshire at South Baddesley. They had also a preceptory, or an estate, at Selborne. The order likewise held the manor of Cerne, near Arreton, in the Isle of Wight, an estate now known as Temple lands at Sherfield on Loddon, and another at Warblington.

The Templars wore a white mantle, or cloak, with a red cross on the left breast, and were commonly known as the Red Cross Knights.

In the reign of Henry II. an annual payment of 13s. 4d. was assigned to the Knights of the Temple out of the fee farm rent of Southampton. A stone coffin-lid, with the insignia of the Knights Templar, may be seen at the present time in the church at Selborne, a relic of their former connection with that place.

The other great military religious order, the Knights Hospitaller, had commanderies at Godsfield, near Alresford, and at North Baddesley. They held also the manor of Woodcot, in the north of the county, and that of Enham, near Andover. This order was also known as that of St. John of Jerusalem, and the members wore a black cloak, with a white cross upon the left breast.

The surplus revenues of the estates of both these orders were sent to Palestine, for their primary objects as crusaders and protectors of pilgrims.

The Hospitallers were an important body in Hampshire, and maintained their peculiar privilege in it when necessary. Thus, in the ninth year of Edward I., their tenant, John de Evineley, was summoned to show cause why he did not make suit at the hundred-court at Andover, and he pleaded 'that he held of the Prior and Brethren of St. John of Jerusalem, and that by charter, 37 Henry III., the prior and his men were freed from scot and geld, sheriffs' aids, and all services at the Hundred Court.'* This exemption was probably claimed for the manor of Knights Enham. The Hospitallers were first established in England in the reign of Henry I., and their chief seat was at St. John's, Clerkenwell. When Bishop Henry de Blois established the hospital of St. Cross, he placed it under the care of the Knights of St. John, and their connection with that great hospital continued for about a century. A survival of the connection of the hospital of St. Cross with the Hospitallers still exists in the dress of the brethren, who wear a black cloak with the cross of the order upon the left breast.

At Godsfield the ancient chapel of the Knights of St. John still exists in a fair state of preservation. In the early part of the twelfth century the land at Godsfield and the hospital of St. Cross were the only possessions which the order held in Hampshire, but when the Knights Templar were suppressed in the reign of Edward II. their possessions in this county were for the most part given to the Hospitallers. In this way the Knights of St. John became possessed of the manor of South Baddesley, the Templars' estate at Selborne, and the annual payment, which had been greatly increased, from the fee farms of the towns of Southampton and Portsmouth. On account of the burning of these towns by the French in 1338, the

* Plac. de quo warranto, 9 Edw. I.

Hospitallers could not get more than £14 10s. in rents in that year, instead of £20 3s. 4d. they had been accustomed to receive.

In 1339, the 'Prior of the Hospital,' or chief of the order in England, was called upon to assist in the defence of Southampton, and to supply esquires and archers to the Earl of Warwick, to whom the custody of that town was then committed. The Hospitallers, as well as the Templars, had the privilege, by ancient grant, of having one man in every borough in the realm, who was quit of common assizes and tallages, *i.e.*, of taxes, within his borough, and who was known as the man of the Hospitallers, or man of the Templars. This privilege must have increased their influence in the Hampshire towns. Monumental remains of the Hospitallers, denoted by the well-known Maltese cross, exist at Selborne, North Baddesley, St. Mary Bourne, Michelmersh, and elsewhere.

The Hospitallers were bound by the rules of their order to relieve casual destitution, and so they dispensed to pilgrims certain hospitality in the places where their estates were situated, as well as in Palestine. In 1185, the Grand Master of the order visited England, and a great council was held at Winchester, at which Henry II. and nearly all the bishops and abbots were present, to receive him with due honour. These knights have left some traces of their former connection with this county as land-holders, in such place-names as Knight's Copse, near South Baddesley, Knightswood, North Baddesley, and Knightsbridge Copse, Selborne.

In order to understand the position which the Knights Hospitaller occupied in the religious life of the country during the Middle Ages, from the twelfth to the sixteenth centuries, we must recognise the important part which the custom of pilgrimage played during that period. Pilgrims to the Holy Land were protected, as far as they could protect them, by the Hospitallers, whose special business was to guard the way to the Holy City; but the expense and fatigue of such a journey prevented all but the rich and the strong from undertaking it. For the mass of the people who desired to go on pilgrimage there were other sacred places and shrines which could be visited. Among these Rome occupied the first place, and pilgrimages to it began as early as Anglo-Saxon time. Some of the kings of Wessex took the pilgrim's staff and went on this journey. Ceadwalla and Ina both died in Rome, where there was a Saxon school or hospital, said to have been founded by the latter king for the reception and relief of needy pilgrims, and for the instruction of young Anglo-Saxons in the faith. A tax of a penny on each house was levied by Ina for the support of this establishment in Rome. This was originally known as Rome-scot, and was the beginning of those payments which in later ages were called Peter's pence. The Saxon kings also established hospitals in many places for the entertainment of pilgrims on their way to Rome. King Cnut, during his famous pilgrimage to Rome, obtained from the Pope the exemption of the English school there from all taxes, and he likewise induced the Emperor and King Rudolf to abolish the barriers and tolls on English pilgrims proceeding to that city.

In later centuries there were other places abroad to which English pilgrims flocked, one of which was the shrine of St. James at Compostella. In the fifteenth century pilgrims for Compostella commonly embarked at Southampton.

There were also many shrines in England which attracted hosts of pilgrims. Hampshire people, no doubt sometimes journeyed to Canterbury, Walsingham, and other noted shrines, but it is certain they more often visited, in company with people from other shires, the sacred places in their own county. Nothing in the history of Hampshire is more certain than the existence of these shrines, which attracted crowds of pilgrims. At Winchester there was first that of St. Swithun, a Hampshire saint, whose fame attracted people from all parts of England. They often brought with them sick folk to be healed by the saint. The enlarged part of he cathedral, between the choir and the Lady Chapel, where the shrine of St. Swithun stood, was often quite filled with them. They entered at the Norman door, now stopped up, but which may still be seen in the outer wall of he north transept. There was in Winchester a pilgrims' guild or fraternity, which had charge of a house where the brethren and sisters received the wanderers. The famous shrine at Canterbury was modern in comparison with that of St. Swithun. Like so many other things in Winchester, a great antiquity hung about it. To it had come many generations of pilgrims long before Becket was born. The traditions of the sacred shrines of their forefathers survived long after the newer shrine of St. Thomas à Becket arose, but many Winchester pilgrims no doubt travelled over the downs eastward to Canterbury along the route known as the Pilgrims' Way.

Winchester had also in the New Minster, and afterwards in the abbey of Hyde, another shrine, that of St. Judocus or St. Josse, whose bones had arrived there early in the tenth century under the circumstances previously mentioned. If a prophet is of no honour in his own country, a saint is, for while St. Swithun's fame as a healing saint increased as centuries rolled by, that of St. Josse, who was of foreign origin, appears to have declined, the healing power of St. Swithun's bones being popularly considered to be far more potent than those of the rival saint.

Pilgrims were also attracted in large numbers to the Chapel of our Lady of Grace at Southampton, which Leland tells us, was 'sometime haunted with pilgrims.' Its ruins still remain near St. Mary's Church. In Southampton there was a pilgrims' quarter near the western shore, a place there having been known formerly as Pilgrims' Pit. The reason for the establishment of this chapel in Southampton is obscure, but it is quite certain that the pilgrims came, for we have documentary evidence that they were sometimes lodged in two small chapels on the marsh which belonged to St. Deny's Priory.

Another place of pilgrimage in Hampshire was South-wick, where there was also a shrine of note. Leland tells us that the fame of Southwick 'stood by a priory of black chanons there, and a pilgrimage to Our Lady.' The seal of the priory, which still exists, has on the obverse the words, ' Sit pro Suthwika mediatrix Virgo pudico et pax angelica, sit nobis semper amica.'

There can be little doubt that pilgrims were also attracted to Christchurch, where the holy beam was pointed out, and the legend told of the strange and wonderful workman, who, during the building of that church, made the beam fit after it had been found too short, and who laboured assidously without pay or reward. A church which was built by the aid of a Divine Carpenter, and consequently named Christchurch, could not fail to attract worshippers from distant places.

Many of these pilgrims were so poor that they often passed the night, while on their journeys, by a fire in the woods, and some few place-names in Hampshire, such as Pilgrims' Copse, near Micheldever railway station, and Pilgrims' Place, East Tisted, still remind us of their wander-ings, and of the part which pilgrimages played in the religious life of our forefathers.

Part of the outcome of the religious revival in England which followed the Norman settlement was the establish-ment of hospitals for the relief of the sick, infirm and poor. The greatest in Hampshire was that of St. Cross. It was founded by Bishop Henry de Blois, in the twelfth century, and enlarged by Cardinal Beaufort, whose statue, in one of the niches over the gateway, may still be seen there. St. Cross is the best example of a medieval hospital which has come down to us. Its noble church, domestic buildings, hall, and gateway, retain all their ancient features. It was spoiled of much of its wealth in ancient days, by some of those whose duty it was to preserve it, and it has been similarly spoiled in modern time ; but great foundations such as this survive those who rob them, and after the

iration of certain long leases of its lands, improperly
ited, the hospital of St. Cross will again be a wealthy
idation. While Winchester was at the height of its
sperity during the Norman period, the want of a hospital
i as this for the relief of the poor and sick among the
it number of people whose business brought them to
royal city must have been much felt. Bishop de Blois'
idation was designed to meet this want. A hundred
r men were daily fed there, and no traveller who knocked
its door was sent empty away. A remnant of this
ent hospitality still survives at St. Cross, where bread
beer are dispensed each day to all who apply for it at
gate.

t. Cross is one of the most precious relics of antiquity
ch Hampshire possesses. It has memories of kings,
ops, and crusaders, of many distinguished men in
rch and state who have guided its fortunes, of countless
rims of high and low degree, and of the poor of more
i twenty generations who have claimed hospitality there
had their claim allowed.

he relief of the sick, infirm, and poor was also provided
it Winchester, by its two great abbeys. Just outside
close of St. Swithun's was an almonry, known as the
ers Hospital, or Sustern Spytal, established for a com-
iity of sisters and a chaplain. Another hospital was
ched to the abbey of Hyde, and in the time of
vard II. the number of sick, infirm, and poor who
rted to it was so great that, with the consent of the
iop, the king allowed the abbey to appropriate the great
es of the church of Micheldever for their relief.

s St. Cross was intended to be the great hospital for
ichester, so that of St. Julian was intended to serve a
purpose at Southampton. It was founded by Gervase,
ealthy merchant, and became known as Maison de
u or Domus Dei, and was popularly called God's House.
Julian Hospitator was the patron saint of travellers,
tmen, ferrymen, and wandering minstrels, and there can

be little doubt that his name being given to this hospital is significant, as showing the purpose of its establishment. It was built close to the beach, and consisted of a church, a gate-house tower, and domestic buildings on both sides. As long as the English connection with Normandy lasted it must have been of great use to poor travellers from over the sea. Afterwards, as long as Gascony still remained a possession of the English crown, it was probably much frequented. Phillipa, the queen of Edward III., induced her husband to give it to her newly-established Queen's Hall in Oxford. Since that time the Provost of Queen's College has been warden of the hospital, and the revenue the college has derived from its estates has apparently increased as the original character of foundation became changed.

The other ancient hospitals of Hampshire were those of St. John the Baptist, at Basingstoke, founded by Walter de Merton in 1261, and one similarly dedicated at Andover, said to have been established by the Conqueror. There was also St. John the Baptist's Hospital at Winchester, founded in 1289 by a citizen named John Devenisshe, and St. Nicholas's Hospital at Portsmouth, founded by Bishop Peter de Roche, early in the thirteenth century, and placed under the care of a prior and brethren. Both of these were also known by the name of Maison de Dieu. There was in addition, a St. John's Hospital at Fordingbridge, which was connected with that of St. Cross.

Besides these general hospitals, there were others which were specially established for lepers, and three of these were dedicated to St. Mary Magdalen. The most important appears to have been the Lepers' Hospital on Magdalen Hill, at Winchester, a part of St. Giles's Hill, which had a very handsome chapel, one of the finest of its kind in the county. This survived until the eighteenth century,* when it was demolished and its materials sold. The hospital for lepers at Southampton stood in the Magdalen Field, now called the West Marlands. There was also a leper hospital

---

* See engravings and description: 'Vetusta Monumenta,' iii., 3-6.

t Christchurch, and another at Newport, to which Isabella
e Fortibus, the Lady of the Isle of Wight, gave an annual
:nt from the town of Newport. In her charter to that
)wn it is mentioned as the Hospital for the Lepers of St.
.ugustine. All these foundations were religious houses,
1e brethren of which probably lived according to the
.ugustine rule. As the hospital at Andover was also dedi-
ited to St. Mary Magdalen, as well as St. John the Baptist,
is probable that it also included a lepers' house.

The legends of Hampshire which have arisen through its
ionastic life are many and curious. There is the renowned
gend of St. Swithun and the forty days' rain, which has
)read all over England. It arose at Winchester, where
1 971, on the completion of the new cathedral built by
ishop Athelwold, the bones of the saint were transferred
om the churchyard to the shrine inside ; when, as an old
ironicler tells us, the saint 'protested weeping.' Nothing
 recorded which tells us of rain falling for forty days. This
as probably of later discovery, and shows how the legend
rew from the accident of a wet day when the translation
f the saint's bones took place.
The legend of King Alfred's ghost haunting the Old
[inster, so that the canons of the church were so much
ightened that they had no peace, is another Winchester
gend. They begged his son, King Edward, to remove
is body to the New Minster, which was done, and after-
ards the canons and their successors had peace until they
ere driven out by Bishop Athelwold.
Some curious old legendary tales hang about Wherwell.
here is the story of Queen Elfrida's remorse, how she was
)rmented by evil spirits, and imagined there was a
ionstrous fiend ever on the watch to drag her down to
)rment, especially in the night, when she felt his grasp.
he establishment of this abbey shows that the remorse
ut of which the legend grew was real enough. A super-
:ition prevails at Wherwell against eating ducks' eggs, and

10

has arisen through the ancient story of a duck which laid an egg in a vault beneath the abbey. On this egg a toad sat, and as a result a cockatrice was hatched, which dwelt in the vault, attained a great size, and killed everything that went there. At last the happy thought occurred of letting a strong mirror down into the vault, a man holding it. This was a new experience to the cockatrice, for he saw his own image, and fought the image furiously, until he was nearly dead, on which the man went down into the vault and despatched him. As a consequence of all this, ducks' eggs are not usually eaten. In 1858, old people were living in the village who remembered seeing a door in a house there with a cockatrice painted in gilt on it to commemorate this legend. At Wherwell, also, a story says that corpse lights may be seen in the churchyard, over the wall of which, in the abbey grounds, was the burial-place of the nuns.

A survival of an old custom which prevailed there is that of the Easter cakes, which are still made in the village, and bear a mark resembling that of some old seal or stamp of the abbey.

At Quarr there is a legend of Queen Eleanor, the wife of Henry II., whom her husband kept a prisoner for so many years. Part of this time she undoubtedly spent in Hampshire, for the sheriff's accounts contain entries of payments made on her account, and therefore she may have spent part of her captivity at Quarr. South of the site of the abbey is a wood known as Eleanor's Grove, which the Ordnance Survey officials, who are not folk-lorists, have named Alender's Grove on the six-inch map. Here, the tradition says, Queen Eleanor, while living in the abbey, used to take her walks, which may have been so ; but the legend also says that after her death she was buried there in a golden coffin, which successive generations of peasants have thought it would be a good thing to find, but which some magical spell has hitherto prevented from being discovered.

CHAPTER XIV.

MANORS AND HUNDREDS.

THE conditions of rural life in Hampshire during the
Middle Ages, and the circumstances connected with it,
form one of the most interesting subjects concerning the
history of the county.

Old English rural institutions had their origin in Anglo-
Saxon time. It was then that manors were first formed.
The organization of country life during the earlier centuries
of our history was not parochial, but manorial. There
must, however, have been a time in Hampshire, as well as
in other parts of England, when agricultural communities
existed without lords of manors. The township and the
tithing were the units of country organization and government in early Anglo-Saxon time. We read of elected
tithingmen and reeves of townships before we hear of
lords of manors. We also hear of the election of a lord by
an agricultural community close to the Hampshire border,
for in his will King Alfred commanded that the community
of Damerham should have their privileges restored, possibly
landed ones, and be allowed to choose for their lord
whom they would. At Pamber the tenants assembled in
their annual court appear for many centuries to have
elected their own lord of the manor, and he had, in virtue
of his office, a right to all the stray cattle and the privilege
of hunting in the forest as far as Windsor.

Long before the time of the Norman Conquest the

manorial system was in full operation, and those manor courts which succeeded the township moots were accustomed to meet, as they have met since, year after year, on many Hampshire manors from that time until our own day. On many old Hampshire manors no courts are now held, and when all the copyhold land has become enfranchised, the manors will only be recognised by the ancient special privileges which belonged exclusively to their lords, and which their successors have maintained.

The manors varied greatly in size. Some of them, such as Andover, Basingstoke, Odiham, Micheldever, and East Meon, were of great extent; others were small, and in some instances so small as to be represented in modern times by only one farm.

The history of the smaller towns and large villages of Hampshire is the history of the growth of the population on these manors. The royal manors of Andover, Basingstoke, Odiham, Broughton, Ringwood, and Eling, were some of the most extensive, and the episcopal or monastic manors of Alresford, Micheldever, Fareham, Havant, and East Meon were also of great extent. Some of these large manors acquired the right of holding markets and fairs at an early period, and so they gradually became the centres to which people went to sell their corn and live stock, and to buy such other commodities as were on sale. These commodities were commonly brought to the fairs and markets by the chapmen, or travelling merchants. Until about the thirteenth century permanent shops were few in number in the present market towns, and in the villages they did not exist.

It was not until the beginning of the present century that such a large village as West Meon had any shops.*

The privilege of opening shops in any place was a market privilege, and if no authority existed for the market no shops could be opened. In the time of

* Thorold Rogers, 'Six Centuries of Work and Wages,' vol. i., p. 147.

Henry III. the men of Basingstoke made a complaint against the Abbess of Wherwell, that her tenants did not frequent the market of Basingstoke, and this because a market had been started at Wherwell. Later on, the abbess established her right to do this, for in 51 Henry III. the king granted her a charter for a market, and the little village shops we now see at Wherwell were then first placed on a legal basis.

During the thirteenth and fourteenth centuries the privilege of holding a market or an annual fair in villages and towns was much sought after, and about this time charters were granted by the kings to the lords of the manors of many places in Hampshire to hold fairs, and in some instances both fairs and markets.

The fairs which are still held, or were at the beginning of this century, at Southwick, Emsworth, Barton Stacey, Kingsclere, Romsey, Wickham, Selborne, Overton, Whitchurch, Petersfield, Hambledon, Lymington, Botley, Christchurch, were all granted to these places by Henry III. Those markets which were held at Neatham, near Alton, at Titchfield, and at Basingstoke, are the earliest recorded markets in Hampshire, and were in existence at the time of the Domesday Survey. Edward II. granted the privilege of holding a fair at Alton to Edmund of Woodstock, who then held the manor. The same king also granted William de Montagu, Earl of Salisbury, the privilege of holding a fair at Ringwood. When the lord of any manor was an influential man in the service of the crown, he generally managed to secure some privileges for his manors. A fair, which has long since passed into oblivion, was granted under these circumstances to William Briwere, to be held on his manor of King's Somborne at a place called Strete, the very name of which is now forgotten. This place was situated on the Roman road near the ford over the Test, and this fair was an attempt to establish an annual mart at a convenient place where local roads crossed the old Roman way.

The local fairs must have been a great convenience to the country people of Hampshire, and also where held a source of profit. The desire to possess these privileges is an evidence of the desire for trading facilities, as well as for increased opportunities of disposing of local produce. The village fair must have been a great event. To it came the travelling merchants to sell their wares with their caravans, and the wandering traders whom we see frequenting fairs at the present day are the surviving and decayed representatives of these medieval merchants. To the fairs also came the mountebanks, the ballad-singers, and the wandering minstrels, to afford amusement to the dull routine of life. Some of the larger fairs also attracted occasionally the wandering companies who acted the miracle plays, or representations of religious mysteries.

During the twelfth and thirteenth centuries fairs were not uncommonly held in churchyards, a custom which led to such serious abuses that it was prohibited by an order drawn up at Winchester in 1285 in these words: 'And the king commandeth and forbiddeth that from henceforth neither fairs nor markets be kept in churchyards.'*

The fairs at Wherwell and Leckford were granted to the abbeys of Wherwell and St. Mary's Winton by King John. The same king also granted to the Bishop of Winchester a market to be held at Alresford. The fair formerly held at Dogmersfield was granted by Edward I. to the Bishop of Bath and Wells, who then held that manor. Edward I. also granted charters for fairs to be held at Thruxton, Boarhunt, and Brading.

Edward III. granted both a market and a fair to the treasurer of the church of York to be held at Mottisfont that interesting manor which belonged to the archbishop of the northern province. The fairs and market privileges at Milton and Hamble were also granted by the same king.

Henry VI. granted or confirmed the right of the Abbot

* Stubb's ' Select Charters.'

f Titchfield to hold a fair at Titchfield, and of the Bishop
f Winchester for a market and fair at Havant.

Beaulieu Fair was granted or confirmed by Edward IV.,
nd the site of the market there is still called Cheapside.

As late as the time of Henry VII. an attempt was made
y the Abbess of Amesbury to establish a fair on Dane-
ury Hill, this being in her manor of Nether Wallop. She
btained from the king a patent authorizing a three days'
air there on July 25, 26, and 27, a very convenient time
f the year for an annual encampment on the hill; but
pparently it did not succeed.

When country people went to the fairs in Hampshire,
hey appear to have usually indulged in a few luxuries.
3eer was no doubt to be had there, and they probably
rank enough of it; but there was also a demand for
ingerbread, and perhaps this is an evidence that their
ives and daughters went to the fairs in ancient days, as
hey are accustomed to do at the present time. Such
ingerbread as was to be had at these old fairs, and which
s still made specially for them in some places, could not
e had every day.

Fairs and markets were not uncommonly held during
he Middle Ages on Sundays, and, notwithstanding the
rder of Henry III., some of them continued to be held
n churchyards, the tolls no doubt being given to the
hurch. By statute 27 Hen. VI., c. 5, it was consequently
nacted that no fair or market be kept on Sunday or in
hurchyards, and after that time the custom appears to have
een discontinued.

As late as the time of Elizabeth such a considerable
lace as Bishop's Waltham had no market, for in that
eign an inquiry was held to ascertain what harm, if any,
ould be caused by the establishment of market privileges
here.*

Until about the middle of the fourteenth century, the
ld system of co-operative farming between all the tenants

* Inq. a. q. d. ; Cal. Inq. p. m. 44 Eliz

on manors commonly prevailed, and the land continued
to be ploughed, sowed, and reaped in the main according
to the system which had come down from Saxon time.

The lord held the demesne land, which was usually that
around his house, or the manor farm, and the under-tenants
farmed the rest in common. The ploughing was usually
done by teams of oxen, which were made up of animals
kept by different owners.

The work the tenants had to perform for the lord was
regulated by the custom of the manor. This varied considerably, and consisted not merely in ploughing, sowing
and harvesting, but in conveying the manure from the lord's
homestead, often in fencing his park, and repairing these
fences, and many other services.

Long after the common arable land had been apportioned
among the copyhold farmers who were the successors of
the villeins, many old customs survived. These small
copyholds usually consisted of a carucate or yardland of
about 30 acres, and many small homesteads with farms of
about this area still exist, or did until quite recently, in this
county. They are the yardlands which on the break up
of the earlier system of agriculture were allotted to the
original copyholders. Much of this land continued to be
subject to common grazing right after harvest, the tenants
of the manor all having the right of turning their live stock
after 'sickle and scythe' on to each other's land, a custom
which was only finally extinguished when the enclosure of
the common lands took place.

The early system' of agriculture has left its traces in
Hampshire. On some of the hill sides we may still see the
lines of the old terrace lands which were formerly cultivated in strips. At Shawford, Easton, Lower Woodcot,
Vernham's Dean, Faccombe, Linkenholt, St. Mary Bourne,
and other places, the lines of these old plough-lands remain,
and many field names elsewhere, such as South Linch,
Hursley, the Linches at Overton, Linch Hill near Alton,
Linch Row, Bishop's Sutton, Linchetts, King's Somborne,

and Linch Hill, Whitchurch, mark the sites where the old linches or headlands of the common ploughed fields ran.

In some places, such as Chilcomb, Worthy Down, Linkenholt, and Woodcot Down, we may see the old rectangular acre plots separated by wide banks, which were also cultivated in common by the tenants of the manor.

Some early references exist to this early system of agriculture in Hampshire, the most remarkable of which is that in Domesday Book relating to the manor of Wallop held by the king. It is there stated that one hide of land belonged to the church, also half the tithes of the manor, 46d. for the villeins' tithes and half the lands, *i.e.*, half the acres cultivated in common, which constituted the villeins' lands as distinct from that of the lord.

The services on the manors which the tenants had to perform for the lords, whether these tenants were villeins who had small farm homesteads and owned a pair or more of oxen, or were labourers who lived in huts or small cottages, were gradually commuted for quit rents, and in this way copyholders arose. Many an old Hampshire cottage, with its thatched roof and garden plot, still pays a small annual quit-rent to the lord of the manor in lieu of the ancient services which far back in the Middle Ages the occupant of that cottage site had to give to the lord. The cottager had, however, certain privileges. After harvest his cow or pigs were free to roam over the stubble land. He and his family had manorial rights, and I cannot doubt that that of gleaning the fields after the harvest wains was one of these rights which had become established by immemorial custom, but which only survives now by the favour of the modern farmer.

The inferior tenants all worked for their lords in return for their common land, and the lords held their manors of the king or of some other great landlord by a variety of tenures. Some of these were of a very interesting kind.

In Hampshire there was less land held by feudal tenure than was the case in many other counties. Consequently there were many estates held by other services, such as sergeantries of various kinds. There were grand sergeantries and petit sergeantries. One of these grand sergeantries was that of aiding in the defence of the castles situated in this county, or near its borders. Thus the manors of Cosham, Wanstead, Boarhunt, and Pury were held by the service of guarding Porchester Castle. The manors of West Tytherley, Rownor, Avon Tyrell, and Stapley were held by service in the defence of Winchester Castle. The manors of Milton, East and West Ashley, and Bayllokefee were held by the service of defending Christchurch Castle. Rotherwick, in the north of the county, was held by service in the defence of Windsor Castle, and Polling Manor was held by a like service at Odiham Castle.

The manor of Woodcote was held for many centuries by the service of keeping Winchester Gaol.

Some of the land at Eling was held in the thirteenth century by the heirs of Cobbe, the smith of the crown, by the annual payment of fifty arrows. At North Stoneham, a tenant named Roger de Mill held a hide of land of the abbey of Hyde by the service of paying the abbot one pound of cummin annually in quit of all demands. At Totton, Roger de Bestesthorn held his land by the service of providing a litter for the king's bed, and hay for his palfrey, when he should sleep at Ives, a place near Fordingbridge. A large manor in Eling was held by the service of carrying the writs sent to the Isle of Wight, and the hundreds of Christchurch, Ringwood and Fordingbridge.

At Warnford, land worth 100s. was held by the service of providing a sparrow-hawk 'to be paid to our lord the king yearly, on the feast of St. Michael, at the Exchequer.'

The crown manors of Basingstoke, Kingsclere, and Hurstbourn Tarrant were linked together in an ancient obligation of providing annually, between them, an entertainment for the king for one day. This appears to have been a Saxon customary payment, and is mentioned in Domesday Book. The manors of Barton Stacey and Eling were held by similar tenures in the time of Edward the Confessor, the obligation being, in each case, that of providing entertainment for the king for half a day. A money payment, or provisions to a fixed amount, was probably made on account of these obligations. The manor of Bury, in the parish of Eling, was anciently held by the service of presenting a brace of white greyhounds, in silver couples, when the king came to the New Forest.

The manor of Sherfield on Loddon was held, in the time of Edward I., by the curious service of finding a sergeant, whose duties it was to look after the laundresses, or female camp-followers of the king's army. Apparently it was thought that this duty was not sufficiently onerous, for in the time of Edward II. the holder of this manor had also to perform other duties, viz., those of dismembering condemned malefactors, and that of measuring the gallons and bushels in the king's household. The manor of Liddesulde was held by the sergeantry of keeping the king's larder. The manor of Fede was held, in the time of King John, by the service of weighing the king's money at the Exchequer. East Worldham was held by the sergeantry of bearing a marshal's wand before the king. A manor known as Comelessend was held, in the thirteenth century, by the service of hunting the wolf with the king's dogs. Eastleigh and Hythe were both held by the sergeantry of being chamberlain to the King's Exchequer.

The manors often reverted to the crown, and were then sometimes granted to other tenants in chief on different obligations, as appears to have been the case at Sherfield on Loddon. Some Hampshire manors were held by an ancient warlike obligation of finding, free of cost for forty days, a man at arms of some kind for service in the king's army—if retained beyond this time he would have to be paid by the king. Thus, West Tytherley was held by the sergeantry of finding one esquire for forty days with a coat of mail, an iron helmet and a lance. Woolston was held by the service of finding an archer, armed and furnished, to serve the king for forty days in England, and part of the land at Bentley was held by a similar service. Steventon was held of the king by the service of finding a man-at-arms and his horse, for forty days' service in Wales.

On the Hampshire manors which were held by knight's service there must have been a greater military training constantly going on, than on those whose lords had to provide only for chamberlain service, duties at the Exchequer, or duties in the king's household. The lords who held by knight-service were liable to be called on by writ to send their service into the field at any time. Thus, after the Norman Conquest, the abbey of Hyde, held the great manor of Micheldever, not on the easy terms by which King Edward the Elder had granted it, but by the feudal tenure of three knights' fees. This feudal obligation was laid on the manor by the Conqueror, after hearing of the mailed monks of this abbey, who fought against him and died at Hastings. The abbot had consequently to have his knights and men-at-arms ready, and in the reign of Edward II. alone, he received at different times no less than eleven writs ordering him to send his service to Carlisle, Newcastle, York, Tweedmouth, or Berwick-on-Tweed, for war against the Scots ; or to Coventry, for war against the Earl of Lancaster ; or to Portsmouth, for service in Gascony.* Alton was also held by the service of three knights, and as often as wars occurred, there must have been the usual preparation for despatching these warriors from that town.

Most of the manors which formed part of the barony of Basing were held of the lords of Basing by knight-service. These lords were the De Ports, and their successors, the St. Johns. The manors are too numerous to mention in detail, but some of the most important were Basing, Sherborne,

---

* Palgrave, ' Parl. Writs,' vol. ii., div. iii.

Portsea, Botley, Church Oakley, West Tisled, Corhampton, Warnford, Bramley, Upton, Wickham, and Ellisfield.*

The manor courts were not merely meetings of the manorial tenants for the benefit of their lords, but the legal assemblies by which disputes between the tenants were settled, and where any other disputes were also settled by ascertaining the custom of the manor. The lord could not, in his dealings with the tenants, go beyond the local customs, which had come down from time immemorial, and what these customs really were was declared by the voice of the court, of which all the manorial tenants were suitors. They were also the jury which gave the decisions, and in a manor court any number of suitors present could form the jury. In this way the weak must often have been protected against the strong.

Many places in Hampshire had the right of holding a court-leet in addition to the manor court. This privilege was highly valued by the lords of manors. It relieved them from certain obligations in connection with the hundred-courts held by the sheriff of the county or his deputy. A manor which had a court-leet could make its own arrangements for the assize of bread and ale, appoint its own ale-taster, and the lord of such a manor usually had also the right of free gallows. So many gibbets existed in various parts of Hampshire at one time, that malefactors could not travel many miles without coming across one or more of these reminders of the majesty of the law, from which the whitened bones of some criminal were perhaps hanging.

During the troubled reign of Henry III., certain encroachments on the royal prerogative occurred in the matter of holding courts and other privileges. The ancient Saxon institution of the view of frankpledge had been held twice a year in each hundred from time immemorial, but where a manor possessed a court-leet, this view of frankpledge was held by the lord on his own estate. The tenants of those manors which had not this franchise had

* Inq. p. m. 21 Edw. III.

to make suit at the hundred-court. Early in the reign of Edward I., a full inquiry into these ancient rights was held in Hampshire, and many lords who claimed the right of free gallows, assize of bread and ale, or exemption of their villeins from making suit at the hundred-courts, had to show on what authority these claims rested. The crown was represented in this inquisition by a very able man, probably one of the early sergeants-at-law, named William de Geselyngham.* Alan Plunkenet, the lord of Eling Manor, had even his right to hold that manor questioned. Master John of Leckford had to show by what warrant he claimed exemption for his villeins from making suit at the hundred-court of Somborne. Similarly the Abbot of Netley had to show his warrant excusing his tenants from making suit at the hundred-court of Mansbridge. The Abbot of Titchfield had to show by what charter he claimed the right of free gallows at Walesworth, and Hugh de Vere by what warrant he claimed the power of hanging criminals at Thornhill. The Abbot of Hyde, who had exercised the privileges of free gallows and assize of bread and ale at Alton, had to prove his claim to the same. In some cases the respondents made a good fight for their privileges, but found William de Geselyngham too clever for them. Thus, William de Valence, Earl of Pembroke, and a relative of the king, was required to show why his villeins at Hook and Strete did not make suit at the hundred-courts of Titchfield and Redbridge. He pleaded exemption in virtue of the grant of the manors of Newton and Hawkley, these manors of Hook and Strete being 'membrum,' or subordinate manors. William de Geselyngham thereupon showed that on October 22, in the thirty-sixth year of Henry III., the tenants did make suit, and demanded inquiry, and the record informs us that after that William de Valence did not appear, and judgment went against him by default.

At the time of the Great Survey, in 1086, Hampshire

* Placito quo warranto.

was divided into forty-three hundreds, and the Isle of Wight into three. By the middle of the fourteenth century these had become somewhat rearranged and reduced in number, for in 1334 the number of hundreds on the mainland was thirty-seven, in addition to the liberties, and in the Isle of Wight two.

The hundreds were in some instances held by important persons or corporate bodies like the manors, and such lords of hundreds held the hundred-courts, these being removed from the sheriff's jurisdiction. To be lord of a hundred was a territorial distinction greater than that of being lord of a manor. In the ninth year of Edward II. the king held the hundreds of Holeshute and Chutely, Bermellesputte, Selborne, the New Forest, Redbridge, Mansbridge, Bosberg, Portsdown, Bountesberg, Meon-stoke, Titchfield, Pacchestrowe, and Thorngate. The bishop held the hundreds of Sutton, East Meon, Over-ton, Waltham, and Fareham. Queen Margaret held those of Andover, Odiham, Alton, Ringwood, and Christchurch, and the liberty of Porchester. The Prior of St. Swithun held the hundreds of Crondall, Fawley, Evingar, and Buttlesgate. The Abbot of Hyde held the hundred of Micheldever. The Earl of Arundel held that of Finch-dean, the Earl of Gloucester held the liberty or burgh of Petersfield, the Earl of Chester held the hundreds of East and West Medina in the Isle of Wight, Henry of Lancaster held that of King's Somborne, Hugh le Despenser held the hundred of Barton, and the Lady Mary, sister of the king, held the liberty of Freshwater.

In addition, there was at that time one other hundred, that of Forde, now Fordingbridge, which was held by William Tracy, and it is interesting to note that his heirs or assigns have continued to hold the title of lord of the hundred of Fordingbridge from that time to the present day. The hundreds, like the borough towns, were amerced for murders and other serious crimes, and as the fines were levied on all the tenants living within them, it was to every man's interest to prevent crime and to catch criminals. Thus, in the fifth year of King Stephen the hundred of Fawley was amerced in twenty marks for a murder, and the sheriff of the county levied it and paid it into the exchequer. About the same time the hundred of Clere was also amerced for a murder.* By the statute of Winchester in 1285, the people of each hundred were obliged to make hue and cry after felons, and if any person, seeing a felon, did not raise the hue and cry, and if others did not join in it, they were liable. It was not sufficient to allow the criminal to depart to another hundred. The hue and cry had to be raised, a chase made, and continued from hundred to hundred until the culprit was caught. Many an exciting chase, with many a cry of ' Stop thief !' or perhaps of ' Murder !' must have taken place across the county in those days. It was no doubt inconvenient to people when they heard the hue and cry to have to leave their work and join in the chase, but this old plan for catching criminals was probably as effective as our modern one of leaving this duty to the rural police.

Some curious examples of the survival of the primitive method of trial by wager of battle occur in the medieval history of Hampshire. In 1246, a dispute concerning some property at Wey Hill was settled by wager of battle. About the same time, also, another case occurred. Two thieves† stole some clothes in the market at Winchester, and could not agree on their shares. William Blowberne, one of them, thereupon turned informer, and charged Hamon le Stare with theft. Le Stare claimed wager of battle, which ended in a victory for Blowberne, whereupon the unfortunate le Stare, probably already half dead, was immediately hanged on the gallows. The last approvers' or informers' duel on record occurred in this county in 1456, between one Fisher, who was falsely charged by a thief named Whitthorn, imprisoned at Winchester. Having some knowledge of the ancient law, he may have invented the charge in order to

* Maddox, ' Hist. Exchequer.'   .† *Ibid.*

et out of gaol. In the duel which took place, however,
'isher defeated the informer, after which he was at once
anged.

Constables of hundreds were first appointed by the
,tatute of Winchester in 1285, and of these officials a few
till survive in Hampshire. In other instances they have
eased to be chosen within the last few years. Thus, until
878, a high constable of Fordingbridge Hundred was
nnually chosen at the hundred court. One of the former
uties of this official was to set the watch each night on the
ridge at Fordingbridge during the fence month in the New
'orest, and to charge the watchman to do his duty accord-
1g to ancient custom. Constables for the hundreds have
een chosen within recent years at Wherwell, Kingsclere,
3arton Stacey, and East Meon.

These were the high officials of the hundred, and as time
rent on constables of the tithings and parishes were also
lected, and these were usually the tithingmen. These
fficials had charge of the village stocks, which apparently
xisted at first only where criminal jurisdiction existed
inder a bailiff and court leet, but later on stocks became
nore numerous. In 1376 the Commons prayed the king
hat stocks might be established in every village. In
his county they still exist at Odiham and Brading.

The ancient system of local administration both of the
1undreds and of the manors is now in a state of extreme
lecay, and must shortly entirely pass away. Some of the
:ourts have been kept alive only by an annual feast. The
1gricultural depression has extinguished one or more to
vhich the suitors have come for the last time. They were
iworn on the jury, addressed by the steward, considered
vhat they had to do, and found nothing. They thereupon
nade their presentment, and waited for the well-known
iounds of the dining arrangements. Since the last court
neeting a change had, however, occurred, and one who
:ared nothing about ancient courts had come, and with him
1arder agricultural times. The suitors waited and waited,

and when at last they realized the sad truth that no dinner was to be had, they resolved before they separated that never again should that court be held, and they have kept their resolution. Thus ingloriously has perished one, if not more, of the ancient courts of Hampshire, which had met annually for perhaps a thousand years, and which, under the ancient conditions of rural life, had no doubt often safeguarded the rights of the inferior tenants.

CHAPTER XV.

REMAINS AND LEGENDS OF THE MIDDLE AGES.

AFTER the loss of Normandy, and the confiscation of the and which had been held by Normans, a number of Hampshire manors changed their owners. Subsequently, when French-speaking lords who resided abroad ceased, and an increase in the number of lords of manors residing on their estates occurred, country life in Hampshire began to assume that condition which it presented during the time of the later Plantagenet kings. A few churches in the county contain monuments of their patrons and lords, dating as far back as the twelfth or early part of the thirteenth centuries. The churches on the manors which belonged to the monastic houses have, of course, no early monuments. Such manors had no resident lords, and in these we usually find no memorials, other than ecclesiastical, earlier than the sixteenth century.

A few parishes which are still designated by personal names attached to the old Saxon place names, such as Strathfieldsaye, Sutton Scotney, Weston Patrick, Stoke Charity, Shipton Bellinger, Sherfield English, Penton Mewsey, Sherborne St. John, Newton Valence, Hartley Maudit, Hartley Wespall, have derived their second names from their ancient Norman or early English lords, and a few manors which are not separate parishes, such as Compton Monceaux, Hinton Daubeney, Barton Peverel, Avon Tyrell, and Binstead St. Clare, have also derived

their ancient personal names from their owners. The old
manorial names have in some instances been superseded by
others of more recent date. Thus, Sherborne Coudray is
now known as The Vyne.

Some of the chief families connected with Hampshire
places in the thirteenth and fourteenth centuries were those
of Monceaux at Compton Monceaux, de la Charité,
Wyndesore, and Hampton at Stoke Charity, Waleraund, at
West Tytherley, Broughton, and Eling, Escotney at Sutton
Scotney, de Pontearche at Newton, Coudray at Sherborne,
de Sacy at Barton Stacey, Gurdon at Selborne and Tisted,
Peverel at Barton Peverel, Maudit at Hartley Maudit, de
Cadurcis at Weston Patrick and King's Somborne, de
Venuz at East Worldham, de Roches at Steventon, de
Brayboef at Cranborne and West Stratton, de Neville at
Vernham, Sturmy at Polling, Liss Sturmy, and Elvetham,
Meoles at Moyles Court, Elingham, and Upper Wallop,
Punchardon at Faccombe, Mortimer at Martyr Worthy,
Plukenet at Tangley and Eling, le Brune at Fording-
bridge, Daubeney at Hinton Daubeney, le Despenser at
Ashley, Bisset at Rockbourne, Grimstede at Brockenhurst,
Paynell at Oakhanger, de Bardolf at Greatham, de
Warblington at Sherfield on Loddon and Warblington, de
Albiniaco at Hinton and Hale, de Buckesgate at West
Tytherley and North Ashley, St. Clare at Binstead St.
Clare, Stures at Wickham, de Borhunt at Boarhunt, de
Welles at Welles near Romsey, le Straung at Chalton, and
de Weston at Middleton.

The rise of middle class landholders in Hampshire during
the latter part of the thirteenth and during the fourteenth
centuries, is seen in such instances as those of Peter
Mathewson, who held land at Warblington, Middleton, and
East Meon in the time of Henry III., of John Johnson,
who held Sopley manor early in the reign of Edward I.,
and of Richard Johnson, who held Lasham manor. The
Johnson family appears to have prospered in Hampshire.
Matthew Johnson held lands or manors at Hunton and

Warblington, and Herbert Johnson at Wolferton. Richard Richardson held land and rents at Amport, and Wallop, and others whose names show that they were known in this age when surnames greatly increased simply as the sons of their fathers, which name thus became their surname, held land elsewhere. The rise of copyhold farms, and the manner in which a number of these farms in some instances became held by one man who was probably not himself of the villein class, is shown by the estate of Richard de Porteseye, who in the time of Edward II. held a messuage and a carucate of land at Portsea and Copnore, also a messuage and a carucate of land at Stanbridge, a messuage and a carucate at North Houghton, a messuage and a carucate at Wanstead, etc. A considerable estate of copyhold land was thus held by Richard, who of course had to make suit of court on the proper manors, and pay the quit rents and other customary dues.

Many large estates in Hampshire were held under the obligation of making suit at the king's hundred courts. Thus the holder of Stapeley manor had to appear at Odiham hundred court, the lord of West Worldham manor at Alton hundred court, the lord of Sherfield on Loddon at Odiham, and the lord of the manor of Enham had to make suit at Chute. Similarly several lords of manors near Basingstoke had to make suit at the hundred court in that town, and of course in all these instances the usual fees had to be paid.

The rise of a family of the merchant class is well seen in the case of that of Devenissche of Winchester.

In the time of Edward I. John le Devenissche came to the front at Winchester, when with other citizens he obstructed the bishop's officers in taking the profits of St. Giles' fair. He was a wealthy citizen and founded the hospital of St. John the Baptist in Winton. Early in the reign of Edward I. we find that one of the same name, probably his son, held houses and land in trust for the master and brethren of the hospital, and later in the century,

we find Nicholas Devenisshe of Winton among the landed
gentry of the county, and holding the manors of Westbury,
Emsworth, Greatham, and Sutton Scotney.

Almost every place in Hampshire has some medieval
associations more or less peculiar to itself, which connect
it with the history of the county, or with some of those who
have played a distinguished part in it. Of such associations a few examples may be given.

Andover was a place of note as early as the time of the
West Saxon kings, who had a residence there. Near that
town were held the early councils of Grately and Enham,
and one was held in the town itself by Edgar. It was the
place also where the Conqueror established a priory, and
whose burgesses grew into importance and acquired
valuable privileges. There for many centuries was held
the hundred court, at which the tithing men of the district
around had to do suit. Its merchants had a guild, and it
was the trading centre for the north-west of the county.
Its market and fairs were held from time immemorial, like
those of Basingstoke, and were part of its privileges as a
royal manor. It has its legends, one of which is that of
the great thunderstorm on Christmas Eve, 1171, when a
priest was struck dead while saying mass, and his fellows
escaped unhurt, but saw the strange sight of a beast in
shape like a pig running about round their feet.

The villages near Andover have their real and legendary
history. West of the town was fought the great battle
between Edmund and Cnut, and in the folk-lore of the
district Cnut's barrow lying about midway between the
great camps of Danebury and Quarley, four miles distant
from each other, marks the line of a subterranean way
between these great fortresses. Quarley was a royal
manor held by Harold, subsequently by the Conqueror,
and later on by the Norman abbey of Bec. In the time of
Henry VI. it belonged to John, Duke of Bedford, but in
1442 it was given to the Hospital of St. Katherine by the

Tower of London, to which it has belonged until the present year.

The neighbouring parish of Thruxton was held at the time of the Great Survey by Gozelin de Cormelies, and the abbey of Cormelies held the church. This still contains a decayed wooden effigy of a mailed knight of about the twelfth century, one of the earliest in the county, and a very fine monument of early fifteenth century date of Sir John Lisle, who held the manor about that time.

The next parish—Amport—has derived its name from the de Port family, and was the Anne de Port mentioned, in Domesday Book. Abbots Anne, another manor in the same valley, was held by the abbey of Hyde, and a curious medieval custom has survived there until the present day. When any unmarried girl of the parish dies, other girls dressed in white carry a garland or virgin crown before her to the burial, and these emblems, now commonly made of coloured paper, are afterwards hung up in the church, which contains many of them. The next parish—Up-Clatford—has its early associations with Adelina the minstrel, the fair singer of the eleventh century, who captivated Roger, Earl of Arundel and Shrewsbury, for he gave her a virgate of land on this manor. Across the downs to the south-west is Over Wallop, which was held in Saxon time of Earl Godwin by the Countess Godiva, wife of Leofric, Earl of Mercia. She was the lady of the Coventry legend, who saved the people of that city from her husband's vengeance by her nude performance on horseback. The next parish down this valley is Nether Wallop, which belonged to the abbey of Amesbury, a sister house to Wherwell, founded by Queen Elfrida, and which, like it, had many royal and noble inmates. On the other side of Andover is Enham, part of which was held by the knights of St. John, and Penton, now called Wey Hill, held by the abbey of Greistain, and later on by the family of Chaucer the poet, whose grand-daughter gave it to the hospital at Ewelme. A little further off is Hurstbourn Tarrant, owned by the

Abbess of Tarrant, who had privileges in the forest of Chute around it. In the extreme north-west of Hampshire is Combe, which belonged to the abbey of Bec, and where medieval criminals could be hanged on a higher gallows than elsewhere in Hampshire—that on Inkpen Beacon, 970 feet high, on the county border. South-east from Hurstbourn Tarrant is St. Mary Bourne, connected with the d'Andeli family, one of whom was a Crusader, and is believed to be represented by a cross-legged effigy still remaining in the church. Southward is Hurstbourn Priors, which belonged to St. Swithun's priory.

Lower down the valley of the Test are the manors which formed part of the possessions of the abbey of Wherwell. Across the river is Chilbolton, which belonged to the priory of St. Swithun at a very early period, having been granted by Æthelstan in commemoration of an important Hampshire event, according to one of its early legends. A Danish giant named Colbrand troubled the city of Winchester, but was challenged by the renowned knight, Guy of Warwick. They fought in a meadow outside the walls, on which the citizens stood eagerly watching the combat. Guy prevailed ; Chilbolton was given to the priory, and the meadow is called Danemead unto this day. A few miles eastward of Chilbolton is the large village of Sutton Scotney, now part of the parish of Wonston, but which had a church of its own, and was quite distinct from it at the time of the Domesday Survey. It has obtained its present name of Scotney from the family of de Scoteney, which held the manor in the thirteenth century. It is singular that the name of this family, stained with a foul crime six hundred years ago, should have clung to this manor. About the forty-second year of Henry III. Richard de Clare Earl of Gloucester, who was connected with Hampshire as the Lord of Petersfield and Mapledurham, and his relative, had poison given to them, from which the earl barely escaped with his life, his hair, nails, and skin coming off, and his relative died. This poison was administered to him by Walter de Scoteney, who was one of his knights. Dugdale* calls him the chief counsellor of the earl. It was believed that he did this for a great sum of money given him by William de Valence, whose name has also come down to us at Newton Valence. Shortly afterwards, de Scoteney was put on his trial, and being found guilty, he was drawn through the city of Winchester and there hanged. A few miles further east is Stoke Charity, a manor which William the Conqueror took away from the abbey of Hyde and gave to one of his Norman followers. Early in the thirteenth century it was held by William de Feritate as part of his Norman barony, and later in that century by Henry de la Charité, the only lord of that name, whose name has since clung to it.

The place of greatest importance in the north of Hampshire during the middle ages was Basingstoke. At the time of the Great Survey its inhabitants already possessed some important privileges, among which was its market. It was the meeting-place for the hundred, and had a moot place, or hall, in a part of the town known in medieval time as Mote Street, but now as Wote Street. It became in time the governing centre for six hundreds, and lords of neighbouring manors had to make suit at its courts. Originally a royal manor administered by the king's bailiff, it acquired in the course of time municipal institutions, and became practically a self-governing community, possessed of more than ordinary authority over the surrounding hundreds. Its church appears to have been given by the Conqueror to the Norman abbey on ' St. Michael's mount in peril of the sea,' the rocky isle near Avranches, which possessed here a hide of land and the tithes of the manor.

Close by is Basing, where the de Ports and the St. Johns had their castle within the earthwork of an old

* Dugdale, Baronage, I., 212 and 676 ; and Rudder, ' Hist. Gloucester,' p. 64.

British fortress. Here, from the time of the Conquest until the decay of the feudal system, was the centre of their great barony, which comprised manors in all parts of the county.

Another important local centre of northern Hampshire in the middle ages was Odiham, a place which has played a part in the history of England, as well as in that of this county. Here the Dauphin of France in his invasion of England in 1216 met with a check. He had taken Guildford, Farnham, and Winchester, and then turned his attention to Odiham Castle, the garrison of which refused to surrender. For a week the siege went on, the defence was vigorously maintained, and some successful sorties were made, after which the defenders came to terms, and were allowed to march out with their arms and horses. This was done before the astonished French army, who counted the defending force and found that it consisted of three knights, three esquires, and seven men at arms, thirteen in all, and they had lost none during the siege. During the next reign Odiham was the favourite residence of Princess Eleanor, who subsequently married de Montfort Earl of Leicester. She kept a large hunting establishment of men and dogs at Odiham, and in the civil war during this reign, in which her husband was the leader of the popular party, the castle was held for him until after the battle of Evesham. The castle and manor formed part of the dower which Edward I. settled on his second wife, Margaret of France; and later on it was also part of the dower of Queen Margaret of Anjou. In the time of Edward III., Odiham Castle was selected as the place of confinement for David Bruce, King of Scotland, who had been taken prisoner at Neville's Cross.

Hampshire was notorious, during the time of Henry III.'s misrule, for its bands of freebooters. Highway robberies were frequent, and the abundance of forests and woods through which many of the roads passed made it comparatively easy for the outlaws to escape. The parliament which was held in Winchester in 1285 enacted that the highways should be widened, so that there might be no bushes, woods, or dykes within two hundred feet of each side of the road, and those proprietors who omitted to cut down underwoods abutting on such highroads were to be held responsible for all felonies which might be committed by persons lurking in their coverts.

The most notorious outlaw of Hampshire in the latter part of the reign of Henry III. was Adam de Gurdon. His family had been settled in the neighbourhood of Alton since the time of Richard I., and he appears to have come into notoriety during the troubles of Henry's reign. For a time he had it all his own way in the eastern forests of Hampshire. The story, or legend, concerning him states that Prince Edward heard of his prowess, and resolved on an adventure against him. The prince met with him in a dell, east of Long Sutton, near Alton, and challenged him. One version of the story is that, after a hard fight, de Gurdon was unhorsed, and that the prince then spared his life. Another is that they fought, and were so equally matched that, during a pause in the fight, the Prince offered de Gurdon his life and advancement, if he would give up his arms. What is certain is that, after this encounter, he became a faithful follower of Prince Edward. We are still reminded of the high hand with which de Gurdon directed matters in this part of Hampshire more than six hundred years ago by a tablet on the cottage, which was formerly a mill, at Hawkley, which tells us that this is ' Hockeley mill, ancient mill of the Bishops of Winchester, taken from them by Sir Adam Gurdon, given back under King Edward, 1280 A.D.'

The fertile imaginings of the Middle Ages have left in Hampshire a store of legends and folk-lore scattered over the county. Ghosts were formerly abundant, and some of them still remain. The ghost of Rufus is of course seen between Stony Cross and Cadnam, at which latter place was a rival tree to that at Glastonbury, an oak which developed its leaves on old Christmas Day. On the eve of that day, also, the cattle in various parts of this county knelt down at midnight. This latter story may be a survival of the medieval Office of the Shepherds, which was held in some churches on Christmas-Eve, and in which the sheep brought into the church by the shepherds were taught to kneel before the altar. Stories of monastic ghosts were formerly common. At Selborne :

> ' Still oft at eve belated shepherd swains
> See the cowled spectre skim the folded plains.'*

Netley Abbey had several ghosts, one of whom was an abbot of that house telling his beads as he walked. At Rockbourne there is a superstition of the occasional appearance of a medieval figure on the interior wall of the church, caused perhaps by some ancient fresco showing its dim outline in damp weather beneath the modern whitewash.

This county has several legends of medieval crawling performances, one of which is that connected with the Bishop's Purlieu, in the New Forest. This purlieu is a great bog, in the forest but not of it, and formerly belonged to the bishops of Winchester, acquired, so the tale says, by one of the ancient prelates being given as much of this forest area as he could crawl round. There is also the well-known legend of the Crawls at Tichborne, which was the origin of the celebrated Tichborne Dole. At Romsey there are legends of Merwenna, the mythical founder of that abbey, and a disciple of St. Patrick. Medieval stories of the devil are common. He evidently frequented the old Roman roads, which have in various parts of the county got the name of the Devil's highway and the Devil's dancing-ground. He leaped as well as danced, for a row of Celtic mounds, near Privet, are known as the Devil's Jumps. In the medieval imagination he was also fond of

---

* Gilbert White.

liquor, for more than one great combe near the border of the county is known as the Devil's Punch-bowl.

Hampshire people still nail old horseshoes to doors in order to bring good luck; and in some remote localities the bees are, or were within recent years, informed of any death which might occur in their owner's family. The fatal incident of the young lady who hid in a large oaken chest from which she could not escape, while the mistletoe hung on the castle wall, is said to have occurred at Marwell, near which place I have been shown the oaken coffer in which her bones are said to have been found. Since the beginning of the present century patients are believed to have been cured of a disease, in which physicians failed, by being drawn through an ash tree—a feat which was accomplished by splitting a young tree, opening the split, and drawing the patient through it. Silchester, of course, has its medieval legends, one of which relates to the famous march thither of King Gurmond and his 160,000 Africans, who landed at Southampton with this considerable army after he had subdued Ireland.

Stories of buried treasure are not uncommon. At Froxfield part of it is reported to have been found by means of a lucky dream, and the remainder awaits discovery, while at Ellisfield, somewhere near the old camp, there is a golden throne buried. Some of the medieval bells occasionally ring out their ghostly sounds. Those at Stenbury, near Preston Candover, a place which has long ceased to exist, are reported to have been heard within one generation; and a submarine peal from sunken bells in Chichester Harbour is still, at times, heard responding to the peal from Bosham church on the Sussex border. Some of the bells of the ancient church of South Hayling, which is said to have been destroyed by the sea early in the fourteenth century, also occasionally send back to the land their ancient sounds. At Rowland's Castle we have still remaining the name of the hero Roland, who slew the Saracen giant Angoulaffre, the name having probably come across the Channel when our kings were more French than English.

The modern representatives of the ancient mummers still perform their version of the Christmas play of the age of the crusades, in which the King of Egypt's daughter is concerned, and the Italian physician educated in the celebrated medieval schools of medicine of North Italy makes his miraculous cure.

King Arthur and his knights were of course connected with such a famous county as Hampshire, and in proof of this we can point to his round table, which hangs on the wall of the County Hall, where it was probably first placed by Henry III., who ordered a 'rota fortuna,' or wheel of fortune, to be made for this building.

A few very old witch stories have survived, one of which is that of Kit Nox, who, tradition says, used to take her aërial journeys near Botley, where a place called Kitnox is said to have been named after her.

Fairy stories have, of course, survived, and these appear to have lingered longest in the New Forest, where the fairies were known by the name of pyxies. The river Avon, which forms the western boundary of the forest, is a stream of clear chalk water. According to the folk-lore of Hampshire, this was the river into which the fair Gwendoline fell while walking with her not very distinguished lover, and from the bank of which, as she sank beneath the water, she gathered a tiny blue flower and threw it to him, saying, 'Forget me not.'

We can read something of the medieval history of this county in many an old wall containing blocks of Binstead limestone worked by medieval masons. The Binstead quarries were the chief source of stone for building purposes in Hampshire from the Saxon period until the fifteenth century, and where we now find it we may feel sure that an ancient building of some kind existed not far away. I have met with this stone as far north as Burghclere. There is not a stone in the fields of Hampshire that has not something of scientific interest beneath it, and there is not an old stone in any wall, whether a local stone or a foreign stone imported as ballast from other lands in ancient ships, which has not an antiquarian interest, and which does not assist us in reading the ancient history of the county.

Among the rarer buildings of the Middle Ages, which have lasted until the present time, are several ancient court houses, such as that of the hundred-court at East Meon, and some disused manorial chapels, such as those at Pittleworth and Upper Eldon. The Cross House, or waiting-place for people, at Southampton, opposite the old ferry at Itchen, is a rare example of its kind. Subterranean passages abound in the imagination of the people—and there are the remains of a real one of the early English period at Winchester. There are traces of several anchorages or recluses' dwellings attached to churches, and the embankment for Alresford pond, made by Bishop Lucy, is an engineering work of the twelfth century.

CHAPTER XVI.

THE ISLE OF WIGHT.

THE history of the Isle of Wight is necessarily closely connected with that of the county of which it forms a part,
and reference has already been made in these pages to
some of the chief points in its early history. There can be
little doubt that it was occupied successively by the same
prehistoric races as those which followed each other on the
mainland. Characteristic remains of the people of the
Neolithic and Bronze ages have been found, and the
weapons, tumuli, and other indications of these prehistoric
races resemble those discovered in other parts of Hampshire.

It was conquered by the Romans under Vespasian, and
the remains of their villas and other buildings discovered
of late years at Carisbrook, Brading, and elsewhere, show
that it must have been occupied and governed by them.
On the withdrawal of the Romans it was, for about a
hundred years, like the mainland, under some system of
government, which resembled that to which the people had
been accustomed during the Roman occupation. Afterwards came the conquest and settlement of the Jutes, the
allies of the original West Saxon settlers in Hampshire.
Then followed the Saxon Jutish wars, which continued
until the island was finally incorporated into the West Saxon
kingdom. The political connection of the Isle of Wight
with Hampshire dates from this time. During the ravages

of the Danes and Northmen, the island was often invaded and occupied. It should, however, be remembered that the islanders were of Jutish descent, and that they were among the last of the inhabitants of the British islands to adopt the Christian faith. Traditions of Woden and Thor must have lingered among them long after their nominal adhesion to Christianity, so that when the Danes appeared, some of whom were allied to them by racial descent, they perhaps found the people of the island nearer them in speech and religious sentiment than the West Saxons on the mainland.

After the Norman conquest, the lordship of the island was given to William FitzOsborne, who was made Earl of Hereford, Seneschal and Marshal of Normandy and England, and was favoured by the Conqueror beyond all the other Norman barons. He is said to have introduced into Wight that modified form of the feudal system which subsequently prevailed there. Some of the principal manors appear to have been given to certain knights, the three chief of these at the time of the Domesday Survey being William the son of Azor, William the son of Stur, and Gozelin the son of Azor.

William FitzOsborne was the founder of the Benedictine abbey of St. Mary at Lira, in the diocese of Evreux in Normandy, and he gave to this abbey six churches in the island, certain lands, and the tithes of the demesne land of the island lordship. At the time of the great survey, the revenue of the abbey arising from the Isle of Wight was stated to be £20.

The entry in Domesday Book relating to the manor of Alvington, shows that the Norman castle of Carisbrook was built between the date of the Conquest and the time of the survey.

William FitzOsborne's connection with the island was short, for he was killed in Normandy in 1070. There is an entry in Domesday Book under the manor of Wilmingham, which shows that his son Roger de Breteuil, who succeeded

12

to his English earldom, was also lord of the island. In 1075 Roger entered into a conspiracy against the Conqueror, as a result of which the remainder of his life was passed in prison. He died in 1086, apparently just before the survey, for on his death his estates in the Isle of Wight and elsewhere were resumed by the crown, and in the Domesday record we find that all the demesne lands of the lord of the island were at that time held by the king. As far as known, the Conqueror visited the Isle of Wight once only, and that was on a memorable occasion in 1085. Odo, his half-brother, Bishop of Bayeux and Earl of Kent, who in his capacity of Regent had oppressed the people and robbed the Church, was preparing an armed expedition of Norman and English knights, with which he hoped to cross the Alps and obtain his election to the papacy. On hearing of these plans, the Conqueror sailed from Normandy and landed in the island, where Odo then was. At a hastily summoned council he accused his brother of his misdeeds, and arrested him with his own hands.

The lordship of the island appears to have been retained by the crown until about the year 1101, when Henry I. rewarded one of his Norman barons, Richard de Redvers, who had assisted him in his contest with his brother Robert, by conferring upon him the earldom of Devon and the lordship of the Isle of Wight. He had married Adeliza, daughter of William FitzOsborne, so that his succession to the lordship of the island was probably a promotion he desired. He died in 1107, and was succeeded by his son, Baldwin de Redvers.

In the meantime an important grant in the Isle of Wight had been made by the Conqueror, and confirmed by William Rufus and Henry I., to Walkelin, Bishop of Winchester, in connection with the great church of St. Swithun he was building at Winchester. This was the gift of half a hide of land at Quarr, and liberty to dig stone there for his building operations. This work went on during these three successive reigns until the Norman Cathedral was finished, and we may see at the present time in its fine Norman transepts some of the stone which was then quarried. We may also see in some of the old overgrown stone pits in Binstead wood the site of these ancient quarries.

This was an age in which great men displayed a zeal in the foundation of religious houses and the erection of churches. Baldwin de Redvers himself founded an abbey not far from the site of these celebrated quarries. From these stone pits it had become known as Quarrera or Quarr, and here a great Cistercian monastery arose, one of the earliest of its kind in these islands. Baldwin placed there a colony of Cistercian monks, whom he brought over from Savigny in Normandy.

The stone quarries had certainly been worked for a long time before. That the Romans had a building of some kind close to the site of Quarr Abbey is very probable, for Roman tiles may be seen built into the stonework of the buttery hatch, and other existing remains of the abbey walls, as if these materials were lying about near at hand when the abbey was built.

Baldwin de Redvers was a supporter of the empress Maud, during the wars of Stephen's reign. He was driven from the island into Normandy, and his possessions confiscated. These were restored to him when peace was made in 1153; but he only lived two years longer. He and his wife and one of his sons were buried in Quarr Abbey, where a number of mural tombs have lately been discovered during the excavations conducted by Mr. Percy G. Stone.

Baldwin was succeeded by his son, Richard de Redvers the second, who further enriched the abbey his father had founded, and granted to the town of Newport its earliest charter. As he died in 1162 that charter must have been given early in the reign of Henry II. He was succeeded by his young son, Baldwin de Redvers the second, who died within a year of his father, and was buried in the

priory of Christchurch. He was succeeded by his brother,
Richard de Redvers the third, who died without issue in
1184. A series of early deaths thus occurred among these
early lords of Wight.

The next to inherit the family honours was William de
Redvers, uncle of the two last lords; but who was more
commonly known as William de Vernon, from a town in
the Cotentin, where he was born. He was one of the
ablest lords of the island, and held it for thirty-two years.
He was loyal to Richard I., and at his second coronation,
in Winchester, in 1194, filled a place of honour. When
John succeeded to the Crown, de Vernon, fearing that his
estates would be confiscated, transferred the lordship of
the island and the manor of Christchurch to Hubert de
Burgh, the Grand Justiciary of England, who had married
his daughter Joan. Hubert de Burgh died without issue
in 1206, and his father-in-law then obtained the restitution
of his estates by paying the crown 500 marks, and placing
his grandson as a hostage in the king's hands. William
de Vernon was one of the barons who forced King John to
sign the Great Charter. He resided much in the island,
was liberal to the abbey of Quarr, where he is said to have
raised a stately family monumental tomb at a great cost,
and where he was himself buried. He died in 1216, and
was succeeded by his grandson, Baldwin de Redvers the
fourth, his son, Baldwin the third, having died shortly
before him.

Baldwin de Redvers the fourth was but a child at the
time of his father's death, and he was placed by King John
as a ward under Fulk de Breauté, a disreputable baron
whom the king constrained the child's mother, Margaret,
to marry. In 1224, Fulk de Breauté was deprived of the
wardship and estates and banished the country, and the
young Earl Baldwin was made the ward of Richard Earl
of Cornwall, brother of Henry III., who was subsequently
elected king of the Romans. This royal guardian took
a great interest in his ward, and by his influence arranged

a marriage for him, in 1227, with Amicia de Clare, daughter of Gilbert de Clare, Earl of Gloucester. When Henry III. held his court at Winchester at Christmas, 1240, Baldwin de Redvers, who is described as having been a youth of noble disposition, and skilful in all martial exercises, was knighted, and formally invested with the lordship of the Isle of Wight. Five years later he died, leaving a son, Baldwin, born in 1235, and two daughters, Margaret, who became a nun, and Isabella. During his minority, Baldwin de Redvers the fifth was made a ward of Henry de Wengham. He married Avicia, a cousin of Queen Eleanor, and had a son, John, who died in childhood. Baldwin died in 1262, it is said of poison administered to him at the table of Peter de Savoy, Earl of Richmond, and was buried in the priory at Breamore.

The lordship of the island appears to have been held by his mother, Amicia de Clare, until her death in 1283, when the honours and estates of the de Redvers family were all inherited by Isabella, who had married William de Fortibus, Earl of Albemarle, and was thus Countess of Albemarle, Countess of Devon, and Lady of the Isle of Wight. At the age of twenty-three, she had been left a widow, and twenty-three years later, on the death of her mother, she succeeded to the domain of the island. She ruled her island lordship for ten years, residing chiefly at Carisbrook, where she maintained a court in almost royal splendour.

She was very liberal to the abbey of Quarr, confirmed the donations of her ancestors, and gave it several other manors. Subsequently, in some dispute with the abbey, she claimed certain lands it enjoyed, and the monks appealed to the king, who commissioned the sheriff of Hampshire to protect their interests. She was an imperious lady, who ruled with a high hand, and she has left traditions of her rule which have survived in the island unto the present day.

As she was on her death-bed, she executed a deed by which, for the sum of 6,000 marks, she transferred all her

powers, privileges, and lands in the Isle of Wight to
Edward I. All her children except one daughter died
before her, and this one, Aveline de Fortibus, who married
twice, left no issue. Her second husband was Edmund
Plantagenet (surnamed Crouchback), Earl of Lancaster,
second son of Henry III.

Thus, while the earldom of Devon passed to the family
of Courtenay, descended from William de Vernon, the
lordship of the Isle of Wight reverted to the crown in
virtue of the deed executed by Isabella de Fortibus. Hugh
de Courtenay, Earl of Devon, who succeeded the Countess
Isabella, declared the deed to be a forgery, and a parliamentary inquiry on his petition took place* in the next
reign, when the validity of the deed was confirmed.

The island had been governed by its own lords as a
peculiar fief for 200 years, and the change which ensued
on the transfer of the lordship to the crown was an
important one for the inhabitants. In one respect it was
to their advantage, for various bishops, abbots, priors, and
others whose estates were situated in the southern counties
were required to assist in its defence, and to equip men for
that service. On the other hand, the change led to
disputes between the chief tenants of the island and the
crown in regard to the nature of the tenure by which they
held their manors and lands. The islanders maintained
that they held, not as feudal tenants, liable to all the
burdens incident to such tenure, but simply of Carisbrook
Castle, being liable to serve for forty days at their own
cost in its defence, and that they were liable for no other
service, except that of conducting their lords into the isle
when they came thither, and out of it when they departed.

The desire of Edward I. that the crown should resume
the lordship of the Isle of Wight must have arisen from a
consideration for the safety of the kingdom. The circumstances were very different at the close of the thirteenth
century from what they were at the end of the eleventh.

* Rot. Parl., 9 Edw. II.

When the lordship was conferred by the Conqueror on William FitzOsborne, or by Henry I. on Richard de Redvers, the island was liable to no menace from Normandy. That duchy had been lost to the English crown. A French expedition, under Louis the Dauphin, had at the beginning of the thirteenth century brought war into Hampshire. If the island should in any future war be seized by any expedition in force, and held by the enemy, its proximity to the English coast would imperil the safety of the kingdom. Edward I. appears, therefore, from such considerations to have made its acquisition part of his far-seeing policy. The additional men subsequently supplied to the king for its greater security included five from the Bishop of Salisbury, seven from the Abbot of Glastonbury, six from the community of Wilts, three from the Abbot of Malmsbury, three from the Abbot of Abingdon, two from the Abbot of Stanley, two from the Abbot of Cirencester, one each from the Abbots of Gloucester, Walton, Romele, and the Prior of Hurle, one each from the Abbesses of Godestow and Wherwell, two from Mary, the king's daughter, a nun at Amesbury, from the revenue of her estates, one each from the Bishops of Worcester and Bath and Wells, and thirty-five others, one each from that number of lords of various manors and hundreds, and other persons, making a total of seventy-three men-at-arms.*

The number of men which the lords of manors and other tenants of lands in the island were, in virtue of their holdings under the honour of Carisbrook, required to supply for its defence was fifty-four men-at-arms and one hundred and forty-one archers. In addition to these, there would be available for the defence of the castle and of the island, such military force as the lord of the island himself might provide, and in cases of emergency all the able-bodied men would be marshalled by their lords in its defence.

In the eighteenth year of Edward II., an inquisition was taken at Shide Bridge concerning the obligations for

* Inquis., 16 Edw. III.

defence in time of war, to which the lords, abbots, priors, rectors, knights, and other free tenants who held land worth twenty pounds per annum, were liable by ancient custom. From this inquisition we learn that a regular organized plan of watches by night and day existed at certain signalling stations, each provided with a beacon-fire, to be lighted on the approach of the enemy. There were thirteen beacon stations in the hundred of East Medine, and sixteen in that of West Medine.

In the early part of the fourteenth century the chief tenants in the island were the families of de Insula or Lisle of Gatcombe, Westover, Westcourt, etc., de Glamorgan of Motteston, Wolverton, and Brook, Russell of Yaverland, de Evercy of East Standen, de Gorges of Knighton, de Albemarle, Trenchard of Chessel and Shalfleet, de Compton of Compton and Atherfield, de St. Martin of Alvington, de Heyne of Stenbury, de Langford of Chale, de Kingston of Kingston, d'Oglandre of Nunwell, de Chekenhull of Whippingham, de Afton of Afton, de Chillingwode, de la Hyde, Urry, le Taillour, Aurifaber, and Tolouse.

The occurrence of such names as le Taillour and Aurifaber among the free tenants is an evidence of the rise of the middle classes, which was going on in the island as elsewhere. The occurrence of the name of Tolouse appears to denote the settlement of a native of Gascony, a subject of the English kings in southern France, who was perhaps rewarded for some service with land in the Isle of Wight.

The most singular of all the smaller landholders in the island from the time of the Domesday Survey until that of Edward III. was the Vavasor. The Domesday entry relating to the manor of Aviston states that a Vavasor was then living there, and that he had two cows. He appears to have been a foreign-born freeman, who had some land given him in the island, and who was of the same status as a minor thane, but, being a foreigner, was described by the foreign title.* In 1279, Roger Vavasor, a tenant who was probably his descendant, held the fourth part of a knight's fee in Weston, and in the time of Edward III. 'The Vavasor' was required to provide two archers for the defensive force of the island.

After obtaining the lordship of Wight, Edward I. kept it in his own hands during the remainder of his life, and appointed wardens for its administration and government. Edward II., in the first year of his reign, made a grant of it to his favourite, Piers Gaveston, but on the remonstrance of the barons he resumed the lordship himself, and conferred it on his eldest son, then a child, Prince Edward, styled Earl of Chester—and afterwards Edward III. It was governed by wardens from 1308, when this grant was made, until 1386, when Richard II. granted the lordship to William Montacute, Earl of Salisbury, for his life. He married Joan, previously known as the Fair Maid of Kent, but the marriage was annulled, she having been married to Sir Thomas Holland, who was still living. She afterwards became Countess of Kent, and her romantic courtship by the Black Prince, after the death of Sir Thomas Holland, is a matter of history. As she was the mother of Richard II., this grant of the lordship of the island to the Earl of Salisbury may have had some connection with her matrimonial affairs.

After the death of the Earl of Salisbury, without issue, Richard II. conferred the lordship of the island, in tail male, on his cousin Edward, Earl of Rutland, son of Edmund de Langley, fifth son of Edward III. The king created him Duke of Albemarle, warden of the New Forest, and promoted him to other dignities. He subsequently became Duke of York. On the accession of Henry IV. he was degraded from the dukedom of Albemarle, but subsequently regained the royal favour, and was made the king's lieutenant for the government of Aquitaine. He married Philippa, a daughter of Lord de Mohun, and was killed at the battle of Agincourt.

* See Du Cange.

Henry V. then granted the lordship of the island, with other possessions, to his widow Philippa, Duchess of York, for her life, and these she held as her dower. At the time of this grant the king appears to have made a grant of the reversion of the lordship after the decease of the Duchess, so that when she died, in 1439, Humphrey, Duke of Gloucester, became lord of Wight in virtue of this reversion. He was its lord until his death in 1446. Shortly before that event, Henry VI. conferred the titular dignity of King of the Isle of Wight, but apparently without any real authority over it, on Henry Beauchamp, Duke of Warwick, son of the Earl of Warwick, late Regent of France. At this ceremonial King Henry assisted in person, and himself placed the crown on the duke's head, but the King of Wight died soon after this empty honour had been conferred upon him.

In 1449 Richard, Duke of York, father of Edward IV., appears to have been lord of the island, as in that year he appointed a steward and lieutenant to act for him, named John Newport.

In 1453 Edmund, Duke of Somerset, who had supplanted the Duke of York as regent in France, obtained from the king a grant of the island to himself and to his heirs male, in satisfaction for certain sums of money due to him from the king's exchequer. He was slain in the first battle of St. Albans, and was succeeded by his son Henry, Duke of Somerset, who, having changed sides from the Lancastrians to the Yorkists, and back again to the Lancastrians, was taken prisoner at Hexham, and beheaded by the Yorkists.

The next Lord of the Isle of Wight was Anthony de Woodville, afterwards Lord Scales, and subsequently Earl Rivers, brother-in-law of Edward IV. He held it from 1464 until 1483, when, as he stood in the way of Richard, Duke of Gloucester, afterwards Richard III., he was seized and, without trial, beheaded in Pontefract Castle.

Two years later Henry VII., in the first year of his reign, made Sir Edward Woodville, brother of Earl Rivers, Captain of the Island. This was the first occasion on which the title of Captain of the Isle of Wight was used, and this title has survived until the present day, the present Captain of the island being Prince Henry of Battenberg.

Sir Edward Woodville's grant, in 1485, as Captain, appears to have included great power. His rule did not last long, for in 1488 he organized a disastrous expedition into Brittany, to assist the Duke of Brittany against the King of France. He first asked permission of Henry VII. to lead this expedition, and received a denial. This, he imagined, was only given to save appearances, and he considered the king would be pleased rather than otherwise by such assistance to the Duke. He depicted the glory which would result from such an expedition to the islanders, and succeeded in inducing forty gentlemen and four hundred of the ablest men of Wight to join in his adventure. The expedition embarked at St. Helen's in four ships and joined the Duke of Brittany's force, but at the battle of St. Aubin's the Duke was defeated, and Sir Edward Woodville and all the islanders slain, except one youth, who managed to escape, and brought home the news of the disaster. Whether Sir Edward was lord of the island as well as captain, as he appears to have been, is uncertain— but it is certain that after this terrible loss no subsequent lord was appointed.

The ancient system of local government which prevailed in the Isle of Wight was similar to that which existed on the mainland. Originally the manors had their courts, where all matters concerning the land held in common were settled. On some of the smaller manors these courts must have become discontinued earlier than on the larger ones, on some of which they have existed down to the present day. There was also the hundred-court, at which the representatives of the tithings or parishes had to attend and pay their fees. There were only two hundreds in the island, known as East Medine and West Medine, the river Medina being the boundary between them. No division of the island into hundreds is recorded in Domesday Book, so that this division was probably a later arrangement. The hundreds are mentioned in the Nomina Villarum, 9 Edward II., the lord of both hundreds at that time being Prince Edward, Earl of Chester, afterwards Edward III.

The ancient place of assembly of the whole body of the freemen of the island appears to have been at Shide Bridge, south of Newport. Hundred-courts in Saxon time not unfrequently met at fords and bridges, the hundreds of Redbridge, Mansbridge, and Fordingbridge, on the mainland of Hampshire, being examples of hundreds which derived their names from such meeting places. It was at Shide Bridge that two important inquisitions were held in the thirteenth year of Edward II., relating to the ancient custom for the defence of the island.

The highest court in the island was that known as the Knighten Court, or Curia Militum, which was probably established by the first lord, William FitzOsborne. It was a judicial tribunal in which the judges were those who held a knight's fee, or part of a knight's fee, of the castle of Carisbrook. The courts of the island were probably varied at different periods of its history. The earliest of all must have been the open air moots, such as that recorded as having been held in the time of Edward II., probably, according to ancient custom, at Shide Bridge. In the Isle of Wight, as elsewhere, the hundred-courts appear in the course of time to have become discontinued, so that in the seventeenth century the knighten-court, which met every three weeks at Newport, discharged functions of a similar kind. It had jurisdiction over the whole island at that time, except the borough of Newport, in such matters as debt and trespass under the value of forty shillings, and in its operations it appears to have resembled a trithing-court, or court having jurisdiction over several hundreds : such as that which existed, in the latter part of the Middle Ages, at Basingstoke, but in the case of this Curia Militum the judges were of knightly rank.

The towns of Newport, Yarmouth, Newtown, and Brading enjoyed exceptional privileges. The earliest charter of Newport, the capital of the island, was granted by Richard de Redvers in the reign of Henry II., and this was enlarged by a charter of the Countess Isabella in the time of Edward I., in which document it is named the New Borough of Medina. This charter was confirmed by subsequent kings, as was usual with corporate towns, until the time of Charles II. James I. substituted a mayor for the ancient bailiff. At Brading the king's bailiff has survived until our own time, and only became extinct in the autumn of 1890. The old court-leet of Brading, over which he presided, had gradually become shorn of its ancient functions by legislative changes, so that for many years its sole use was the administration of certain corporate property belonging to the place. Under the old town-hall the ancient stocks and whipping-post may still be seen, and in the open space of the street close by a large iron ring, to which in olden time the bulls were fastened for the purpose of being baited. The stocks have long been disused, the ring is now only an antiquity, and the bailiff of Brading has gone for ever.

The ecclesiastical life of the island was complicated by the connection of some of its churches and religious houses with Norman monasteries. William FitzOsborne founded the Abbey of Lira, in Normandy, and he gave to that abbey the priory of Carisbrook, which he also founded, and the tithes of six churches, as mentioned in Domesday Book. The charter of William de Vernon, confirming this grant, tells us that these churches were Arreton, Whippingham, Newchurch, Godshill, Niton, and Freshwater. Subsequently the tithes of other churches in the island, and of all the demesne land of the lord, were granted to the same abbey, so that this Norman monastery must have drawn a very considerable revenue from Wight, and the churches of the island must have been proportionally impoverished.

Disputes arose between the Abbey of Lira and the Bishop of Winchester concerning the presentation of vicars to these benefices, and the general question was referred to Pope Alexander IV., who expressed an opinion against the appropriation of parochial churches by religious houses, by which ' the worship of God was lost, hospitality was intermitted, episcopal rights were detained, the doors of charity were shut against the poor, and the encouragement of studious scholars was abated,' etc.

In 1307, and again in 1340, the monks who looked after the interests of Lira Abbey, in the island, took forcible possession of the church of Godshill, and the Bishop of Winchester petitioned the king on both occasions to order them to be removed.

For more than two hundred years during the reigns of the Norman and early Plantagenet kings the island was free from invasion. Subsequently it was much troubled by the French, so much so that it was necessary for its inhabitants to be all trained in the art of war. Land was held in other parts of Hampshire by many kinds of tenure. In the island it was held by tenure of one kind only, that of home defence, and this appears to have been of very ancient origin. All the land was held by the obligation to assist in the defence of Carisbrook Castle. The origin of this fortress must be ascribed to a very remote antiquity, probably the pre-Roman period. A British earthwork probably existed here, and this appears to have been adapted by the Norman lords of the island for the inclosure of the castle, which was built during the Norman period. The earthworks of many British fortresses were utilized by the Normans in this manner.

As long as any organized community existed in the island, some system of defence must have prevailed, and the ancient British castle of refuge, represented by the earliest fortification at Carisbrook, was probably a similar defensive work to those which I have mentioned on the mainland.

To such earthworks the people of the country round would flee in case of attack. In the Isle of Wight such a castle of refuge, in the defence of which all the inhabitants would be interested, must have been a necessity in British time, and it may be that the obligation to defend the castle, which we find prevailed throughout the island in medieval time, was a survival of a far more ancient custom.*

The abbey of Montesberg, in Normandy, had a prior and two monks at Applederwell in 1340. They had probably been sent there from the parent house, which received the revenues of the priory after the expenses of the small establishment had been paid. At that time England was at war with France. The French had recently attacked Southampton in force, had looted the town, and had set it on fire. The organization which prevailed in the island for watch and ward, at that time, was extensive. Armed men were stationed, by night and day, at twenty-nine places round the coast, and in other parts of Wight, each place being provided with materials ready laid for beacon-fires to be lighted on the approach of the enemy, which would flash the intelligence through the island, and call the people to arms. The militia was organized in eleven companies under the command of the most able men, including the bailiffs of Newport, who commanded the trained band of that town. In view of these elaborate preparations for defence, it was thought to be unsafe to allow foreign monks of Applederwell, a priory situated near the sea, to remain there, and consequently the king issued an order to the Bishop of Winchester, to provide for the prior and his monks residing on the mainland at Hyde Abbey or at Salisbury, during the war with France. In the same year a French force landed at Bembridge, but was driven back by the militia, under Sir Theobald Russell of Yaverland, who was mortally wounded in the hour of victory.

* See paper by the author on 'Early Boroughs in Hampshire,' *Archæological Review*, vol. iv., No. 4.

During this century the French made several other attacks on the island. In 1377 they destroyed Francheville, afterwards rebuilt and known as Newtown, burnt Yarmouth, and captured Newport. This encouraged them to attack the castle of Carisbrook, which was defended by all the available force of the island under Sir Hugh Tyrril, who repulsed their assault with great slaughter. It is said that Newport had been so devastated during this invasion that it remained unoccupied for two years. A few years later we read that another invasion was expected, and the Earl of Salisbury, who was in 1386 appointed lord of the island, was intrusted specially with its defence.

During the lordship of Edmund, Duke of York, the French made another descent on Wight, in 1404. Waleram, Count of St. Pol, assembled at Abbeville a force of 1600 fighting men, among whom were many of noble birth, for an invasion of Wight. He embarked his troops at Harfleur, and sailed straight across to the island. He landed without opposition, and the inhabitants retired. The count appeared confident of success, and made several new knights among his followers. Meanwhile, we are told, an astute priest of the country came to treat for the ransom and safety of the island, and named such a sum as a possible price, that the count and his knights were induced to continue the parley. During this conference the forces of the island had been assembled, and when these preparations were completed the negotiations were broken off, and the count then realizing that he had been outwitted, embarked his men with all convenient speed, and returned to France.

In the latter part of the year 1418 another body of French landed, and plundered the inhabitants of their cattle, but as they were driving them towards their ships the islanders suddenly attacked them, forced them to leave their spoil, and killed many of them before they could embark. The next year another party came 'with a great navie, and sent certain of their men to demand tribute in the name of King

.ichard and Queen Isabell.' The islanders replied that ie king was dead, and that the queen, sometime his wife, id been sent home to her parents without any condition ˙ tribute, 'but if the Frenchmen's minde were to˙fight, iey willed them to come up, and no man should let iinder) them for the space of five hours, to refresh them- ilves, but when that time was expired they should have ittayle given to them.' The invaders declined this iivalrous invitation and returned to their own country.

No other invasion of Wight occurred until 1545, when great armament, consisting of 150 large ships, 25 galleys, id 50 other vessels and transports appeared off St. Helen's, id took up their position in a line stretching from Brading arbour almost as far as Ryde. The main object of the rench was an attack on Portsmouth, and as their fleet far itnumbered the English ships which lay in and near irtsmouth Harbour, the French commander landed veral parties of his troops on Wight, and set fire to veral places, hoping thereby to draw the English ships it. The islanders gave a good account of themselves, and / retiring before the invaders led them into difficulties, id many of them were slain when caught in small detach- ents. The French, however, caused considerable destruc- in the island. It was during this invasion that 'olverton, on the south of Brading Harbour, was burnt, d has ever since remained an overgrown, ruined site.

This invasion caused the king to strengthen its defences, d about this time the forts at Cowes, Sandown, Sharp- ide in Freshwater, and Yarmouth, were built under the rection of Sir Richard Worsley, then captain of the island d constable of Carisbrook castle. He also induced the anders to adopt more modern warlike appliances. During e invasion of 1545 they harassed the French from their ibuscades in the woods with the ancient weapons to iich they were accustomed, bows and arrows. Sir chard Worsley persuaded them to provide a train of artillery at their own expense, every parish purchasing its own gun. This artillery, with the additional forts, gave them greater security. Cowes seems to have derived its name from the guns placed in the forts there, the noise of the discharge of which was supposed to resemble the lowing of a cow.

> ' The two great cows, that in loud thunder roar,
> This on the eastern, that the western shore.'*

The remains of the fort at West Cowes, which now forms part of the Royal Southern Yacht Club house, was the more important. All traces of the eastern fort, such as it was, have long since disappeared.

The invasion of 1545 was the last appearance of an enemy in Wight. Its proximity to Portsmouth and the increase of its own defensive power subsequently kept it free from attack. In 1625 its military muster was 2,020 men, of whom only 196 were armed with ' bare pickes.' The militia was mustered twice a year for training in the time of Queen Elizabeth, and this custom appears to have been long continued. All the able-bodied men were enrolled in this militia, so that the enemy, knowing of this preparation for war, kept away from the Isle of Wight. During the wars of the seventeenth and eighteenth centuries the islanders were continually expecting invaders who never came, and in the folk-tales and island songs of this period they appear to have taken some credit to themselves for this immunity from attack. In 1781 the militia only numbered one company of sixty men, but eighteen of the cannon made in the sixteenth century still remained, some being kept in the churches.

The gun which was made for the parish of Brading is still preserved, and bears the inscription ' John and Robert Owine, Brethren, made this pese, 1549, Brerdynd.'

The folk-lore of the Isle of Wight comprises many legends. An island story which somewhat resembles that

---

* Gibson's ' Translation of Leland's Latin Verse.'

of the pied piper of Hamelin who decoyed the rats and children away is sometimes told.

There are stories about haunted houses at Wootton, which the ghost of a former rector in gown and cassock sometimes revisits, and at Knighton, where the former manor-house was haunted by one of its previous owners. A very curious tradition hangs about Carisbrook as to the way the old island family of Oglander obtained their estates. It is to the effect that a former possessor of Carisbrook was walking on the ramparts of that fortress, when a knight appeared in the fields outside, and challenged him to fight. The combat of course took place, but the story is somewhat doubtful as to the result, except that the strange knight fought so well that he was rewarded with certain lands, and being the first to introduce pigs into the island, he was called Oglander. The native folk-lorist will also sometimes point out to a stranger the forest of Parkhurst, and tell a hazy story about some lady, who, a good many years ago, 'was done out of that wood,' which, as Parkhurst was a forest of the lordship, can, I think, only refer, through the mist of ages, to the supposed wrong done to Isabella de Fortibus by Edward I.

The defence of the island appears always to have been considered a sacred duty by the people of Wight. We cannot, therefore, feel surprised at the terrible fate of the mythical Sir Mordred, the father of Sir Bevois of Hampton, who is said to have been boiled to death beneath the keep of Carisbrook Castle for a conspiracy to betray it.

On the side of the high down between Ventnor and Bonchurch is St. Boniface's Well or the Wishing-well, which was in olden times visited by young people for the purpose of having their wishes fulfilled. This well or spring is said to have been first discovered by a certain bishop, who was riding along the precipitous slope of the down, when his horse began to slip, and the soft ground round the spring alone saved him. The bishop thereupon vowed to St. Boniface that if he reached the bottom of the down in safety he would dedicate an acre of land to him. The Bishop's Acre, which is part of the glebe of Bonchurch, is still pointed out in evidence of his safe descent. In the Middle Ages this Holy Well of St. Boniface, the site of which was visible from the sea, was an object of reverence to sailors, who sometimes lowered the topsails of their ships on passing near it.

In the folk-lore of Wight, Lot's wife finds a place. The rocks known as the Needles have no needle-shaped mass rising above the other rocks now, but a very remarkable rock of this shape, about 120 feet high, existed there until 1764, when it fell with a great noise heard for many miles. This rock was known for ages as Lot's wife.

A curious example of the survival of astrological lore exists at Newport. The church there contains a fine carved wooden pulpit, dated 1636, and having on the panels the names of the seven liberal sciences as they were then understood : Grammatica, Dialectica, Rhetorica, Musica, Arithmetica, Geometrica, and Astrologia.

One of the most persistent of the legends of the Isle of Wight is that concerning the connection of the island with the mainland, as late as the time when the Greek traders from Marseilles frequented it, in order to buy tin, which, the tradition says, was brought across from the mainland in carts at low water.

During the latter part of the sixteenth century the captains or wardens of the island were Sir Richard Worsley, Sir Edward Horsey, a gallant sea-captain, and Sir George Carey, who appears to have been styled governor as well as captain. During his captaincy Carisbrook Castle was repaired and considerably enlarged, under the direction of Gainibelli, an eminent Italian engineer. The Spanish king was at that time fitting out the great Armada. The queen gave £4,000, the gentry of the island £400, towards the cost of this work, and all the able-bodied men in the island gave their labour. The ther forts were strengthened, and an additional small fort, called Carey's Sconce, built near Yarmouth.

In 1603 the Earl of Southampton was appointed captain and governor of the island. He was the friend and patron of Shakespeare, and resided much in Wight, and at his seat on the opposite side of the Solent at Titchfield. During his captaincy King James and Prince Charles, who were his guests at Beaulieu, crossed over to the island and paid a visit to Carisbrook. The earl died in 1625, and the Isle of Wight was governed successively by Lord Conway, Lord Weston, the Earl of Portland, and the Earl of Pembroke, until the time of the Civil War. The people of Wight sided with the Parliament so strongly that they would not allow the Countess of Portland to remain in Carisbrook Castle, where she had taken refuge after her husband's removal from office. The Earl of Pembroke, who was favourable to the Parliamentary party, held the captaincy for several years, and was succeeded in 1647 by Colonel Hammond. Two months after his appointment, Charles I., who was residing at Hampton Court, suddenly left that place, hoping to find a place of greater security in Hampshire or the Isle of Wight. The result of this sudden journey was to find himself after a short time a prisoner in Carisbrook Castle. Hammond was thanked and rewarded for his action in this matter by the Parliament, which also made a liberal provision for the king's expenses. Then began the captivity of the king in the island, which lasted from the autumn of 1647 until that of 1648. He was strictly guarded at Carisbrook, but allowed such freedom within the castle as was consistent with his safe custody. There he appears to have employed his time in religious studies and some literary pursuits. The verses known as 'Suspiria Regalia' and 'Majesty in Misery' were written by him at this time. Two attempts at escape were made by the king, aided by some friends outside the castle, but these failed.

In August, 1648, the Conference of Newport took place,

between fifteen commissioners appointed by the Parliament and the king, in the hope of securing a settlement for the troubles of the kingdom. The restrictions on the king's personal liberty were largely removed. He was allowed to assemble some of his adherents around him, and to live in Newport. The conferences took place in the town-hall, where he sat on a raised daïs under a canopy, attended by his lords and other advisers, and the Parliamentary commissioners sat at a table apart. The negotiations were prolonged for three months, when a treaty was signed by the unhappy monarch, under which the prerogatives of the crown were practically conveyed to the Parliament. After this the commissioners returned to London, and orders were soon issued for the king to be removed and conveyed a prisoner to Hurst Castle.

Colonel Hammond was succeeded in the island government by Colonel William Sydenham, a brother of the celebrated physician of that name, and a zealous parliamentarian.

In 1650 Carisbrook Castle became the prison of two of the unhappy king's children, the Princess Elizabeth and the Duke of Gloucester, who were conveyed thither for safe custody in August of that year. The princess died there from the effects of a sudden chill a few weeks after her arrival, and was buried in the church at Newport. When the church was rebuilt in 1856, Queen Victoria erected a fine monument, with a reclining figure of the princess and a suitable inscription, over her grave.

On the restoration of Charles II., Lord Culpeper was made governor of the island, and he was succeeded in 1667 by Admiral Sir Robert Holmes, who held the office for many years. He resided at Yarmouth, where in 1671 he entertained Charles II. and his court. He died in 1692, and was buried in Yarmouth Church, where a very fine monument to his memory was erected by his son in a chapel attached to the church.

The succeeding captains and governors during the next

century were Lord Cutts; Charles, Duke of Bolton, who resigned in 1710; Lieutenant-General Webb; William, Earl of Cadogan; Charles, Duke of Bolton, who resigned in 1733; John, Duke of Montagu; the Earl of Portsmouth; Thomas, Lord Holmes, a grandson of Sir Robert; Hans Stanley, Esq.; Henry, Duke of Bolton; Sir Richard Worsley, and the Right Honourable Thomas Orde. By the middle of the eighteenth century the office appears to have become a sinecure, such as it still remains.

The first parliamentary representatives from the Isle of Wight were those sent by Yarmouth and Newport combined as one borough, in 1295. The island received some parliamentary writs subsequently, but apparently made no returns until the time of Queen Elizabeth.

The representation of the three boroughs of Newport, Yarmouth and Newtown began in 1584, and was continued until the first Reform Act, when the two latter were disfranchised. By the last Reform Act also the representation of Newport has been merged in the general representation of the island. In 1640 Lord Falkland sat for Newport, and in 1678 John Churchill, afterwards the first Duke of Marlborough, sat for Newtown.

CHAPTER XVII.

WINCHESTER.

As long as the English race lasts, Winchester will be classic ground. English-speaking people from distant parts of the world come year by year in increasing numbers to see the mother country, to visit Oxford and Cambridge, to view Shakespeare's house, and to gaze on the greatness of London, and many of the more intellectual of these also find their way to the Hampshire city to see the home of so many early kings, and the cradle of those early institutions of the Anglo-Saxon race, which are their inheritance as well as ours.

Winchester was founded in a prehistoric age. The compressed layer of peat which underlies a great part of its area near the river and the branch streams marks the site of the original settlement. Bronze implements have been found in this peat layer. The original site appears to have been selected on account of its water defences. Nature had marked it out as a place for human occupation in a primitive age. It is in the most remarkable opening in the downland of Hampshire, where the forces of nature have cut through the chalk almost to its base, and where ridges of river gravel made one or more natural fords.

Marks of extreme antiquity lie around it. Human bones, marking the site of a burial by contracted inhumation, were found in a chalk cist on the slope of St. Giles' Hill when the railway was made there. St. Catherine's earthwork cannot be of later origin than the Bronze period, and the round barrows on the downland east of St. Giles' Hill probably mark the site where some of the chieftains in the Bronze Age were cremated. On the opposite side of the city is Seven Sleepers' Hill, a name derived from that venerable legend which clings also to other cities of extreme antiquity in several parts of Europe and Asia.

Winchester was built, like many other towns of Roman date, in the form of a parallelogram, and was surrounded by a wall made of flint and concrete. Part of this wall remains in the eastern part of the city, where the town wall is formed by the wall of Wolvesey Palace. In this structure there are some bricks and other material of Roman origin worked in with the layers of flint, as if the old material was used up when the wall was built. The existing remains of the wall which surrounded the close is a good example of a concreted flint wall, and shows that when the city was surrounded by such a structure its defensive power must have been great. The river flowed just outside the wall on the east, and a branch stream washed the northern wall along the greater part of its course. A ditch, which could for the greater part be filled with water, formed an outer defence along the north-west, west, and south. The castle was built at the south-western part of the fortified area, the highest ground being selected for its site. The city had six gates, in addition, probably, to one which led directly into the castle area, by a drawbridge over the western moat. The west gate at the upper end of the High Street, and the King's Gate on the south, which led into the close, are all that now remain of these.

For the maintenance of the walls a heavy outlay must have been necessary from time to time. King John gave the citizens the two mills in Coitebury for the repair of their walls, and other repairs were necessary about the end of the reign of Henry III.* Early in the reign of

---

* Muragium pro civitate Winton. Cal. Rot. Pat., 56 Hen. III.

Henry IV. also the king remitted a portion of the fee ferme of the city for the repair of the walls, and Henry VI. also did the same.

Some very early guilds existed at Winchester, the oldest, and at one time the most influential, of which was probably that known as the knights' guild, originally established in Saxon time, and comprising young men, sons of nobles and thanes. In Domesday Book we read of many thanes who, continued to hold their lands in Hampshire. It was the sons of such as these who came to Winchester and joined the knights' guild, and later on, no doubt, it comprised youths of Norman descent. In the West Saxon capital these knightly youths would see something of the world and learn important duties. They had their halls, one in the east of the city and one near the west gate. This guild appears to have been quite a Saxon institution, and to have become obsolete long before the decay of the trade guilds. The ancient West Saxon capital was so important in Saxon time that Wintonia and London are the only cities in England marked on the Anglo-Saxon map of the world discovered among the muniments of Hereford Cathedral.

During the Saxon period Winchester was under a system of government similar to that which prevailed in other important towns at that time. There was a head townsman who was known by the title of præpositus. He was assisted by others known as burgesses, the præpositus being also mentioned as the port-reeve or wic-reeve. In the first survey recorded in the Liber Winton we are told that, in the time of King Edward the Confessor, the præpositus, or provost, was named Aldelwold, and that he was succeeded by others who bore the names of Warine, Geford, and Richard. At the time of the second survey the præpositus was named Herbert. The Saxon organization for the government of the town of Winchester was only an enlarged modification of that which prevailed in many smaller places in Hampshire.

Winchester was part of the ancient demesne of the West Saxon Kings, all the land in the town having originally belonged to the king. At the time of the surveys recorded in the Liber Winton, some of the tenements were held as freeholds ; but others paid various rents, or the holders were liable for certain customary services. These payments and services were, a small ground rent known as 'langabulum,' 'brigbote,' an ancient tax for maintaining bridges, the land tax, or 'Danegeld,' a tax on tenements known as 'fripene' or frith penny, a tax on goods sold known as ' venta,' a liability to supply a certain amount of food for the king's prison, known as 'pascere,' the service of watch and ward, probably in rotation, known as 'wata,' and a fixed service with plough and cart called 'avere.'

The earliest charter of the city is that of Henry II., which conceded the liberties and customs it had under Henry I., and restored those which might have been lost in Stephen's reign. During the Saxon period the privileges of places such as Winchester were based on ancient custom, so that in time they were acknowledged as prescriptive rights. Subsequently, when towns began to receive charters, they found it desirable to get them renewed by each succeeding king on his accession. This was done at Winchester for many centuries down to the time of James II.

After the Norman Conquest, when bailiffs appear to have been first appointed under that name, in the towns which belonged to the king, the præpositus was still mentioned, and at Winchester as late as the date of the charter granted by Henry III. The senior bailiff during this time, and until the full recognition of a mayor, may have been also the præpositus of the city.

The history of Winchester is so much identified with the history of the county, that it is not possible to write a general sketch of the latter without including much of the former. In the previous chapters I have already narrated much of the early history of this city which it is not necessary to recapitulate. To understand its history aright, it is necessary to bear in mind the dual character of the government which prevailed in it. There were for all practical purposes two Winchesters, existing side by side, and one indeed partly containing the other. There was the municipal Winchester, the city properly so called, and there was the ecclesiastical Winchester, which was quite distinct from it in civil as well as in ecclesiastical government. This was the Bishop's Soke, sometimes described in old records as 'The Bishop's Soke in the suburbs of Winchester.'* Such a separation of the ecclesiastical from the municipal part of the town was not peculiar to this city. In London a similar example occurred, where the Bishop's Soke included the ward of Cornhill. In the Soke the bishop had his own court and his own civil officers. All the tenements that existed beyond the Eastgate were in the bishop's jurisdiction, and formed that part of it known as the East Soke. The Soke also included the Cathedral precincts, the College, the Hospital of St. Cross, part of the parishes of St. Faith, St. Thomas, and Chilcombe, the ville of Milland, part of the parish of St. Bartholomew, and the small manor of Godbiete in the middle of the city itself. There is a reference to the Soke in Domesday Book, under the entry relating to Basingstoke, which place had four suburbani, *i.e.*, Soke men, in Winchester; but as the name Soke is derived from the Anglo Saxon *sóc*, a liberty, its origin must be ascribed to Saxon time.

Before the time when the chief city official became known by the name of mayor, the government of the city rested with a præpositus or provost, and the bailiffs were of much importance for centuries after the first appointment of a mayor. In the time of Edward I., the bailiffs were chosen by the community and twenty-three chief citizens. The chief citizens were required to choose four of

* Maddock, 'Hist. Excheq.,' 496.

their own number, and from these four the community elected one bailiff, and the chief citizens the other.*

The burghmotes, which were held regularly during the Middle Ages, were certainly as old as the time of King Edgar, by whose laws these courts were ordered to be held three times a year.† At a later period they met twice a year only, and were held in Winchester at Hocktide and Michaelmas, and at the latter meeting the officers for the ensuing year were chosen. The earliest record of these courts is in the Black Book, which Winchester has lost, and which is now preserved in the British Museum. This burghmote court was probably at one time held in the open air. Certainly a Husting or open air court, after the Danish custom, existed in Winchester,‡ perhaps in the time of Cnut.

In the Soke the bishop had his court, over which his deputy, the bailiff of the Soke, presided, and the jurisdiction of this was as independent of that of the city as if it had been many miles away. He had three tithingmen and a constable to assist him, and he had his own prison at Wolvesey, and stocks for malefactors standing a little east of the bridge over the Itchen. In the manor of Godbiete, north of the High Street, a manor court was held by the steward of the priory, in the same way as he held courts on other manors belonging to St. Swithun's. The court of the Soke, which became known as the Cheney Court, was, however, a superior court to this, and had a criminal jurisdiction.

When Queen Elizabeth granted her charter to Winchester, the bishop's rights as lord of the Soke were safeguarded, and so the two Winchesters existed side by side, the mayor of the city and the bailiff of the Soke being in later centuries the chief magnates of their respective jurisdictions, until the year 1835, when, under the changes then

* 'Abbreviatio Placitorum Edw. I.,' p. 187.
† Merewether, 'Boroughs,' i. 38.
‡ Gomme, ' Primitive Folk Motes,' 252.

introduced, the Soke for all practical purposes disappeared.

The character of the population of Winchester was considerably changed during the Norman period. In the earlier years of the Conqueror's reign it must have had a large majority of English, as shown by the secrecy and details of Waltheof's execution. We find that a change had occurred between that time and the date of the compilations made in the Liber Winton. In the first of these inquisitions, made in 1115, out of 238 owners of 288 tenements, 86 only, or 36·1 per cent., bear Saxon names, and about 5·1 per cent. of the others are recorded whose fathers had Saxon names; 126 owners, or 52·9 per cent., bore Norman or French names, the latter class holding 60 per cent. of the tenements, and the former 35 per cent. Winchester at that time had a majority of Norman-French inhabitants. In the second inquisition, made in 1148, and also recorded in the Liber Winton, the house owners bearing Norman or French names outnumbered those bearing English names by two to one. Winchester by that time had become a Norman-French city.

Although Winchester is not included in the Domesday Survey, we learn something about it at that time from the entries relating to other places in Hampshire, the manors of which had houses in this city. Thus a manor at Preston Candover, which was held by a fraternity described as 'The Clerici,' had a house in Winchester. Dummer and Norton manors, which were held by one of the king's thanes named Odo of Winchester, had respectively three and five houses in the city.

The Archbishop of York, who held the manor of Mottisfont, had a house belonging to the manor in Winchester, which was probably of much use to him on the occasion of any national assembly there to which he was summoned. The manor of Woodcote, which was held by the tenure of keeping the gaol in the city, had also a house there. Eversley Manor, which belonged to Westminster Abbey, had another. A house in Winchester was also attached to the manor of Stratfield. The bishop's manors of West Meon and Meonstoke each had eight messuages in the city. The manor of Minstead had a house there. The royal manors of Clatford, Paccombe, and Wallop had two or more houses each in the city, and the Abbess of Wherwell had thirty-one messuages there, which were free from all customary dues except the king's geld, and the abbess's own house was also free from that. Fourteen burgesses of Winchester paid twenty-five shillings rent to the abbey of Romsey, and at Clere the abbey of Hyde held the church and four and a quarter hides of land, which were given to it by King William for land in Winchester, on which he built his town house. This was the palace the Conqueror erected near St. Lawrence's Church, and west of the New Minster, adjoining which, and within the inclosure of this royal residence, were the offices for the state officials and the church of St. Lawrence itself. A curious survival of the connection of this church with the Conqueror's palace has come down to our own time. Before the enthronement of each new bishop, he goes to St. Lawrence's Church and tolls a bell there, a custom which is believed to have had its origin in Norman time, when the bishop went to the palace to which this church was attached, to perform some act of homage to the king.

The ancient mills which existed within the city were important. At the time of the Domesday Survey the Abbess of Wherwell had in Winchester the best mill in all Hampshire, its annual value being assessed at that time at forty-eight shillings. Later on we read of the great fullers' mill in Coitebury, that part a little north of Eastgate, and in the time of King John, Coitebury had two mills. Another mill also existed at Durngate, and another, known as Seagrim's Mill, outside the wall in the Soke, on the site of Wharf Mill.

The cloth manufacture required plenty of water facilities, and these existed in abundance in the north-eastern part of the city, where the cloth-workers were located.

During the Saxon, Norman, and early English periods Winchester was the chief trading centre of this part of England. Among its inhabitants in the time of Edward the Confessor were those who followed the trades of gold-smith, swordsmith, shoemaker, hosier, and the dealers in hay, soap, and herrings. In the time of Henry I. others are mentioned who followed the occupations of tailor, baker, cook, butcher, tanner, linen-draper, embosser, net-maker, old clothes dealer, and barber (probably barber-surgeon). In the time of Stephen the second inquisition shows that in addition to these there were others who followed the occupations of mercer, clothseller, weaver, fuller, dyer, shieldmaker, furbisher, currier, saddler, mason, carpenter, painter, miller, brewer, innkeeper, writer, parch-ment-maker, physician, and dealers in grease and wax. Several of these trades gave names to the ancient streets in which the crafts were carried on. There was Flescmangere Street, or that of the butchers, Alwarene Street, where the mercers were located, Snithelinga Street, or that of the tailors, Scowertene Street, or the shoemakers' quarter, Tanner Street, where the tanners lived, and Scyldwortene Street, where the shieldmakers pursued their craft. The present High Street was known as Cyp, or Cheap Street, where the shops of the merchants, or dealers, were situated.

Some of these crafts had fraternities of their own, such as the weavers and fullers, who were concerned with the cloth trade, which was very considerable, some of the cloth being exported from Southampton. The subordinate brother-hoods, craftsmen and traders of other occupations who had no special guild of their own, were all united in one trading association, known as the Guild Merchant. The members of this guild enjoyed important trading privileges in other places as well as in their own town, and if disputes arose in their business transactions, or they suffered wrong in any other town, the members of the Winchester Guild Merchant had an organization of considerable power to see that right was done them. None of its members, except the moneyers and royal servants, could be impleaded out of their own city. The Guild Merchant of Winchester was one of the earliest of these trading fraternities which existed in England, and in the charters which other towns gradually obtained, its constitution is often mentioned, the burgesses of such towns being commonly granted all the liberties and free customs 'which the citizens of Winchester have.' The traders, or merchants properly so called, had a distinct organization from the artificers and craftsmen, such as the weavers and fullers, and their guild is mentioned as the Cypmanna-gild, or Chapmen's guild.

These chapmen must have been an important class, who made Winchester their headquarters. They had there their place of assembly, known as the Chapmen's Hall, for the farm of which they paid twenty marks* in the time of King John. These merchants were the commercial travellers of the Middle Ages, who took their goods with them, and they supplied an important want in the country places where no shops existed.

The trade of Winchester appears to have been connected with the navigation of the Itchen from a very early time. It is but ten miles from the city to the tidal water at Wood Mill. Flat-bottomed boats could without much difficulty pass along the natural stream to and from the sea, and there can be little doubt that the stone used in building the cathedral, much of which is Bembridge limestone, probably from Binstead in the Isle of Wight, was conveyed to Winchester by water. 'The old Itchen upward to the orchard on the new river' at Stoneham is mentioned in a charter of Edward the Confessor in 1045. The water transit was greatly assisted by the canal cut by Bishop Lucy, in recognition of which King John granted him a charter authorizing the levying of certain tolls on vessels passing through the Soke. When the trade of the city

* Maddox, Hist. Exch., 234.

declined the canal was neglected, and became useless until the time of Charles II., when an Act of Parliament was passed, empowering a company of undertakers to improve it. A new Act was obtained in 1767, and for nearly a century afterwards the traffic on it was kept up, but it is now in a ruinous state.

The ordinary commercial life in Winchester during the Middle Ages was annually interrupted by St. Giles's fair, which was the great annual mart for this part of England. This fair was established by charter granted by William Rufus to Bishop Walkelin. It originally lasted three days, and was held on St. Giles's Hill, where rows of booths and huts arranged in streets, such as may now be seen at Wey Hill, were erected. The profits went to the bishop, and were used by him in completing the cathedral church and other parts of the convent of St. Swithun. While the fair lasted trade was suspended in Winchester, and in the country seven leagues round. The fair became very much frequented by merchants from many parts of England, and also from over the sea. In addition to the revenue arising from the tolls, the bishop obtained for St. Swithun's, of which he was the titular head, another source of revenue, for on the occasion of the fair the convent engaged in trade, and dealt largely in foreign wines, furs, spices, and other commodities. The concourse at this annual mart was so great that three days were found to be not time enough for it, and so it was increased by successive kings to eight, fourteen, and ultimately to sixteen days.* The people of Winchester, whose ordinary business was suspended during this time, may have recouped themselves in other ways, but the Southampton traders, who were also compelled to suspend their ordinary business, could not do this, and they found the fair very oppressive. The monks derived a great profit from this commercial gathering on the hill. During the fair the bishop not only became the commercial lord of Winchester, but the civil lord also, for the power

* Cal. Rot. Pat., 2 Edw. II. ; and Charter of Edw. III.

of the city authorities ceased. His officers took possession
of all the gates, set their own watch, and dismissed those
belonging to the city. The mayor and bailiffs were suspended from their offices ; all civil jurisdiction ceased, and
offenders were tried in the bishop's pavilion court on the
hill, and by his justiciars. The fair-time must have been a
proud time for the bailiff of the Soke, for his ordinary
jurisdiction would usually at this time be much enlarged.
The bishop's officers walked round the city, and compelled
the mayor and bailiffs of Winchester to accompany them,
in order to proclaim the fair at certain spots. It is quite
clear that all who attempted to forestall the trade on the
hill by intercepting and buying goods cheaply on their way
to the fair must have been severely dealt with, and the
suspension of the civil authority and the business of the
city and neighbourhood was, of course, for the purpose of
causing a roaring trade to be done on the hill.

The country people of Hampshire must have regarded
St. Giles's fair as a very great institution, for it afforded
them an excellent opportunity of buying in the cheapest
market the stores they required for the winter. They
must also have found some pleasure there, as probably
Langland did, who, writing about 1365, makes Piers
Plowman say :

'At Wy and at Winchester I went to the fair.'

The ecclesiastical history of Winchester is largely represented by the cathedral itself. Beneath its floor lies the
dust of many of the kings and queens who were its early
benefactors. The bones of some of these are preserved in
the chests on the screen of its choir. Here also rest the
remains of most of its Saxon bishops, some of whom were
canonized : St. Birinus, St. Hedda, St. Swithun, St. Frith-
stan, St. Brinstan, St. Alphege, St. Athelwold, St. Brithwold,
and others. The present building probably contains no
architectural remains of the church built by St. Athelwold,
but there is every reason to believe that some of the stones

14—2

of the existing cathedral formed part of the Saxon minster church. The mass of the stone is that of the Bembridge formation, a fresh-water limestone which occurs only in the Isle of Wight, and was quarried by the Romans. The Norman bishop, Walkelin, has left his monument in the great transepts, and in the timber roof above the stone-groined nave. Bishop Lucy has left his monument in the Lady Chapel, which was built further eastward in order to accommodate the crowd of pilgrims who came to the shrine of St. Swithun, between it and the choir. Bishop Edington has left his monument in the transformation of the Norman nave into the Early Perpendicular style, which was begun in his time and completed in that of his successor, Bishop William of Wykeham, the greatest architect of his age, who perhaps himself designed the alteration in his predecessor's time. The chantry-chapels of Wykeham, Beaufort, Waynfleet, Langton, and Fox, still remind us of the distinguished parts which these prelates played in the history of their country, as well as in the ecclesiastical history of Winchester.

A great part of the history of Hampshire is centred round Winchester. Similarly, as the bishopric and priory of St. Swithun's were so important, they overshadowed in later centuries the commercial importance of the town, and the later history of the city is consequently centred round the cathedral rather than round its municipal institutions. The castle, while it continued to be a royal residence, was of course of greater importance than the bishop's residence at Wolvesey ; but, after the thirteenth century, the castle was less frequented, while Wolvesey Palace continued to be a residence of the bishop in the city. The ecclesiastical importance of Winchester has endured until the present day, while its political importance has for centuries ceased.

Life at Winchester during the Middle Ages must have presented many aspects. In addition to its permanent residents, the city always had a fluctuating population. During the times when the king, or his family, were in residence, there must necessarily have been much coming and going of messengers, visits of noble personages, high officers of state and their retinues. During the Norman period these often came from France, as well as from distant parts of England.

While the Exchequer and the Records continued to be kept at Winchester, there must have been a staff of officials connected with them, and visits of sheriffs, bailiffs, and stewards of the royal estates would be of frequent occurrence. Whenever great councils, synods, and other assemblies met there, the old city would receive a larger number of temporary residents; and when parliaments began to be held, on the occasions when they met at Winchester, the influx of temporary residents must have been larger still. The old capital must have also attracted many adventurers and needy persons, who hoped to repair their fortunes by some lucky chance in a city which possessed so many opportunities. To it doubtless came military adventurers and landless knights, desirous of employment in the field, as well as political attendants on the wheel of fortune, seeking for civil offices or employment of some kind under the state.

In addition to all these, there were the crowds of pilgrims whom I have already mentioned, many of whom brought their sick friends to be healed at the shrine of St. Swithun. If they could not get material relief at the shrine of the Old Minster, they could try the shrine of St. Josse, in the abbey of Hyde, and at least they could carry away with them spiritual comfort. The visits of pilgrims to Winchester went on during the whole of the Middle Ages, and did not wholly cease until 1539, when the shrine of St. Swithun was destroyed.

Winchester must have also had a constant stream of persons seeking sanctuary. As early as the tenth century we read of female slaves fleeing there to take refuge at the tomb of St. Swithun. In the eleventh century Queen Emma, the wife of Cnut, granted to St. Swithun's the manor and liberty of Godbiete, in the middle of the city, as a 'Privilegium Deo datum,' in which stood the church of St. Peter in Macellis, which was a sanctuary, where accused persons, whether innocent or guilty, were free from the writ of the king or the civic authorities, and this sanctuary presented a curious and anomalous picture of the seamy side of life, down to the middle of the sixteenth century.

There were also wandering minstrels, mountebanks, and other travellers whose occupation must have led them rather frequently to the old capital. It was perhaps in the fertile imagination of one of these minstrels that two famous Hampshire legends had their origin, or, at least, took their present shape. While Bishop Adam de Orlton was visiting the Prior of St. Swithun's, in 1333, he was entertained in the great hall of the priory, by a celebrated minstrel, who sang to him the legendary songs of Guy, Earl of Warwick, overthrowing and killing Colbrand the Danish giant, under the walls of the city, and of Queen Emma walking unhurt over the red-hot ploughshares in the Old Minster.

Of ecclesiastical personages, Winchester must have seen a great variety. Here, on many occasions, came papal legates, archbishops, and other prelates to State functions, with great retinues. Its resident population included Benedictine monks at St. Swithun's and Hyde, Benedictine nuns at St. Mary's, Dominican, Franciscan, and Carmelite friars, calendars, parsons or secular priests of parishes, and chantry priests of various kinds, including those who sang masses for the souls of former well known citizens, and those of the Fraternity of the Holy Trinity, who sang masses in the chapel of the Carnary, or charnel house, over the bones of the unknown dead collected from all parts of the city. The Cistercians from Beaulieu, Netley, Quarr, Waverley, and other abbeys, must have had business occasionally which called one or more of their Order to the city. The Præmonstratensians also, the White Canons of Titchfield, and the Augustines or Black Canons of South-

wick and St. Denys, must sometimes have found it neces-
sary for some of their order to visit the episcopal city.
Here, also, were to be sometimes seen the Knights of the
Temple, who rode over from Selborne or South Baddesley,
and the Knights of St. John of Jerusalem, who came from
Godsfield and Woodcott, or at one time from St. Cross.

There must have been, in Winchester, many occasional
residents of the villein and borderer class, who came,
perhaps, from other counties, on business for some lord of
a manor, and who sought for opportunities of remaining
for the year and a day, which would give them borough
rights and free them from manorial services for ever.
Among the crowds of country people who came to sell
their produce must have been others who came to sell the
village medley cloths and other country manufactures,
smiths from Odiham and elsewhere with their iron goods,
salt-makers from the salterns along the coast, and charcoal
burners from the New Forest. Purkis, the charcoal-burner
who found the dead body of Rufus, knew where to take
the corpse of the king. Doubtless he had often found a
market for his charcoal among the minters, metal-
workers and others in the city of Winchester.

In the streets would be seen other forest people, those
who had the care of the dogs or the hawks—the huntsmen
and the falconers. Just outside the west gate was the
king's 'domus hafoc,' or hawk's house, where the falconers
kept their birds.

Winchester had, during the Middle Ages, a considerable
colony of Jews, who must have carried on profitable trades
and occupations and have been well-conducted citizens, for
they were protected by the king when persecuted elsewhere.
A city which was visited by so many strangers must have
required money-lenders and people who would buy jewel-
lery and other valuables of those whose funds ran short, and
some of the Jews were perhaps men of this description.
Winchester was, during several centuries, one of the few
places in England where the Jews met with fair treatment.

CHAPTER XVIII.

WINCHESTER IN DECAY.

THE prosperity of the city began to decline in the time of Henry III., who was born there, and was, unfortunately for the place, much connected with it. He was often at the castle, and took quite a native interest in its municipal and religious life. It was the centre of his misrule. During his long reign, trouble followed trouble for the monks and for the citizens. His exactions on the city were oppressive, and his coercion of the convent of St. Swithun was such as it had never before experienced. His father, King John, had lost Normandy ; but Henry was still Lord of Poitou and Aquitaine. The Normans had ceased to trouble England, and the English estates of the Norman nobles had been confiscated ; but this opened the way to a host of adventurers from southern France, who crowded round the king and were the cause of much trouble with his English subjects. During his minority, Peter des Roche, Bishop of Winchester, was the chief man in the kingdom. He surrounded himself with his relatives and other foreigners from Gascony and Provence. Some of these have left their names in Hampshire. Roche Court, near Fareham, still reminds us of the influence of the bishop in the affairs of this county. Henry married Eleanor of Poitou, and this increased the foreign influence, the troubles of England in general, and of Winchester in particular. Henry made several attempts to force the

nonks of St. Swithun to elect a foreign bishop, and on
he second vacancy during his reign, in 1250, he succeeded
n forcing on them his young half-brother Aymer de
Valence, the fourth son of his mother, Queen Isabella, by
ier second husband. The Valence family played a
>rominent part in this reign, and their name at Newton
Valence still reminds us of their influence in Hampshire
iffairs. During this reign, which was so disastrous for
Winchester, a building arose in the city which is one of
he chief architectural treasures of Hampshire, the County
Hall. It was originally built as the Castle Hall, and its
:onstruction is probably connected with a change in one of
he Hampshire forests, for the king issued a writ to Peter
les Roche, ordering him to cut down and sell all the
inderwood in the forest of Bere, and to apply the proceeds
o the making of the great hall in the castle of Winchester ;
ind about this time, the forest began to be curtailed in
:xtent. On the raised daïs at the west of the hall the
:ing loved to feast, with a great crowd of nobles and
:ourtiers. Here he held Parliaments of the magnates of
he realm in 1261, 1265, and 1268. While the building of
he hall and other work at the castle was in progress, the
custos operationum,' or director of the work, was named
Master Gerard, who had a messuage in the city.*

It was during the oppressive reign of Henry III. that
he glory of Winchester as the ancient governing centre of
he kingdom began to wane. Kings came and Parliaments
net there after his reign ; but it was not the same
vealthy city it had been during the Saxon and Norman
)eriods. With the loss of Normandy, the trade and
:ommercial importance of Winchester declined. The cost
)f making a brave show on the occasion of royal and
lational gatherings was too great for the impoverished
:itizens. The treasury had gone to London, and with it
heir prosperity. During the reign of Henry of Winchester,
he citizens sided with the king in the civil war which

* Inq. p. m. 56 Hen. III.

raged. In doing so, they probably judged this to be the safest side for them. On the other hand, the convent of St. Swithun, which had been so much oppressed by the king and his foreign friends, took the other side, so that when Simon de Montfort the younger appeared before the town, the citizens were arrayed on one side and the monks on the other, and when the citizens refused him admittance, the monks assisted him and his men to get in through the King's Gate, which they held, and so he forced his way through the close into Winchester. He gave the city up to plunder and slew all the Jews he could find, these being friends of the king and a prosperous body in the city, where the name of their quarter, Jewry Street, survives unto the present day.

The civil and ecclesiastical troubles of Winchester lasted until the close of Henry's life. In the fifty-sixth year of his reign,[*] the town was seized into the king's hand for not accounting at the exchequer, but the impoverished citizens, who were compelled to pray for relief from the payment of the 'fee farme' rent due to the king, still clung tenaciously to their ancient privileges, hoping for a return of more prosperous days. They disputed with the citizens of London the right of serving the king in the royal cellar as cupbearers, when he wore his crown after the ancient fashion at Westminster, and a few years later they carefully safeguarded the honour of the ancient city by successfully claiming against the city of York the right forequarter of the body of the brother of the Welsh prince who was executed and quartered at Shrewsbury, which they brought to Winchester, and, no doubt with much satisfaction at their victory, set up over one of the gates.

After this time Winchester never recovered its former importance. It was in succeeding reigns visited by kings, who on some occasions summoned Parliaments to meet there; but its day as a capital city was past. In 1285 a notable Parliament, which passed the 'Statutes of Win-

[*] Maddox, 'Hist. Excheq.,' 701.

hester,' relating to the administration of justice and the
reservation of the public peace, met within its walls.
Forty-five years later Edward III. summoned a Parliament to meet there, and letters and writs to this assembly
were issued to the two archbishops, to nineteen bishops,
twenty-seven abbots, two conventual priors, the Prior
of St. John of Jerusalem, eleven earls, fifty barons, nine
councillors, the sheriffs of the counties to send knights,
and the Warden of the Cinque Ports. Later on in the
same reign, Edward III. held a council there in 1371, to
which the sheriffs of thirty-seven counties were required to
send the specified knights, citizens, and burgesses who
were at the last Parliament. In 1393 Richard II.
summoned a Parliament to meet at Winchester, the writs
being sent to the prelates, the dukes, and earls, to forty
barons, and to all the sheriffs. In the same year the
convocation of the clergy in the province of Canterbury
assembled at the Church of St. Swithun, the two assemblies
being in session at the same time. The Parliament was
held in the present County Hall, while the convocation
of the clergy met at the cathedral, probably in the
chapter-house.

During the greater part of the fourteenth and fifteenth
centuries Winchester had for its bishops a series of able
men, who were statesmen of the highest rank as well as
ecclesiastics. It was the wealthiest see in the kingdom, and
its occupant during these centuries was often the Chancellor
or Treasurer of England. John de Stratford, who had
been treasurer under Edward II., was consecrated bishop by
the Pope in opposition to the king's wishes, whereupon the
king seized the estates and revenues of the bishopric, and
for more than a year this contest between the king and the
bishop went on. The bishop at first sided with the queen and
Mortimer, against Edward and the elder Despenser, whose
title of Earl of Winchester shows his connection with this
city. After the queen's party had executed the earl, his head
was sent to Winchester, to be set up over one of the gates

as a warning to the citizens whose sympathies were with the king.

Mortimer, the queen's paramour, acquired great power during the latter part of the unhappy reign of Edward II. The leader of the barons, Edward, Earl of Kent, was seized and attainted at an assembly held in Winchester Castle, at which he was condemned to death. The bishop had to flee for his life, and did not recover his position until the overthrow of Mortimer by the young king, Edward III.

Some years later, his successor, Bishop Edington, rose to high office in the state, and became treasurer of the kingdom. His successor in the bishopric, William of Wykeham, who took his name from his native place of Wykeham or Wickham, in this county, was one of the greatest men Hampshire has produced. He was Treasurer, and subsequently Chancellor, of England. He is remembered also as the founder of the earliest of the English public schools. His great school known as St. Mary's College, which he established near the close, was in existence nearly a hundred years before Henry VI. founded Eton College. Wykeham was a great reformer of ecclesiastical discipline at St. Swithun's, of abuses at St. Cross, and of irregularities throughout his diocese. Although he had no sympathy with the reform movement under Wycliffe, he withstood the undue claims of the Papacy.

Edward III. made Winchester one of his ten staple towns for wool and leather, and did what he could to revive its prosperity; but in vain. Richard II. was favourably disposed towards it, and was a great friend of Wykeham. Henry IV. honoured the city, by selecting it for the celebration of his marriage, which took place in the cathedral. It was in Winchester also that Henry V. entertained the ambassadors from France in 1415, just before he started on his French expedition, to carry war into their country. At that time Beaufort, a son of John of Gaunt, whose high position, wealth, and experience made him a great power in the state, was Bishop of Winchester. After him came Bishop Wayneflete, who lived in the troublous time of the Wars of the Roses, but managed to steer his course clear of both the contending parties. Henry VI. exhibited a great interest in the progress of Wykeham's educational foundations. His reign was an age favourable to the progress of educational ideas, and Wykeham's colleges at Winchester and Oxford became the models from which the king founded Eton College and King's College, Cambridge. Bishop Wayneflete, emulating the educational zeal of Wykeham and of the king, founded Magdalen College, Oxford, which became endowed with the estates of Selborne Priory, and other ecclesiastical lands in this county.

In the meantime, the prosperity of the city continued to decline. The kings had ceased to live there, and the ancient channels by which trade and wealth had formerly flowed into it were now changed. Owing to the outbreak of the plague in London in 1449, Parliament was summoned once more to meet in the great hall at Winchester. The session lasted a month, and during this time the decayed old capital must have experienced a brief return of its former stately importance ; but the king and his Parliament soon left, and poverty again settled in the place. Two years later, on account of its ruined condition, the citizens sent a petition to the king for help, in which they stated that, owing to the great charges in connection with its walls and defences, the poor city was become 'right desolate, insomuch as many notable parsons ben withdrawen out of the saide citee.' They stated that the number of households had greatly decreased, that some of the streets had fallen down for want of inhabitants, and also gave a list of the ruined churches. The king granted the petition by restoring the annual payment of forty marks. The political and commercial importance of Winchester was, however, doomed. Kings could give temporary relief to its distressed inhabitants, but they could not bring back those ancient political and commercial conditions under which Winchester had prospered. There was no stream now of wealthy subjects of English monarchs coming from their great French fiefs, for the reception of whom Winchester had been so convenient. Normandy had long been severed from the English crown, and Gascony, the last great English province in France, had lately been lost. The king and his court, with all the state officials, had left the West Saxon capital as a permanent place of residence for ever. The map of Europe and the conditions of English political and commercial life had become greatly altered. Henceforth there could be no progress for Winchester but a down-ward progress until the bottom should be touched, after which great decline—a decadence unparalleled among the cities of England, during which, however, she continued to be the county centre—Winchester should again revive, under altered circumstances, and take her place among English county towns as one of the pleasantest of them for residence, having historical memories and traditions in which she far surpasses them all.

The gradual decadence of the city, which thus began in the thirteenth century, and went on for more than three hundred years, was occasionally broken by royal visits and important state events that took place within its walls.

We look upon Winchester now as the ancient capital with an interest which is historical only; but during the centuries of its decline, although that decline could not be arrested, its historical associations had a stronger hold on the popular mind, so that more than one of our kings, whose title to the crown was not undisputed, turned towards the place, as the home of so many of his ancient predecessors, with a kind of instinct, and sought to invest himself and his house with any advantages from associa-tion with it in the popular mind which such a connection could give. It was no doubt from a motive such as this that Henry VII. journeyed to Winchester with his queen, Elizabeth of York, and took up his residence there, in order that their eldest child should be born in England's old capital. In addition to its long list of real sovereigns, Winchester has its more ancient legendary kings, the earliest of whom is the renowned King Arthur, whose table still hangs in the great hall, as it did in the time of Henry VII. The table itself cannot be older than the time of Henry III.; but the legend goes back into the mist of ages. Henry VII. probably attached more importance to this legend than it obtains now. He was of Welsh descent, and King Arthur was a Celtic chieftain. He may have thought that his son, born in the old West Saxon capital, where so many kings had been born, would gain something thereby in the eyes of his subjects, and would not only be the representative of both the rival houses of York and Lancaster, but, as a future king of Welsh descent, would finally heal the ancient race feud between the Saxon and the Celt. In any case he caused him to be named Arthur, and a splendid state ceremonial at his christening and confirmation in the cathedral followed his birth. The cathedral was richly decorated for the ceremony, which was attended by the high officers of state. Under the same roof lay the remains of Henry's great relative, Cardinal Beaufort, beneath the richly adorned effigy and chapel which still remain there. Pipes of wine were set up in the churchyard, that all might drink, and great rejoicings followed. The people of Winchester must have sighed for a return of the good old days when it was all over, and the king and his court had left.

In the next reign the city was honoured by a week's visit of Henry VIII., in company with the Emperor Charles V., who was entertained there in a manner suitable to his rank. The two monarchs visited the college and other objects of interest, and we are told that Charles was shown King Arthur's table.

In the time of Queen Mary, Winchester was selected by

the queen to be the scene of her marriage with the emperor's son, Philip, Prince of Spain, which took place in the cathedral in 1554. The great church had, however, been much changed since the time when the emperor visited it. Its gorgeous shrine had been destroyed, the priory had been dissolved, the costly ornaments of the church, which had been accumulated from the gifts of kings and bishops during many centuries, had disappeared, and, although decorated for the occasion, it must have appeared, to those who had known it twenty years before, a bare and desolated place, shorn of its former grandeur.

The decadence of Winchester must have been completed by the Reformation. After it had ceased to be a royal residence, its episcopal state still remained, and its wealthy monastic houses still enjoyed the revenues of their great estates. A considerable part of this income would necessarily be spent in the place, but when the monastic houses were suppressed, and the bishopric shorn of a great part of its revenue, Winchester must have reached its lowest point. Its citizens, who had inherited only traditions of its past glories, must then have despaired of better days; but perhaps some of them, like John Claptone the alchemist, who lived there about this time, hoped to find the philosopher's stone or some other potent remedy for their distress. Claptone made elixirs, one of which, according to his own account of it, might have renewed the prosperity of the place if it could have been successfully worked. He says: 'Augment the fire even to the second degree to a citrination of the matter; then fortify the fire to the fourth degree, till the matter be fused like wax in the colour of a jacinth; and it is high matter, and a royal medicine, which readily cureth all the infirmities of a diseased body, and converts every metal into pure gold.'

Queen Elizabeth took little interest in Winchester, and did not visit it until 1570, when she was welcomed with many loyal addresses. She visited the college, and was greeted there with many Latin verses composed for the occasion, and a few in Greek, which shows that the study of the latter language had made some progress.

James I., soon after his accession, made some use of the old capital of his new kingdom. He came there with his court in the autumn of 1603, and it was the scene of the state trials which then took place, in which Lord Brooke, Cobham, Grey of Wilton, and Sir Walter Raleigh, were implicated. The Winchester people hailed their new king with delight, and pelted Raleigh with tobacco-pipes. One of the most remarkable travesties of justice followed, and before it was over, the want of fair treatment of Raleigh was so manifest that the citizens changed their opinions, and Raleigh became a hero in their eyes. During this time that unfortunate lady, Arabella Stuart, was kept about the court at the castle in a kind of captivity. King James's court was not a lively one, and its temporary connection with the place had no effect on its decay. Taylor, the water poet, described it in the seventeenth century as a 'city which had almost as many parishes as souls.'

In the civil war of this century Winchester was held for the king, and finally taken by Oliver Cromwell in the autumn of 1645, after which the castle was mined and blown up.

Charles II. took a fancy to the old place, and began to build a magnificent palace on the site of the ruined castle. He was in Hampshire on many occasions, and there are traditions of him and Nell Gwynne still told in Winchester and at Avington, a few miles away, where she often resided. The great palace was never completed. James II. had other matters to attend to, and it was not until the time of Queen Anne that any thought was given to it. The idea of completing it for the Prince of Denmark, the queen's husband, was then considered, and finally abandoned. That part of the palace which Charles II. built, with suitable additions, has for many years been used as a barrack.

All hope of the restoration of Winchester to its ancient dignity as a place of royal residence died out after the seventeenth century. It has since that time revived, and has now become a prosperous county town with a population of about twenty thousand.

CHAPTER XIX.

SOUTHAMPTON.

THE reasons for thinking that the present site of Southampton was inhabited in Romano-British time, and perhaps
earlier, have already been mentioned. Its situation is such
as would naturally invite a settlement. It was certainly
one of the first settlements of the West Saxons. The
earliest Saxon coins which have been found are sceattas
and pennies of the eighth century, which were discovered
with others of later date, and many articles of early Saxon
manufacture, in the refuse-pits, or kitchen middens, brought
to light about fifty years ago in St. Mary's field. This has
since been covered with buildings, but the site of one or
more of these pits is marked by the situation of an inn,
known as the Edinburgh Hotel. The site of these pits is
about half a mile outside the ancient enclosed area formed
by the medieval walls. Coins of Offa, King of Mercia and
overlord of Wessex, in the latter part of the eighth
century, were also found many years ago on the site of the
castle keep, when its artificial mound was levelled. This
site is within the medieval fortified enclosure, so that there
can be little doubt that the Saxons occupied the medieval
site as well as other parts of the borough area.

History dawns on Southampton in the ninth century,
an early reference to the town being that in 837,
when the Danes were repulsed. In 840 Ethelwulf
dated a charter from the 'royal town called Hamtun.'

From this brief record we learn that Southampton was a royal town of ancient demesne more than two hundred years before the date of the Domesday Survey. Various entries relating to the place occur in Saxon documents. We may estimate the importance of this town to the West Saxons from the circumstance that it gave its name to the county. Hamtunscire is mentioned towards the end of the ninth century, and 'Suthamtune,' a name probably given to it to distinguish it from Northampton, first occurs about 962. The West Saxon conquest of Hampshire took place from the sea. The invaders penetrated into the county from Southampton Water. On its shores they founded their home town, or Hamtun, which they made their base, and although history is silent concerning the details of the conquest, the naming of the county after the name of this town is significant.

The ancient alternative name 'Hantun' may have been derived in part from the Celtic period, 'an' being a Celtic water word of frequent occurrence among the place-names of the county, and the situation of Hantun at the junction of the Test and the Itchen would justify such a name. On the other hand, the name Hantun may, of course, have had its origin merely in a variety of spelling, but, however derived, it still survives in part in the short name of the county, 'Hants.' Hampshire and Hants are but common customary names, the legal name being the 'County of Southampton.'

Southampton still possesses a considerable area of land which in former centuries formed its common fields and pasture. The pasture known as the Common still remains, and forms an attractive appendage to the town, its modern area, including the cemetery, being about 365 acres, well diversified with wood. The hay, or boundary hedge of Hampton, is mentioned as early as 1045 in the boundaries of land at Millbrook granted by King Edward. From this reference to the boundary of the borough liberty, and from circumstances connected with the holding of the court-leet in the open-air at Cuthorne, where the ancient mound, or burh, still remains, we may conclude that the area of the town liberty was as considerable in the time of the Saxons as it is now.

Nature has made an excellent port in the Southampton Water, and the town has always been a commercial channel. The glimpses we get of its condition, and its history before the Norman Conquest, show that it was governed like other Saxon towns, and that its inhabitants were engaged in both commercial and agricultural pursuits. It had considerable traffic with Normandy before the time of the Conquest, and after that event its trade greatly increased.

Southampton must have been much used as a port in early Saxon time before the chroniclers began to record events in detail. Egbert is said to have landed here on his return to Winchester after his exile at the court of Charlemagne. There must have been considerable intercourse across the Channel in those days, for coins of Charlemagne have been found in this town. In 837 it was attacked by the Danes with a considerable fleet, but they were driven off after a severe fight. In the charters which Ethelwulf and his successors dated from Southampton, it is in one or more instances described as the 'celebrated place called Heamtun,' from which it is evident that it was a place of note early in the ninth century. The Danes, from the frequency of their visits, evidently considered it a desirable place. In 860 they landed near Hampton, and did much damage in the county before they were repulsed. Southampton was probably the seat of King Alfred's shipbuilding operations, which were certainly carried on conveniently near to Winchester for the king to personally visit and direct the work. Towards the end of the tenth century the Danes and Northmen attacked it in force on several occasions, and in 994 Olaf of Norway and Swein of Denmark wintered there. Olaf was bought off at Andover by the unhappy King Ethelred, but Swein continued to harass the town for many years. The inhabi-

tants at last apparently welcomed the Danes, and gave
their support to Cnut. It was at Southampton that Cnut
was chosen king, while his rival Edmund was in London.
With the troubles of Edward the Confessor's time this
town had but little connection, but it was a port by
which communications were kept up between the English
and Norman courts. Both Earl Godwin and his son
Harold, before he became king, were connected with
the neighbourhood, and held several large manors in the
southern part of the county.

At the time of the Survey its population was partly
French. We are told that sixty-five French-born inhabitants and thirty-one English-born inhabitants were lodged
or settled in Southampton after King William came into
England. The Domesday record also states that the king had
seventy-six men in demesne, who paid £7 in land gable.
These were the old demesne tenants of the borough, and
quite distinct from the new settlers after the Conquest.
The old demesne tenants paid the same land-tax they or
their predecessors paid in the time of Edward the Confessor, and in addition to their commercial pursuits, such as
they were, constituted the agricultural community which
cultivated the land in St. Mary's field, Highfield, and
other parts of the borough liberty. Of these seventy-six
agricultural tenants, we are told that twenty-seven paid 8d.
each, two paid 12d. each, and fifty paid 6d. each. The
new settlers brought into the town by King William paid
£4 0s. 6d. for all customs. These were perhaps wholly
engaged in that increased trade which followed the
Norman Conquest, and we may in all probability see some
of the results of the activity of these new settlers in the
remains of the Norman vaults, in the doorways, and other
remains of substantial Norman houses, and in the Norman
work of the church of St. Michael, situated within the
French part of the town. Two streets in this part of
Southampton—French Street and Bugle Street—still bear
names whose origin dates from this period.

The Norman Conquest brought great changes to Southampton. Its fortifications, which in the time of the Saxons
probably consisted only of an earthen rampart and one or
more ditches, were greatly improved. A stone wall was built
almost round it, the parts which were not inclosed by the
new wall being only those sites which were occupied by the
king's houses at the West Quay, and the south side including the site of St. Julian's Hospital, the buildings which
existed on these spots being perhaps considered sufficiently
strong for effective defence. A Norman castle was built,
the great mound which the Saxons had thrown up as their
burh being utilized as the site of the castle keep. As this
mound was composed of a loose material, and was situated
near the slightly elevated sandy cliff, close to the western
shore, it was necessary for the safety of the castle buildings
raised on the mound and the edge of the cliff to strengthen
the sea wall, which was done by constructing a very strong
arched vault or vaults near the water-gate of the castle.
Part of this strong vaulted structure, which was utilized
as a storehouse for the castle, still remains. The original
Bar Gate was then built, and this apparently was a Norman
gateway with a tower or gatehouse above, in which the
machinery of the portcullis was worked. The central arch
and part of the two flanking turrets of this Norman gate-
house still remain, incorporated with the additions of a
later date.

Soon after the Conquest a church was built in the French
quarter of the town, and appropriately dedicated to St.
Michael, the patron saint of Normandy. The four massive
tower arches of this Norman church, which has been much
altered at later periods, still remain, a monument of the
rugged masonry of the early Norman period.

Many stone vaults for the storage of wine were built in
Southampton in the time of the Normans, some of which
are still in existence. It is quite clear from the architectural remains of this period which have come down to us
that much money was expended on the fortifications and

on the buildings which were then erected. The stone used was chiefly the Bembridge limestone, and the conveyance of this from the Isle of Wight must have given employment to many ships.

Municipal changes also came in with the Conquest. The Saxon præpositus, or portreeve, was superseded by the king's bailiffs, officials of Norman origin, whose authority was for centuries very great. Their ancient functions have disappeared, owing to the changes which have occurred during the last few centuries, but they are still annually elected.

During the rule of the Norman and Angevin kings, certain ecclesiastical changes also occurred in Southampton which had a great influence on its religious life. The priory of St. Denys was founded by Henry I. within the borough liberty, and endowed with land and other property. He gave to this priory the four churches of Holy Rood, St. Lawrence, All Saints, and St. Michael, described in the charter as chapels, the mother church being that of St. Mary, outside the town walls. The Augustine canons of St. Denys were subsequently much concerned with ecclesiastical matters in Southampton. At St. Denys they conducted a school, where young men, among others, were educated for the priesthood. In subsequent centuries the canons also officiated at the chapels of the Trinity and St. Andrew, outside the walls of the town.

The greater trade and commerce which came in with the Normans also brought with it an increased number of lepers, and so, in 1173, the hospital of St. Mary Magdalen for these infirm people was founded in the West Marlands, about half a mile outside the town walls. The Franciscan friars also settled in Southampton, and their convent was founded about 1237.

Another institution of a conventual nature was founded in the twelfth century, the hospital of St. Julian, or the Maison de Dieu, commonly called God's House. This hospital was an important institution in Southampton. In the latter part of the thirteenth century one of its priors, or wardens, Henry de Bluntesdon, conferred a great benefit on the town by conveying water into it from the friars' conduit, or spring-head, at Hill, about a mile outside the town walls. This spring had been given to the friars by Nicholas de Barbeflet, lord of the manor of Shirley, and by the liberality of the warden of God's House Hospital, it was conducted into the borough in a leaden pipe, and placed at the service of the inhabitants at several town conduits. The hospital was fairly wealthy, and, unfortunately for Southampton, the wardenship was given by Edward III. to the provost and scholars of Queen's Hall, now Queen's College, Oxford, under whose management its original purposes were forgotten and changed in subsequent centuries.

The oldest institution in Southampton is its court-leet, which it certainly possessed long before the Norman Conquest, and which was the earliest guarantee of its liberties. It exempted the town from the jurisdiction of the hundred-court, held by the Sheriff of Hampshire, and was the basis on which the subsequent privileges of the borough grew. The old court-leet is still held on Hock Tuesday, and is a venerable relic come down from Saxon time. During the Saxon period the reeve, or præpositus, was probably chosen at this court. Although he was subsequently superseded by the bailiffs, he is mentioned long after the Conquest in the chartulary of the priory of St. Denys, founded by Henry I., in which it is stated that the tenants of the priory had to perform the same customary services which they had performed for the king, and among these was that of carrying rushes to the house of the reeve, or bailiff, of Hampton, on the vigils of the chief Church festivals.

Early in the reign of Henry I. Southampton received what was, as far as is known, its first charter. Towns such as this, which enjoyed privileges under the Saxon kings, generally possessed these liberties by custom and pre-scriptive right. In later times the inhabitants sought to confirm these customs and liberties by royal charters. The liberties of the borough of Southampton were con-firmed by successive kings until the time of Charles I. The charter of Henry I. is referred to in that granted by Henry II., who confirmed to the burgesses the possession of all 'the liberties and customs by land and by sea which they held in the time of King Henry, my grandfather.' Richard I. granted the burgesses the important privilege of not being impleaded out of their own borough. The earliest town charter which has been preserved to the present time is that of King John.

During the time of the Norman and Angevin kings Southampton was a very prosperous town. As it was the most convenient port for traffic between Winchester and Nor-mandy, the Norman kings had houses in the borough. The remains of one of these, situated close to the ancient quay, known as West Quay, constitute one of the best examples in the kingdom of domestic architecture of the Norman period.

It was no doubt a convenience to those who had occa-sionally to pass to or from Normandy, or to send their servants, to have houses in Southampton, and at the time of the Domesday Survey we find that forty-eight houses were held in this town free of tax by various barons, officials of the royal household, and others, including one each held by the Norman abbeys of Lira and Cormelies. These abbeys subsequently had a grant of tithes in Southampton given to them by Henry II., amounting to £18. A certain small payment was also ordered by that king to be made out of the revenue of the town to the Knights Templars.

Some of the principal historical events which happened at Southampton before the fourteenth century have already been mentioned in the earlier chapters of this volume. In 1338 the most disastrous event in the annals of the town occurred. War had broken out with France, and Edward III. was invading that country. The French retaliated by suddenly attacking Southampton in force on October 4 in that year, landing early on a Sunday morning at West Quay. The inhabitants were entirely unprepared for an attack, and for the most part fled. The enemy plundered and burnt the houses at their pleasure. It was at this time that the king's houses at West Quay were destroyed, except those fine Norman walls, doorways, and windows which have lasted until the present day. The destruction of property on this occasion was so great that for years afterwards the inhabitants were unable to pay their rents due to the king, the Knights Hospitaller, the abbey of Lira, the Queen Dowager Isabella, and others. After this great disaster the fortifications were strengthened, and a trained defensive force for the town was organized. In 1346 Edward III. and the Black Prince embarked at Southampton with the greater part of the army, with which he then invaded France. The fleet sailed on July 14, and the battle of Crecy was fought on August 26. Three years later, in common with the rest of the county, Southampton suffered greatly from the first visitation of the pestilence known as the Black Death, which is said to have entered England at this port. In the first year of Richard II.'s reign, the French fleet again appeared in Southampton Water. They had devastated part of the Isle of Wight, but the town was now in a condition to withstand an attack, and with the aid of the English ships under the Earl of Salisbury, the enemy was driven off.

In 1378 John of Gaunt, with his expedition for the invasion of Brittany, sailed from Southampton, and after an unsuccessful attack on St. Malo returned to this port.

In 1415 a notable expedition was mustered here. Henry V., having resolved to invade France, assembled his army in and around this port. He came to the town while the preparations were going on, and it was here that the conspiracy took place against him just before the expedition sailed. The king's cousin, Richard, Earl of

Cambridge, Lord Scrope, and Sir Thomas Grey were convicted by a jury of conspiring against the king. Sir Thomas Grey was beheaded the same day, and an assembly of peers, presided over by the Duke of Clarence, confirmed the judgment against the earl and Lord Scrope, who had appealed to their own order. They were condemned : the earl was permitted to walk to the place of execution outside the North Gate, but Lord Scrope was drawn thither on a hurdle. The earl, who was buried within the chapel of God's House Hospital, was the fifteenth ancestor of our present queen in the Yorkist line. During the work of restoring the chapel about thirty years ago, a skeleton was found in the chancel, with the skull lying near the bones of the legs. These remains were reinterred, and are believed to have been those of the unfortunate earl.

The fleet of Henry V. sailed for France on August 11, 1415, and the battle of Agincourt was fought in October.

In the following year a fleet of French and Genoese ships appeared in the Solent, and a naval battle was fought not far from Southampton, in which the English had the advantage. There was much activity in this port in the embarkation of troops during the subsequent years of Henry V., and this went on during the early part of the next reign. In 1445 Margaret of Anjou arrived at Southampton, and was lodged in God's House Hospital previously to her marriage with Henry VI., which ceremony took place at Titchfield, a few miles distant.

When the events of the Wars of the Roses had made Edward IV. king, he enlarged the foundation of God's House Hospital, by providing an endowment for three priests there, to pray for the souls of his father, Richard, Duke of York, and also his grandfather, Richard, Earl of Cambridge, buried in that hospital, a circumstance which shows the interest he took in the place, and that he had not forgotten the incidents of his grandfather's time which had occurred in Southampton.

Wine and wool formed the chief articles of trade in Southampton during the Middle Ages. Many of the ancient stone vaults, in which the king's prisage and other wines were stored, have been destroyed during the street improvements of the last fifty years. The 'prisage of wine,' afterwards known as 'butlerage' was an ancient duty under which the king claimed out of every shipload of wines of more than twenty tuns, two tuns of wine at his own fixed price. In Southampton, where the importation of wine was great, this was a source of considerable revenue to the crown, until early in the fourteenth century, when it was commuted by agreement with foreign merchants for the payment of two shillings per tun. Subsequently, in the reign of Henry VII., an Act of Parliament relieved the burgesses from the payment of this duty.

The wool trade, which was also very considerable in Southampton, grew into importance during the thirteenth century, when regulations were made for just weight. The old Woolhouse in which the wool was weighed still remains, and the custody of the weighing beam, or tron, was for a long time vested in the family of the Earl of Warwick, who held a house in the town by the service of weighing goods in Southampton.

The great foreign traders to Southampton from the early part of the thirteenth until the middle of the sixteenth century were the Venetians. Their ships were commonly known as the Flanders galleys, from trading also to Flanders. These trading expeditions were organized by the Venetian senate, the galleys being under the command of an admiral or chief captain, whose flagship was often anchored in Southampton Water, while the other vessels of the fleet proceeded to other parts of the English coast, and to Flanders. They brought spices, Indian cotton, silks, and other commodities, and took away wool, leather, Winchester and other cloths, and tin.

The trade of the town was carried on during the Middle Ages under the regulations of the Guild Merchant. These regulations or ordinances are of early date. A copy written in a book made by W. Overey, town clerk in 1473, is preserved among the muniments, and in this it is stated that the 'auncient fathers made the said booke of olde tyme in French tonge, and this is now translated out of Frenche into Englishe.' The ordinances of the Guild Merchant,* show that some of its rules were derived as much from Saxon borough customs as from the later usages of the Normans, and the regulations appear to have been compiled from both sources. The two discreets of the market referred to in these ordinances are still annually appointed by the town council. Another ancient officer, the Alderman of Portswood, who was the representative of law and order for the tithing of Portswood, is also still annually elected.

The jurisdiction which the town gradually acquired over the port was one of its chief privileges. The port of Southampton originally extended from Langstone on the east to Hurst on the west, and thus included the whole of the north of the Solent in addition to Southampton Water. King John granted the town to the burgesses at a fixed payment, together with the port of Portsmouth, then much smaller than Southampton, and in a trial in 1324 with the burgesses of Lymington, concerning petty customs, it was set forth that all places from Hurst to Langstone were within the port of Southampton. Henry VI. granted to the borough, in 1451, admiralty jurisdiction within the port, in right of which grant the burgesses held an admiralty court, claimed all wrecks, regulated fishing, had a prison for the punishment of offenders on the water, and erected an admiralty gallows close to the shore for the execution of criminals, in addition to the town gallows, more than two miles away, at the northern boundary of the borough liberty. It was in virtue of this old admiralty jurisdiction that the Mayor of

---

* See 'History of Southampton,' by the Rev. J. Silvester Davies, pp. 132-151.

Southampton, as admiral of the port, had an oar carried before him, and the silver oar which still exists among the town regalia is the emblem of this ancient dignity.

From the Conquest until the middle of the fifteenth century, when the French provinces were finally lost to the English crown, Southampton was a busy port. Many Normans and other subjects of the Norman kings made it their home. Norman-French became the language of its chief inhabitants, and the government of the town was practically in the hands of burgesses of foreign birth and their descendants. Its older Saxon institutions became merged into a municipal system of government which was largely of French origin. In the time of Henry II. and his sons, Angevins, Poitevins, and Gascon merchants became closely connected with the port. The chief shipmasters at this period bore such names as Vitullus, Wasceline, Fitz-Geldewin, De Baion, De la Wicha, De Braiose, Trenchemere, Vitalis, Fitz-Alan, Mansel, Berenger de Hampton, and Humphrey Hai.* These were the men who were largely concerned in the commercial traffic across the Channel, and whose ships were very frequently hired for the royal service. Later on, as the Norman traffic died out, there came an increased number of merchant ships from Bordeaux and other ports of Gascony, and the Venetians, who among their other commercial transactions bought wool produced on the estates of many of the Cistercian and other monasteries, including Beaulieu, Netley, Quarr, and Titchfield in this county. In the fifteenth century alum was brought to this port by the Genoese, and other Italian merchants rode about the country buying up at first hand wools, woollen cloths, and tin. The relative prosperity of the port in the middle of the fifteenth century may be estimated by a loan of £1,000 which was ordered to be levied in 1454, of which London was assessed at £300, Bristol £150, Hampton £100, and Norwich and Yarmouth together £100. This

* See 'The Court, Household and Itinerary of King Henry II.,' Index.

pro rata levy probably included Lymington and other places within the ancient port.

The customs arising from the port of Southampton were on many occasions assigned by the crown as security for various loans, such as in the time of Henry V. to the Chancellor Beaufort, and in that of Henry VI. to the feoffees of the duchy of Lancaster. By a charter granted in 1447 the town was made into a county, under the name of the 'County of the town of Southampton,' and the burgesses were permitted to choose a sheriff, a privilege they still exercise. From about this time the bailiffs began to decline in importance, as the town gradually became more independent of the royal control, and as the mayor and sheriff became invested with increased authority.

In the Middle Ages the burgesses grew corn on their common arable lands at Highfield, St. Mary's field, and elsewhere, and ground it into flour with other corn, brought into the town, at the tidal mills on the Itchen and at the outlet of the moat. Two of the old trade quarters of the town are still designated by the names of Simnel Street, which was probably a place where bakers pursued their craft ; and Pepper Alley, where groceries or spices were sold. Brewing was an occupation which was largely carried on in and just outside the town, and much of this beer was probably supplied to ships. The brewers were accustomed to dig clay in the salt marsh to make bungs for their beer barrels. The fish market was held in St. Michael's Square, and the market for poultry, eggs, and other country produce near the market-cross in the High Street. Southampton had four ancient fairs, of which only one now survives in a modified form, viz., that on Trinity Monday, granted or confirmed by Henry VII. to the burgesses and to the hermit of Holy Trinity Chapel. Its streets in the Middle Ages were frequented by motley groups of foreign merchants, sailors, and travellers—Normans, Poitevins, Gascons, Flemings, mariners from the Low Countries and from the Hanse towns, Venetians and sailors from their dependencies, such as the Sclavonians, who had a guild of their own in this town and a burial-place at North Stoneham, a few miles away. Here came crowds of pilgrims on their way to foreign shrines, such as that at Compostella, or to the English shrines at Winchester and Canterbury, and as long as the connection lasted, monks and other ecclesiastics to and from foreign abbeys and their dependent English priories.

During the sixteenth century the maritime trade of Southampton declined, and during the seventeenth it had few ships and very little commerce. The Venetian galleys left the port for the last time in 1532, and although other ships from Venice came after that date, their voyages were private undertakings, and not commercial expeditions organized by the Venetian state. The opening of the newer trade route to India was one of the causes of the decline of the Venetian trade with this town, and the opening of another route to India, *via* the Suez Canal, has in our own time also taken away part of the traffic of this port with Eastern countries.

During the eighteenth century, Southampton became a fashionable seaside resort. Assembly rooms were built after the model of those at Bath, and their present dilapidated state and decayed gilded decorations remind us of that time.

The latest commercial development of the town began about fifty years ago, since which time it has rapidly grown, and populous suburbs have sprung up around it. Including its suburbs it has now a population of about one hundred thousand.

CHAPTER XX.

THE earliest record relating to the island of Portsea, on which Portsmouth is situated, is a grant by King Ethelred, the son of King Edgar, of Frederington, now known as Fratton, with four hides of land, to the New Minster at Winchester.

Portsea Island is not mentioned by name in Domesday Book, but the manors of Copnor, Fratton, and Buckland included within it are named, and also the manor of Applestede, which is believed to have included lands in and adjoining the harbour. From this survey we learn that Copnor and Buckland formed part of the great lordship of Earl Godwin in the time of Edward the Confessor, and were held of him by Saxon thanes named Tovi and Alward. Fratton was held by a thane named Chetel, of King Edward, and Applestede was held also directly from the king by a thane named Goding. The tenures of Applestede, Buckland, and Fratton were allodial, the holders being only liable for the repair of local defences, the repair of bridges, and for military service in case of invasion. Copnor was held of Earl Godwin by a thane of a lower grade, who could not remove from the land. At the time of the Norman Survey, Hugh de Port was the superior lord of Applestede and Buckland ; Robert, the son of Gerold, was the superior lord of Copnor ; and William de Warren was the superior lord of Fratton; and these manors were held respectively of them by tenants named Tezelin, Heldred, who had both Buckland and Copnor, and Oismelin. These estates were entirely agricultural, except that of Copnor, which had also a saltern.

The harbour of Portsmouth was used by the Romans, who built the fortress of Porchester on its northern shore. Many traces of Roman occupation have been found near Porchester. Nothing positively is known of the early history of this Roman station, but there are traditions, derived from the Chronicles, and repeated from age to age, of a battle being fought near Portsmouth, the leader of the invaders being named Port, who is supposed to have given his name to the place. This tradition must be taken for what it is worth. All that is certain about the Port or de Port family, at Portsea or Portsmouth, is that at the time of the Domesday Survey Hugh de Port, the greatest Hampshire baron, who held many manors in the county, held Applestede and Buckland.

In 1101 we read of Portsmouth as the place where Duke Robert of Normandy landed with his troops. Subsequently the advantages of the harbour as a port in passing to or from Normandy became recognised. Henry I. was at Portsmouth at Whitsuntide, 1123. The Empress Maud and Robert Earl of Gloucester landed there in 1139. It was much used by Henry II., who landed or embarked at Portsmouth on ten occasions. King Richard and King John both made use of the port, the latter king passing through it on ten occasions during his reign.

The old church of Portsmouth is dedicated to St. Thomas à Becket, and was founded as a chapel in the parish of Portsea soon after the murder of the archbishop and his subsequent canonization, on a site in Sud mede or South mead given by Richard de Gisors.

In a grant made by King John in 1201 of two mills at Portsmouth to the abbey of Fontevrault, we see what was perhaps only part of the gift made at that time by the king to this abbey, where his brother, Richard, was buried. In the time of John the history of Portsmouth as a shipbuilding place appears to have commenced, and there are numerous subsequent references to its trade and shipping.

Portsmouth was used by Henry III. as the place for the assembly of his expeditions to Gascony. In 1229 a great army of English, Irish, Scotch, and Welsh was mustered there. Again in 1242 and in 1253 Henry III. was at Portsmouth with troops destined for his great province in southern France. In 1272 the town was seized into the king's hand for not accounting at the Exchequer.*

In 1260, an endowment was provided for the church of St. Thomas à Becket, originally founded as a chapel, which after this time was placed in a more independent ecclesiastical position.

The increase of traffic between Portsmouth and the ports of Gascony in the thirteenth century was apparently the cause of the establishment of the hospital of St. Nicholas, or God's House. This was founded by Bishop Peter de Roche, and was subsequently endowed with lands and messuages in the town. The hospital played an important part in its early history and enjoyed special privileges. In 1229 provision was made that the privileges of this hospital should not encroach on the rights of the town, to which, by way of fealty, the hospital was bound to pay five shillings quarterly. During the wars of Edward III., Portsmouth was on several occasions concerned in the despatch of troops across the Channel to northern France. Expeditions sailed from the harbour for these wars in 1346, 1369, and 1386. In 1377 the French retaliated by capturing the town and burning it, and it is probable that many of its early muniments were lost or destroyed at that time. During the troubles of Henry VI.'s reign, de Moleyns, Bishop of Chichester, who held office under the king, was murdered

* Maddox, 'Hist. Exchequer,' p. 701.

by an infuriated mob at Portsmouth in 1450. In 1475 there was a great encampment of troops on Southsea Common, Edward IV. himself being present. That king and his successors, Richard III. and Henry VII., did much for the fortifications of the town, which were enlarged and strengthened during these reigns. The dockyard may be considered to date from 1509. Southsea Castle was built by Henry VIII., and when Leland visited Portsmouth during this reign, he found the town defended by 'a mud waulle from the Est Tour armed with tymbre, whereon be great pieces of iron and brasen ordinaunce, a wall of mud like the other going Est, a gate of tymbre at the north end of the town, and by it a hille of erthe dichid, whereon be guns to defend entry to town by land.' About that time the entrance to the harbour was defended by a great chain made of large iron links stretched across it from tower to tower on either side. This is shown in a plan of the town made in the time of Queen Elizabeth, and now preserved among the Cottonian MS. in the British Museum.

A naval battle which lasted two days was fought off Portsmouth in July, 1545, between the French fleet, commanded by d'Annabaut, and the English, commanded by Lord Lisle, whose flagship was the *Great Harry*. The French were finally driven off, or abandoned their attack, but during the operations the large English ship named the *Mary Rose* went down with 600 men, many of whom were lost. Henry VIII. was at Portsmouth at this time. After this engagement a large fresco, commemorative of the event, was painted by Holbein on a wall at Cowdray House in Sussex. A very large engraving of this painting was made by Basire in 1778 for the Society of Antiquaries, and as Cowdray House was shortly afterwards burnt, the engraving now alone remains to commemorate this famous engagement. Illustrations of the *Great Harry*, the *Mary Rose*, and other ships which took part in this engagement, are preserved in the Pepsian Library at Cambridge.

One of the greatest fleets which assembled at Portsmouth in the sixteenth century was that in the time of Edward VI., when fifty-three ships of 6,655 tonnage, manned by 5,136 seamen, 1,885 soldiers, and 759 gunners, were mustered there. During the time when Sir Henry Radcliffe was Captain of Portsmouth, in the reign of Elizabeth, the fortifications were much improved.

Many notable old ships of the English navy have been launched at Portsmouth, and many others have ended their career in its harbour. When Leland visited the place, the old ribs of Henry V.'s famous ship, the *Grace Dieu*, which was built at Southampton 120 years before, lay rotting on the mud. Her timbers were apparently pointed out to the old antiquary, with sentiments akin to those with which the *Victory* is shown at the present day.

In August, 1627, a fleet of ninety ships was assembled at Portsmouth, intended for the relief of Rochelle. This fleet was commanded by the Duke of Buckingham, who was assassinated on the morning of August 22 by Lieutenant Felton. The king was at Southwick, a few miles away, and was attending morning prayers in the chapel at that place, when Sir John Hippesley entered the chapel and whispered to him the news of Buckingham's death.

During the early part of the political troubles of Charles I.'s time Portsmouth supported the Royalists. On August 2, 1642, Colonel Goring, who was in command, openly declared for the king, and the town was shortly afterwards besieged by the Parliamentary forces. The siege lasted from August 12 to September 7, the town garrison consisting of 300 soldiers, 100 townsmen, 100 men of Portsea, 50 officers and their servants, and 50 horses. After about a month's siege the garrison was obliged to surrender the town, and after its surrender it was held during the remainder of the war for the Parliament. During the Commonwealth an important naval event occurred. Off Portsmouth, in 1652, Admiral Blake captured eleven Dutch men-of-war and thirty merchant ships. The town stood a short siege in December, 1659, when it supported the Parliament against the army in the political struggle which preceded the restoration of Charles II. That king was fond of Portsmouth, and visited it several times. In 1661 he was at Portsmouth with his mother, Queen Henrietta, and in 1662 he was married there to Catherine of Braganza, the Portuguese princess who brought Bombay to the crown as part of her dower. Portsmouth and its neighbourhood was selected by Charles II. for the territorial titles he conferred on his mistress, Louise de Querouaille, the Madam Carwell of Hampshire folk-lore. He created her Baroness of Petersfield, Countess of Fareham, and Duchess of Portsmouth, and she gave to the corporation the fine pair of flagons of silver gilt which is still preserved among the town plate.

The earliest charter granted to the borough, as far as known, was that of Richard I., although a charter of Henry I. is mentioned in a record of the Visitation of Hampshire in the books of Heralds' College ;* but this is not mentioned in the inspeximus of any one of the numerous charters of confirmation afterwards granted to the borough. King Richard, in his charter, discharged the burgesses from tolls, gave them a market and an annual fair, exempted them from suit at the hundred-court, and gave them other privileges. A charter granted by King John confirmed most of these liberties. Henry III. granted the town four charters, in the last of which, dated 1256, he allowed the establishment of a merchant guild. Subsequent charters of confirmation were granted by Edward I., Edward II., Edward III., Richard II., Henry IV., and Henry VI. Edward IV. confirmed the charter of Richard II., ignoring those of the Lancastrian kings. Richard III. granted a charter in the second year of his reign. Henry VII. confirmed the charter of Edward IV., and this was confirmed by his son Henry VIII., by Edward VI., and Elizabeth.

---

* 'Extracts from the Portsmouth Records,' by R. J. Murrell and R. East, p. 382.

In the forty-second year of the reign of Queen Elizabeth an extended charter was granted to Portsmouth incorporating the mayor and burgesses, and giving the town the same legal recognition of ancient privileges by a new charter, as Southampton, Winchester, and other towns received about the same time. The corporation was first legally styled 'the Mayor and Burgesses of the Borough of Portsmouth' in this charter. The office of Mayor of Portsmouth appears to have become first recognised as such in the time of Edward IV., the more ancient bailiffs having been previously the governing officials. An important reservation of the rights of the military governor of Portsmouth and his successors was made in this charter.

Charles I. granted another charter to the town in the third year of his reign, and this was the last legal document of the kind Portsmouth received. In the next reign Charles II. granted the borough another charter towards the end of his reign, varying its privileges and adding Gosport to it, for no doubt a money consideration, and on the surrender of the charter of his father, Charles I. Then occurred a curious episode in the history of Portsmouth. The new charter was received and was acted upon for some few years. In the meantime someone, perhaps in the interests of the town, obtained possession of the old charter and kept it until after the Revolution of 1688, when it was found that the charter of Charles II. had not been enrolled, nor that of Charles I. cancelled. This being then discovered accidentally or otherwise, the town reverted to the franchises it possessed under the charter of Charles I., much to its own satisfaction, and Gosport has since ceased to be incorporated with it.

Portsmouth continued to be governed under its ancient charters until 1836. The old town-hall and markethouse stood in the middle of the High Street. This was demolished as soon as the new corporation came into existence, when a new guildhall was built, and this latter building has lately been superseded by a very handsome modern town-hall, which has cost upwards of a hundred thousand pounds, and is the finest building of its kind in the southern counties.

The records of the Portsmouth court-leet, which have been preserved, date from 1562, and they contain many entries of presentments by the jury for offences of various kinds against the laws and customs of the borough in the sixteenth and seventeenth centuries. From the large influx of temporary residents, sailors and soldiers, which had begun in the sixteenth century, Portsmouth must have presented difficulties to the constituted authorities in the matter of local government from which boroughs which had no such part to play in national affairs were free. Municipal life in Portsmouth was also somewhat complicated by reason of its position as a fortified town, held by a military force, under the command of a governor or captain. The municipal and military authorities not unfrequently came into conflict. This occurred as early as the sixteenth century, and in the charter of the forty-second year of Elizabeth, the rights of the military commandant and his successors were expressly safeguarded. In the matter of local government Portsmouth had thus a price to pay on account of its greatness as a national arsenal and naval station, but its inhabitants must have been recompensed for any troubles of this kind which they experienced by the prosperity which the town enjoyed. While fleets and ships were being fitted out in the harbour, soldiers and sailors coming and going, the inhabitants generally prospering, and some of them becoming rich, the ancient court-leet fulfilled its functions in the local government of the place, and looked after those of the community 'who lett their chymnes be affyer,' who left their cattle in the fields and commons after sunset ; those brewers 'who did not sell their beer at the price the clark of the market set down,' and others who did 'their washing at the town pumps.' The court was also concerned with 'forestallers and regrattors' of the market, with the maintenance of the pillory and the stocks, the keeping up of the fences round the common lands, and such-like matters. It fined those who broke open the pound and took impounded cattle out, and the jury made presentments against those who did not go to church. Some were presented to the court for not attending divine service at all, some for only going now and then, and some for only putting in an appearance occasionally at the time when the sermon came on. Some of the female part of the community were also included in these presentments.*

When Jack was afloat in the harbour, he must have been a more manageable inhabitant than when ashore. The presentment of the court jury made in 1704, 'that the anointing of ratts and putting fire to them is of dangerous consequence, especially in this Towne, where there are Magazeens of Powder, and tends to the setting the dwelling houses of the inhabitants on fire,' is a singular one, and looks as if intended to repress the sailors' freaks while on shore. The presentment, however, says nothing about cruelty to the rats.

The great beer question was always an important one in this town. Beer was brewed for the ships of the navy in four large brewhouses erected by Henry VII., and these were distinct from the town breweries. The great number of alehouses, victualling houses, punch-houses, and other tippling places in 'the Back streets and By places of the town and its liberties,' was seriously considered by the court - leet in 1702. The presentment then made says that the daily increase of such houses 'tends to the impoverishment of some, gives too great a liberty of intemperance to others of the inhabitants, and is a common nuisance, and of ill consequence.' In 1716 there were in Portsmouth 129 public-houses, 20 brandy shops, and six coffee-houses.

One of the most important of the early institutions of Portsmouth was its annual fair or free mart, which lasted fifteen days. This was established by the charter of

* 'Extracts from the Portsmouth Records,' by Murrell and East.

Richard I., and appointed to be held at the time of the feast of St. Peter ad Vincula, *i.e.*, August 1. It was free to all people, natives and foreigners, without tolls, duties or imposts of any kind. The date at which it was held was varied in subsequent centuries, and it was continued until 1846. From being a trading institution of an exceptional kind granted by King Richard as a special favour to the town with a view of adding to its prosperity, this fair, as time went on, became its greatest nuisance, until, within the recollection of people now living, it had degenerated into a scene of demoralization and turmoil such as could no longer be tolerated, and it was abolished by Act of Parliament, to the entire satisfaction of the great majority of the inhabitants.

During the seventeenth and eighteenth centuries, when old customs and old conditions of life were gradually giving place to those of modern date, those ancient instruments of punishment, the pillory, the cucking-stool, and the stocks, which had been of frequent service in Portsmouth, fell into disuse there, as they did elsewhere. The preservation of the peace and the maintenance of order were always difficult matters in this town, owing to its large and varying population. The disorderly houses, which are described as having been sinks of debauchery and corruption, gave the borough authorities much trouble as early as the beginning of the eighteenth century. The town records tell us that it was from them that riots, disorders, violence against his majesty's subject, and contempt of justice, proceeded. From a circumstance which occurred in 1733, we may perhaps surmise that some of his majesty's tars had, while on shore or while subject to the civil authority, conducted themselves badly, and been put into the stocks, for in that year the stocks were surreptitiously taken down, as the records tell us, ' by some offenders in their nightly rowells' and thrown into the churchyard, ' in order to be buried among the monuments of the dead.'

The later history of Portsmouth, like the earlier history of Winchester, has been national in its interest. The narrative of the expeditions and chief events of Portsmouth history during the last two centuries would, for the most part, be a narrative of national affairs. The whole British Empire now feels an interest in this famous town. Its growth has been commensurate with the growth of the navy and of the empire. It is now a place of upwards of 159,000 people, having the populous suburb of Gosport close to it. The reconstruction of the navy by the substitution of steam for sailing ships, and the later reconstruction by the substitution of the latest type of battle ships for those ironclads of earlier date, have necessitated a great extension of the dockyard, and have contributed to the growth of Portsmouth. It is a great military station as well as the chief naval port. Its connection with India, as the home port from which the trooping ships sail, is considerable, and of advantage to it. Public money is freely spent in Portsmouth, and part of this comes from the Indian Exchequer.

In the time of the Saxon kings, when Winchester was the governing centre of the kingdom, Portsmouth was practically unknown. It was of such small account in Norman and early English time, that the corporation of Southampton claimed and exercised maritime jurisdiction in its waters. From this obscurity, it has risen to a position of supreme importance to the nation. Its fortified lines extend for many miles around it, and are perhaps the most extensive of any within the United Kingdom. About the time when Winchester began to decline, Portsmouth began to grow. The national interest in Winchester is an ancient one. The national interest in Portsmouth is of another kind, and is modern.

CHAPTER XXI.

LATER MEDIEVAL AND GENERAL HISTORY.

HAMPSHIRE was first represented in Parliament in 1295, when four knights of the shire attended at Westminster. Two burgesses were also sent to this Parliament for the first time by Winchester, Southampton, Portsmouth, Andover, Alresford, Overton, Alton, Basingstoke, and Yarmouth and Newport combined as one borough. In the Parliament of 1297 only two knights of the shire were summoned, and burgesses from Winchester, Southampton, and Portsmouth. In the early Parliaments which met between 1297 and 1306-7, Alresford, Basingstoke, Odiham, Overton, Alton, continued to receive writs. Odiham made no return to the Parliamentary writ in 1300. The Isle of Wight sent no representatives to this and several succeeding Parliaments, although writs appear to have been issued. Petersfield was first summoned to send burgesses to the Parliament which met at Carlisle on January 20, 1306-7, and to this assembly Fareham also sent representatives. Christchurch received a writ, but made no return.

After 1307, until 1552, the usual writs for the attendance of representatives appear to have been received only by Winchester, Southampton, and Portsmouth, in addition to the writ for knights of the shire.

In 1552-3 the representation of Petersfield was renewed, after an interval of more than 240 years. In 1562-3 Stockbridge was made a Parliamentary borough. In 1572

Christchurch also received a writ. In 1584 Lymington and Newtown received writs for the first time, and the representation of Newport and Yarmouth was renewed. In 1586 Andover was again summoned to send representatives, and Whitchurch received a writ for the first time. After this date until the first Reform Act, the county and twelve boroughs in Hampshire continued to send members to Parliament. After 1832, Whitchurch, Stockbridge, Yarmouth, and Newtown lost their Parliamentary privileges.

As long as the English kings retained any provinces in France, the Hampshire ports were necessarily much connected with the despatch of troops to Rochelle, Bordeaux, and other ports of Gascony. Many musters of troops for service in France took place in Hampshire during the fourteenth and fifteenth centuries, and at these times there was a constant passage of knights, with their men-at-arms, archers, and followers, along the main roads of the county converging towards Southampton and Portsmouth. The Channel Islands, that remnant of the Norman duchy which the English kings managed to retain after the loss of their territory in northern France, have since that time been more closely connected with Hampshire than with any other English county, and are, for ecclesiastical purposes, still part of the diocese of Winchester.

In 1445 an event of considerable national interest took place at Titchfield, viz., the marriage of Henry VI. to Margaret of Anjou. No events of very great importance occurred in this county during the wars of the Roses, but it contained adherents of both sides, and some minor skirmishes took place in Hampshire. One of these was that near Southampton in which Lord Scales defeated the Duke of Clarence and the Earl of Warwick, took the ship *La Trinité*, and some prisoners. Edward IV. then came to Southampton, and caused a court to be held on the prisoners, who were hanged and impaled. In April, 1471, the Countess of Warwick, wife of the king-maker, landed at Southampton, but soon afterwards, on the day after the battle of Barnet, in which her husband was slain, she hastened to Beaulieu Abbey, and there took sanctuary. To this same privileged refuge Perkin Warbeck fled in 1497, after his failure in the West and the desertion of his troops. He was closely pursued, and the abbey was surrounded. Believing the promises made to him on behalf of the king, he left the sanctuary, and was conducted a prisoner to the Tower.

Hampshire played such an important part in the early history of England that the record of events connected with it after the fourteenth century is of much less general interest than those of earlier date. A tradition survives in the south-west of the county concerning Milford and the landing of Henry Tudor, afterwards Henry VII. He was known to be in France, and it was rumoured that he would land at Milford ; but this turned out to be, not the Milford in Hampshire, where the tradition says Richard III. expected him, but Milford in South Wales, a much more likely place for his arrival, among his own countrymen.

The Tudor sovereigns all passed through the county on various occasions, and spent some time in various parts of it. In his youth Henry VIII. was fond of hunting, and a place in Woolmer Forest now called Lode Farm was a favourite hunting-box of this prince. From the frequent visits he paid to it, we are told he got the name of Harry at Lode. The young king Edward VI. journeyed leisurely through Hampshire shortly before his death, in the hope of restoring his health ; and in the next reign Southampton Water was the scene of the arrival in state of a great fleet of Spanish ships, which escorted Philip, Prince of Spain, to this country, on the occasion of his marriage to Queen Mary. His landing took place on the beach outside the Water Gate of Southampton, where he was met by the mayor, who humbly gave up the keys of the town to him as an act of homage. The prince and a gorgeous procession of English nobles and Spanish grandees proceeded through the Water Gate to Holy Rood Church, where high mass was sung in thanksgiving for his safe arrival, after which we are told the Spaniards regaled themselves with the beer for which the town was noted, and some of them became drunk.

During the progresses of Queen Elizabeth the county received its full share of attention. She journeyed through it on various occasions. The base of one of the ruined pillars of the great church of Netley Abbey still bears the name of the virgin queen, cut into it on the occasion of one of her visits to the Earl of Hertford, who then resided there. The inscription begins : ' Elizabetha Rex Angliæ,' the queen being styled ' Rex,' not ' Regina.'

The finest entertainment this queen received in Hampshire was, however, provided for her by the same earl at another of his seats in this county. This was at Elvetham, near Odiham, where, in 1591, he received his sovereign with much pomp, and organized for her entertainment a series of princely sports such as she delighted in, after the manner of those for which Kenilworth became famous. At Elvetham the earl caused new buildings to be specially erected for the use of her majesty and her attendants. Bowers were constructed, and a poet clad in green appeared, who, of course, was able to versify in the Latin tongue. He addressed the queen in a Latin oration, which much pleased her. Water pageants were got up on the lake in Elvetham Park. Nymphs appeared, and Neptune put in an appearance, and even condescended to conduct a pinnace on the water, which contained three virgins who, as they passed by the queen, delighted her by playing Scottish jigs. All this is amusing to read, and it happened in Hampshire three centuries ago, but it belongs to the history of the court rather than to the history of the county.

During the Civil War of the seventeenth century Hampshire was the scene of several important events. At the beginning of hostilities it was soon apparent that the feeling of the county was much divided. A majority of the inhabitants of the towns and some of the gentry of the county sided with the Parliament. On the other side was a considerable party of Royalists, the most notable of whom was the Marquis of Winchester. The great struggle which ensued caused divisions even in the county families, such as in those of the Paulets and the Tichbornes, some of whom took up arms on opposite sides.

In December, 1642, Winchester was captured by the Parliamentary force under Sir William Waller, and then it was that such irreparable injury was done to the cathedral muniments, many of which were scattered and lost. The cathedral itself was much injured in the interior ; many of its monumental chapels which had escaped destruction a hundred years before were then defaced. The Parliamentary soldiers profaned the sacred edifice, broke down the organ, opened the tombs, smashed the windows, and rode through the streets of the city, bearing with them such trophies as surplices, hoods, and other ecclesiastical vestments, organ-pipes, pieces of carved work, and copies of the Book of Common Prayer. During the summer of 1643 Winchester again suffered. It was attacked on several occasions, and was occupied about this time by both the contending parties more than once. At the outbreak of hostilities Winchester, like other old defensive positions, was not prepared to stand a siege, so that it was taken and retaken during this year. By the end of this year it was securely held by the Royalists, under Lord Hopton, who had under his command about 3,000 foot and 1,500 horse. The military importance of the city, and the part it played during the next two years, were due to its ancient fortifications. Although its castle was somewhat dilapidated, it was a strong defensive place, and the old city wall still remained. Winchester Castle was soon put into a position to stand a siege ; it was provisioned, and its defences repaired.

During this war, the towns of Southampton and Portsmouth were held for the Parliament, while from the end of

1643 to the end of 1645 Winchester was held for the king. In the North of Hampshire, Basing House was also held by the Marquis of Winchester for the Royalist cause. This house possessed many of the features of a castle. It took the place of the medieval castle which had been burnt in the time of Queen Elizabeth, and, like its predecessor, was built within the lines of an ancient British fortification. Basing House was close to the main road from London to the West, while Winchester was on the main thoroughfare between the south-western counties and the south-eastern. During the Civil War Hampshire was linked with Surrey, Kent, and Sussex by the Parliament for military purposes. The chief Parliamentary general in this part of England, during the greater part of the war, was Sir William Waller. Opposed to him at the end of 1643 was Lord Hopton, whose headquarters were at Winchester. Southampton was held by Colonel Norton, while Waller's headquarters were at Farnham Castle. The last battle fought on Hampshire soil took place in March, 1644, on the downland between Cheriton and Bramdean, between the forces under the commands of Sir William Waller and Lord Hopton. This has been since known as the battle of Cheriton, and its importance has scarcely been sufficiently recognised. Several thousands of men were engaged on both sides ; the fighting lasted from ten in the morning until darkness came on at night, and the slaughter was great. Waller gained a decisive victory, and Hopton, aided by the darkness, retreated towards Basing, which the greater part of the remnant of his force reached, while the remaining part retired to Winchester. Both Winchester and Basing House continued to be held for the king for more than a year and a half longer.

Basing stood several sieges, and skirmishes went on round Winchester and Southampton. After the fall of Bristol, Cromwell marched into Hampshire. The Parliament held Portsmouth, Southampton, and Christchurch, while Winchester and Basing held out for the king. Cromwell appeared before Winchester with a strong force early in October, 1645, and summoned the city to surrender. After some parleying and artillery practice in battering the castle wall, the place was surrendered. The final siege of Basing then took place. The force with which Cromwell surrounded it a few days after the fall of Winchester was too strong for successful resistance, and Basing was taken. It has been calculated that during its sieges more than 2,000 lives were lost by skirmishes and various attacks upon it.

Many stories of the period of the Civil War, more or less real, survive in the county. Hursley, near Winchester, was the seat of Richard Cromwell, who acquired it through his wife, Dorothy Major. Traditions of the greatness of the Cromwell family, and of Richard during his brief period of office as lord protector, survive there, and traditions of his fall survive in the name of the public-house bearing the name of Tumbledown Dick at Farnborough, which, with others of a similar kind, was probably adopted as a tavern sign at the time of the restoration of the monarchy. At West Tisted, a hollow oak-tree is shown near the old manor-house in which Sir Benjamin Tichborne concealed himself after Cheriton fight, and which is still known as Sir Benjamin's oak. Cheriton and its neighbourhood abound in chalk springs, which are usually very active in the month of March. The tradition that one of the lanes there leading from the battle-field ran with blood may have had some foundation from the fact of the blood from some of the slain being mingled with the spring water. At East Wellow the ghost of Colonel Norton, the regicide, is still said occasionally to walk from the site of the old manor-house, formerly a seat of his family, into the parish church.

The effects of the Civil War in Hampshire were considerable. The royal castle at Winchester was demolished, and the bishop's fortified palace at Waltham was reduced to the state of ruin in which it now remains. Old Basing

House, which had stood out so long in the royal cause, was burnt and destroyed. The Royalist families in this county became impoverished by the heavy fines laid upon them in order to save their estates.

The Marquis of Winchester and his family became greatly reduced after the fall of Basing, and the Earl of Southampton, the last of the four earls, who died in 1667, sank into a position of less importance in the county than his father and grandfather had occupied.

The imprisonment of Charles I. at Carisbrook Castle, and the negotiations which took place at Newport a short time before the trial of the king, are well-known events of our national history.

After the battle of Worcester and the suppression of the rising under Prince Charles, the estates of a considerable number of Hampshire Royalists were confiscated by the Act of 1651, which ordered the lands and estates forfeited for treason to be sold, and by the Acts of 1652, which ordered forfeited estates to be sold for the use of the navy, or for other purposes. The families which lost their lands in this way were those of Fowel of Abbots Ann, Chamberlain of Lyndhurst and Nash, Budding of Clinton, Gosling of Morestead, Hide of Woodhouse, Laney of Petersfield, Linkhorn of Bowyet, Mallet of Portsmouth, Phillipson of Throp, Pinchin of Shalden, Sir Charles and Sir John Somerset, Sir Richard Tichborne, and Wells of Eastleigh. The manors of Blendworth, Catherington, Chalton, and Clanfield were also sold under these Acts of Parliament.

In 1651 Charles II. passed through Hampshire in disguise, during his adventurous wanderings before he reached Shoreham and escaped to France. Being unsuccessful in finding a ship in Dorsetshire, he arrived at Hale, in the south-west of this county, in the company of one Robin Philips, and was lodged for one night in the house of Mrs. Hyde, a widow lady living there. She arranged for Charles and his companion to ride off openly the next morning, and to return secretly in the evening, when she contrived that the servants were all absent. They spent the day roaming over Salisbury Plain, viewing Stonehenge and counting the stones there, and in the evening, when they returned, Charles was conducted to the secret chamber, such as many houses at that time contained. There he remained four or five days, and Philips rode off to Salisbury. Subsequently Philips brought word that Colonel Gunther had provided a vessel at Shoreham, and he and the prince left Hale at two o'clock the next morning. About fifteen miles from Hale they met Gunther, with whom the prince rode on to Hambledon. They lodged that night at the house of the colonel's brother-in-law, who came home to supper, having, after the fashion of the time, been spending the day as a good-fellow-well-met with his neighbours at an ale-house. He did not like the look of the disguised prince, and declared he was like some 'round-headed rogue's son'; but the colonel reassured his relative, and said that Mr. Jackson (the name by which Charles went) was not such an one. Later on in the evening, when the host let fall an oath, Mr. Jackson took occasion modestly to reprove him. The next day they reached Shoreham, and Charles escaped across the Channel to Fécamp.*

The marriage of Charles II. to Catherine of Braganza took place at Portsmouth on May 22, 1662.

He was much in Hampshire in subsequent years, with various members of his dissolute court, and he selected Portsmouth, Petersfield, and Southampton for the names of titles which he conferred on his mistresses and one of his illegitimate children.

A later event of this king's reign, in which Lord William Russell was implicated, has more than a local interest. Lord William Russell's devoted wife was Rachel, a daughter and co-heiress of Thomas Wriothesley, fourth

* Boscobel Tracts.

Earl of Southampton. She had been brought up at Titchfield, where the ruin of the family mansion of the Earls of Southampton, on the site of the earlier abbey, still remains. There also, attached to the church, is the chapel containing the fine monuments to the founder of the family and his wife, Thomas Wriothesley, lord chancellor under Henry VIII., and his son the second earl, which Henry the third earl, the friend and patron of Shakespeare, reared at a very great cost. Some of Lady Rachel Russell's well-known letters were written from Stratton Park in Hampshire, where her memory still survives in the name of an avenue of trees known as Lady Russell's Walk.

In 1685 the troops raised by James II. moved through Hampshire towards Somersetshire to suppress the rising under Monmouth, and after the battle of Sedgemoor the duke was captured as a fugitive on the south-western border of Hampshire, near Ringwood. This border-land is a country of heaths and woodlands, and it was on the edge of one of these woods that the unfortunate duke was taken, disguised as a shepherd, in July, 1685. He was conveyed to Ringwood, where, a local tradition says, he was lodged in the White Hart Inn, an ancient hostelry, whose sign still survives, and which preserves this and other traditions. At Ringwood the captive duke was kept a close prisoner for two days, and from this place he wrote his abject letter to the king, in which he begged piteously for pardon, and sought to extenuate his offence to no purpose, for he was hurried on through Romsey and Winchester to London, and thence to the scaffold.

The neighbourhood of Ringwood was the scene of another event of national interest connected with Monmouth's rebellion a few weeks later. Fugitives from the duke's army were hiding, and were being hunted down. On the evening of July 28, 1685, two of these, named Hickes and Nelthorpe, arrived at Moyles Court, three miles from Ringwood, and sought hospitality for the night.

The lady of the house was Dame Alice Lisle, the widow of Colonel Lisle, who had taken a prominent part on the side of the Parliament in the troubles of the time of Charles I. The reception of these fugitives, and their capture the same night by Colonel Penruddock and his troop of soldiers, is a matter of history. Then followed the arrest of the lady of the house and her removal to Winchester. Subsequently followed the 'bloody assize,' under the infamous Judge Jefferies, and the so-called trial of the venerable lady. She was convicted, and condemned to be burned. The only indulgence shown her by the king was one in accordance with her own petition, that she might be beheaded, which sentence was carried out at Winchester on September 2, 1685. The tomb of this notable woman may be seen close to the south door of Ellingham Church, inside which the family pew as it was in her time still remains. At Moyles Court, also, the memory of these events is well preserved. The house has been carefully restored by its present proprietor, and a collection of portraits of the chief personages connected with the rebellion and this judicial murder has been formed there.

Three years later Hampshire was the scene of other events in which James II. was the chief actor. His son-in-law, William, Prince of Orange, had landed at Torbay on November 5, 1688. The king moved his troops to the south-west to meet him. Then followed delays, irresolute action, and desertions from the royal cause at Salisbury. James retired from Salisbury in December towards London, and halted for the first night at Andover, where he invited his other son-in-law, Prince George of Denmark, and the Duke of Ormond to supper. We shall never know the subjects which were discussed at that supper, but we know what followed. As soon as it was over the prince and the duke mounted their horses, and rode off through the winter night to join the Prince of Orange.

A change occurred in Hampshire agriculture about the time of James II., which had a far greater effect on its

economic history than all the visits and patronage of the
Stuart kings. This was the introduction of the turnip,
which led to improvements in the system of sheep-farming,
so extensively carried out on the downlands of the county.
No considerable changes from the early methods of agriculture had been made in Hampshire until about the end of
the seventeenth century. At that time waggons were made
without beds or boards,* like the Anglo-Saxon wains, and
were left exposed to the weather, cart-sheds not being
commonly provided. Oxen were harnessed to ploughs
with hempen traces, and continued to be much used for
field work until the end of the eighteenth century.

The turnip, by providing a winter crop, finally brought
about improvements in the rotation of crops, and led to
the gradual disuse of the system of annually allowing a
third of the land to lie fallow. By supplying winter food,
it also led gradually to the disuse of the custom of killing
live stock at the beginning of winter, and the consequent
large consumption of salted meat. At the beginning of
the eighteenth century farmers in Hampshire were accustomed to lay in a stock of salt in the summer, because at
that time it was cheap, owing to the salterns on the coast
making more than they had storage room for.†

* Lisle, 'Observations on Husbandry,' p. 33. † *Ibid.*, 413.

CHAPTER XXII.

CONCLUSION.

THE connection of Hampshire with the navy has been long and close. In most of the naval battles of England since the Middle Ages, ships built of Hampshire oak have been engaged. In the fifteenth century many noted ships, such as the *Trinité, Grace Dieu*, and the *Holy Goste*, were built on the Itchen. The clays of various kinds which abound in Hampshire form a congenial soil for the growth of oak. The natural growth of the New Forest provided timber for the navy for centuries, until the time of William III.; but in 1698 it was found necessary, in order to keep up the supply, to enclose 6,000 acres of that forest as a nursery for young oaks, which was done by Act of Parliament, and some of the trees then planted now form part of the ornamental woods in that forest. The forest of Woolmer and Alice Holt also supplied much wood for the navy. In 1608 there were growing in that forest 13,031 trees fit for shipbuilding, and in 1783 it contained 38,919 oak-trees. In 1777 a fall of 300 loads of timber for the navy was ordered in that forest; in 1784 a fall of 1,000 loads was ordered; and in 1788 a further fall of 500 loads. During parts of the seventeenth and eighteenth centuries, owing to great peculations which went on by rangers and others, the country did not get half the value of the timber in the Hampshire forests. Mrs. Ruperta Howe, who certainly had no special knowledge of forestry, was appointed Ranger of Woolmer and Alice Holt in 1699, and held the office for forty-five years, during which time the country got little and the ranger got much of the profit from the timber on these crown lands.

The Hampshire forests have played an important part in its history. The pleasures of the chase have attracted to the county many kings and notable personages. There have been few of our monarchs who have not taken part in hunting and other sports in this county. Long after most of the forests in other counties had been inclosed, the royal forests of Hampshire, though diminished in extent, still remained, and in some instances their ancient courts of Attachment and Swainmote met. In the national records during the middle ages, we obtain glimpses here and there of the gradual inclosure of some of the old forest land of this county. As early as Henry III.'s reign, the cultivation of newly assarted wood land in the forests of Pamber, Freemantle, and Chute had begun. The great northern forest disappeared gradually, and this was followed by the disappearance of Buckholt and West Bere, and the diminution in area of the other crown woods and forest land, so that in the seventeenth century, the New Forest, Woolmer, Alice Holt, Bere, and Parkhurst, in the Isle of Wight, were all that remained. Royal grants of land which had been within the area of some forest, and the permission to make parks, were the origin of many private estates in the county, and of some of the villages of later origin. For example, permission was granted by Henry III. to Patric de Cadurcis to inclose and make a fence round parts of the forest of Odiham at Weston, called Heydon and Haselmangrave,* which appears to have been the origin of the manor of Weston Patrick. The inclosure of forest land went on for centuries, in the interests of the crown and those to whom the land was granted. Gilbert White, writing towards the end of the eighteenth century, tells us that the forests near Selborne were then of much less

* Cal. Rot. Chart., 42 Hen. III.

extent than they were at the time of the perambulation made in 1635.

As we wander through Hampshire at the present time, we observe inclosed fields and pastures in all directions, not only in those parts of the county which in the early Middle Ages were forest land, but in those where forests did not exist. The modern aspect of the county is quite different from its ancient aspect. In olden time areas of uninclosed fields and pastures extending for miles were attached to the larger manors and parishes. These extensive areas were commonly joined by other similar areas belonging to other manors, so that hedgerows and other fences only existed round the lord's homestead or manor house. Then in the thirteenth century arose the desire of the lords for making inclosed areas, called parks. By the Statutes of Merton and Westminster, 20th Henry III. and 13th Edward I., the lord of a manor was allowed to inclose a portion of the common pasture, in so far as the pasture rights of the commoners were not damaged thereby. Under this legal sanction the transformation of the surface of Hampshire began, and this did not cease, until in the present century some of the latest inclosures of the remaining commons have been made under comparatively recent Acts of Parliament.

In 1785 the common lands of Andover, comprising 2,954 acres, were inclosed. 15,000 acres of Christchurch parish were formerly common land, and the Act for their inclosure and appropriation was obtained in 1803. One of the earliest of the modern inclosures was that of the common land of Ropley, made about the beginning of the eighteenth century. The long parallel fields at the east of this parish denote the situation of these lands, while the old tenements, lanes, and gardens at the west of the parish show where the ancient village existed. In 1787 1,981 acres in Over Wallop, and in 1797 2,236 acres in Nether Wallop, were inclosed. The common lands of Headbourn Worthy, comprising 1,472 acres, were inclosed in 1791,

302 acres at Upton Grey in 1796, 650 acres at Kilmiston in 1805, 923 acres at Bentworth in 1799, 2,700 acres at Broughton in 1790, 1,790 acres at King's Somborne in 1784, 1,566 acres at Leckford in 1780, 778 acres at Hurstbourn Priors in 1787, 764 acres at Froxfield in 1805, 760 acres at Longparish in 1804, 1,036 acres at Michelmersh in 1797, 1,382 acres at Shipton Bellinger in 1793, 1,335 acres at Upper Clatford in 1786, 1,683 acres at Whitchurch in 1798, 447 acres at Dibden in 1797, 1,432 acres at Rockbourn in 1802, 484 acres at Maplederwell in 1797, 923 acres at Easton in 1800, and 436 acres at Grateley in 1778.

For more than a thousand years the appearance of the old settled parts of the county had remained practically unaltered, except in the formation here and there of parks during the Middle Ages; but after the eighteenth century the Hampshire landscapes began to present those characteristics of inclosed meadows and fields, hedgerows and private woodlands, with which we are now so familiar.

One effect of the inclosure of the common lands has been the rise of many new hamlets and villages in those places where the commoners received their apportionments in land, and built themselves cottages. In this way it has happened that the ancient dwelling site, commonly near the parish church, has in numerous instances become almost deserted, and newer clusters of dwellings have arisen at some distance on the old common lands. In other instances the commoners appear to have sold their several apportionments to the lord of the manor for a money payment, and in these cases no newer hamlets have sprung up at a distance from the ancient villages, which still remain the habitable sites of these parishes.

During the early part of the eighteenth century this county became notorious for its deer-stealers, and subsequently its smugglers. A gang of lawless men known as the 'Waltham Blacks' committed great depredations among the deer in the Bishop's Chase at Waltham. After they had practically exterminated that herd, they extended their operations eastward to the forests of Bere and Woolmer, until 1723, when the Black Act was passed, so named from including more felonies than any other previous statute.

During the eighteenth century the occupation of smuggling possessed attractions for many Hampshire people. After the lapse of many years, during which smuggling has practically been extinct, the tales and traditions of the smugglers of last century still survive in the south of the county and far into its interior. Emsworth, Hayling Island, Rowland's Castle, Yarmouth, Lymington, Hordle, Christchurch, and the New Forest, all have traditions of smuggling adventures, hairbreadth escapes, and the capture of contraband goods landed during the last century, with tales of caves, secret cellars beneath cottages, and stores for spirits, tobacco, and other smuggled goods as far north as Ropley.

Squatting on the commonable crown lands was also followed during the eighteenth and preceding centuries. Where a cluster of huts and wattle and dob cottages existed on the fringe of a forest, it was difficult for bailiffs and wardens to detect the addition of one or two to the number, and in this way the fringes of the Hampshire forests became gradually occupied by an increased number of small tenements. The forest officials were not themselves over-scrupulous about the crown rights, and thus, under a loose system of administration, and what was locally known as keyhold tenure, the huts, in some places, grew in number. Under the keyhold custom, if a man could erect his hut during one night, and get his fire lighted before morning, he had a right to his hearth and habitation.

It was during the latter part of the eighteenth century that a quiet country clergyman was living in Hampshire, who combined with his ministerial functions such a love for the study of Nature, as exemplified in the natural history of his native parish of Selborne, that the name of

Gilbert White has become a household word among English-speaking people in different parts of the world.

Hampshire had at that time its leading men in county affairs, men of some importance in their day; but the names of these have been forgotten, while that of the quiet student of Selborne appears likely to live for centuries in the affections of English people. The 'Natural History of Selborne' has gone through many editions, and is read in England, America, and the colonies at the present time, with as much interest as it was read during the lifetime of its author. Gilbert White was for many years curate of Farringdon, a neighbouring parish to Selborne, where he lived.

His writings have caused Selborne to become one of the minor places of modern English pilgrimage, and his house, although now considerably altered, attracts many visitors. The pulpit from which he preached to the rural congregation at Farringdon may still be seen in the church there.

The old manufactures of cloth and silk survived in this county until the present century. About a hundred years ago a brisk trade was carried on at Alton in barragons, serges, bombazines, and other woven fabrics, which found a market at Philadelphia. At the same time shalloons were made at Andover, and worsted yarn was spun in many Hampshire villages. The silk manufacture, which has not yet quite died out, was at the same time carried on profitably at Overton, Whitchurch, Andover, Alton, and Odiham.

During the latter part of the eighteenth century the agricultural population of the county was in a distressed condition. Labour was abundant, work was scarce in winter, and wages low. The poor rates were consequently high, and a system prevailed in some parishes of paying certain low wages out of the rates, for the work of men who could not obtain ordinary employment on the farms at the usual rate of pay. This system led to various abuses, demoralizing alike to the labourers and to the farmers who obtained part of their labour under the ordinary rate. These circumstances were urged as a reason for the inclosure of the common lands, which, by increasing the area under cultivation, afforded increased employment for the people. At that time, the only country schools were those known as charity schools, and these humble institutions were few and far between. The bulk of the agricultural population of Hampshire remained practically untaught until the State came to their assistance. Consequently, when labour-saving appliances, such as the thrashing-machine, were first introduced, the labourers, who found employment in winter in thrashing corn with the flail, as their forefathers had done from Saxon time downwards, were too ignorant to see anything in such an innovation except ruin for themselves and their families, and riots occurred in some places, in which the machines were smashed and other acts of lawlessness were committed.

The ancient royal hunting establishment in the New Forest was nominally maintained for centuries after kings and courtiers had ceased to hunt there, and some of the old hunting appointments, such as that of bow-bearer, were regarded as honourable distinctions long after they had become sinecures. The New Forest stag-hounds were of a peculiar breed which had long been identified with the forest, and dogs of this kind were last kept about thirty years ago by the late Mr. Tom Neville, a noted Hampshire sportsman who lived at Martyr Worthy. One of the most famous of English hunting men made Hampshire his home in the earlier part of the present century—Mr. Thomas Assheton Smith, who lived at South Tidworth. The achievements of him and his hounds in the field have for many years formed part of the folk-tales of north-western Hampshire.

The game of cricket was played in this county at an early date. Near the picturesque village of Hambledon, the ground of one of the earliest cricket clubs in England existed. It is a local tradition there that cricket had its origin at Hambledon. Near the site of this old cricket ground an inn still bearing the sign of the Bat and Ball remains, and proud stories are told in the neighbourhood of the matches, more than a century ago, in which the Hambledon club could easily beat All England.

An annual event of considerable interest in some parts of this county is the rising of the May-fly. The Hampshire streams have from time immemorial been noted for trout, and are of great value as angling preserves. Isaac Walton often fished in these streams. He died at Winchester in 1683, and was buried in the cathedral. The fishing season is an important time for many people in the districts adjoining the upper parts of the Hampshire rivers, where the appearance of the May-fly is an important local event.

Along the coast, sea-fishing provides a subsistence for a large number of families. During the yachting season many of the younger fishermen abandon their boats to take service on board the numerous yachts which are fitted out at Southampton, Cowes, Gosport, Lymington, and other places. Aquatic pursuits occupy the attention of a large number of people in the southern part of Hampshire during the summer months. The yacht races round the British coasts are followed with great interest, and the numerous regattas and yachting events which take place in the Solent and Southampton Water are regarded as important annual occurrences.

The course of national events and the growth of London, which led in the Middle Ages to the removal of the seat of government from this county, the decay of its trade, and the extinction of its home industries by the competition of the midland and northern counties, which all contributed to diminish its prosperity, have, however, brought some compensation to Hampshire. As the national wealth increased, the residential advantages of its coasts, its forest and woodland scenery, its dry gravel subsoil, and its chalk downs, have attracted an increasing number of settlers from other parts of the kingdom. The mild climate of the Undercliff has led to the growth of Ventnor. Shanklin and Sandown, also on the south coast of the island, are now considerable towns, while Ryde, on the northern coast, has had a rapid growth, and has become the most populous place in the Isle of Wight. Ryde and Cowes have attractions of their own as yachting places, which bring them an annual summer supply of temporary residents. Southsea, the fashionable part of Portsmouth, has grown with the growth of the great naval station, and also from attractions of its own. In the south-west of Hampshire a great town is rapidly rising into importance. Half a century ago the Bourne was but the name of the beautiful little stream which now flows down the wooded vale into the sea, through the ornamental public grounds of Bournemouth. The town which has risen on both sides of this Bourne is already miles in extent in both directions. Its stately buildings, wooded drives, and its beach, which is scarcely surpassed by that of any other place, attract to it a never-ending stream of visitors, of which those in the winter are as important to its prosperity as those in the summer. The modern necessity for an improved military training of the army has been the cause of the growth of a considerable town in the east of the county, where Aldershot has risen from the condition of an insignificant village, and has become the chief training place for the army.

The population of the county, including the Isle of Wight, has increased from 593,000 in 1881 to 690,000 in 1891.

In this volume I have endeavoured to place briefly before the reader the outlines of the history of Hampshire, with a sketch of the conditions and institutions under which its people have lived in past ages, rather than attempt to chronicle in detail all the historical events which have happened within it. Its local history is that of an agricultural county which is also a maritime county. The considerable home industries of which it was the seat during the middle ages have for the most part left it, and the question is sometimes asked, ' Have these industries gone for ever?' Having regard to the progress of modern science, he would be a bold man who would, without hesitation, reply in the affirmative. Hampshire possesses in its steadily flowing chalk streams, which never vary much in volume, and in its tides, enormous sources of power which are only utilized at present in driving a few river and tidal mills.

Coal has been discovered at Dover, and its occurrence there points at least to the probable former existence of the Coal Measures along a line between the Somersetshire coal-field and that of Belgium. The practical geological question, whether any part of these Coal Measures still remains, covered by formations of later date, is one of much importance to the people of this county. The lowest geological beds which exist on the surface of any part of the mainland of Hampshire are the Gault and the Lower Greensand. What there may be even five hundred feet below these beds no one can safely say, still less can it be predicted what beds may exist at a depth of two thousand feet. Some people in this county have been greatly interested in the experimental investigations which have been made further eastward. A good case for trial borings has already been made out. If such trial borings, which must sooner or later be made, should lead to the discovery of coal, Hampshire will again become a manufacturing county, and its commerce will be greatly expanded.

INDEX.

Elliot Stock, Paternoster Row, London.

www.ingramcontent.com/pod-product-compliance
Lightning Source LLC
Chambersburg PA
CBHW020847020726
47497CB00005B/1298